Apple Training Series

iWork '09

Richard Harrington

Apple
Certified

Apple Training Series: iWork '09
Richard Harrington
Copyright © 2009 by Richard Harrington

Published by Peachpit Press. For information on Peachpit Press books, contact:

Peachpit Press
1249 Eighth Street
Berkeley, CA 94710
(510) 524-2178
Fax: (510) 524-2221
http://www.peachpit.com
To report errors, please send a note to errata@peachpit.com
Peachpit Press is a division of Pearson Education

Apple Series Editor: Serena Herr
Editors: Bob Lindstrom, Serena Herr
Contributing Writer: Brendan Boykin
Copy Editor: Elissa Rabellino
Technical Editor: Michael Greenberg
Proofreaders: Darren Meiss, Elissa Rabellino, and Karen Seriguchi
Technical Review: Brendan Boykin, Heather Christy
Compositor: Danielle Foster
Indexer: Jack Lewis
Cover Illustration: Kent Oberheu
Cover Production: Happenstance Type-O-Rama
Media Producer: Eric Geoffroy
Lesson File Media Production: Mark Weiser, Emmanuel Etim, Xi Lin, Megan Tytler, Kevin Bradley, James Ball, Bemnet Goitem, Pamela Vinal, and Ian Pullens—RHED Pixel

ISBN 13: 978-0-321-61851-1
ISBN 10: 0-321-61851-3

9 8 7 6 5 4 3 2 1

Printed and bound in the United States of America

Contents at a Glance

Table of Contents

Pages: Publishing Made Easy

Getting Started

Welcome to the Apple-certified training course for the iWork '09 suite of products: Keynote, Pages, and Numbers.

This book is about creating presentations, publications, and spreadsheets—but it's also about how to take those documents a little further into the creative realm than they normally go.

iWork '09 features three powerful applications for producing everything from school newsletters to business presentations. With Keynote '09, you can produce cinema-quality presentations and slideshows. With Pages '09, you can quickly create a variety of stunning documents. With Numbers '09, you can produce innovative spreadsheets with over 250 functions to help you organize data, perform calculations, and manage lists.

Whether you are a student, a business owner, or a creative pro, iWork can help you organize your ideas and information and then publish them in compelling, accessible ways. The lessons in this book teach you how to use iWork '09 to express yourself with style.

The Methodology

This book emphasizes hands-on training, with practical step-by-step lessons and project files. The lessons advance by progressively increasing the complexity of the media you use and the projects you create. For example, you start by working with text in a Keynote slideshow, and then add images, animations, video, and more. The exercises are designed to help you learn the best features of the applications. Above all, these lessons are meant to be practical—not esoteric projects to show off the software, but real-world projects for real-life people with time constraints, well-worn equipment, and concerns about budget.

If you are new to iWork, it's best to start at the beginning and progress through each lesson in order, because each lesson builds on information learned in previous ones. If you have some experience with the application, you can choose to start with the section that addresses Keynote, Pages, or Numbers directly.

Course Structure

The book is divided into three sections: Keynote, Pages, and Numbers. Each of the 16 lessons in this book focuses on a different aspect of project creation and distribution.

Keynote: Making Great Presentations

▶   In Lessons 1 through 7, you'll work with presentations in Keynote. You'll learn how to create compelling presentations quickly; how add photos, graphics, charts, video, and web links; and how to animate elements of your slides to keep your presentation moving. You'll also take advantage of the versatility of Keynote, importing and enhancing documents from other applications and publishing your presentation in a variety of formats.

Pages: Publishing Made Easy

▶   In Lessons 8 through 12, you'll work mostly with printable documents—letters, reports, newsletters, brochures, posters, classroom materials, and more. You'll learn how to design, produce, and publish great documents that communicate clearly in print and on the web.

Numbers: Working with Spreadsheets

▶   In Lessons 13 and 14, you'll learn your way around Numbers, working with spreadsheets, reports, and budgets, creating beautiful charts and graphs, and designing a wedding planner to track the big event from beginning to end. Lessons 15 and 16 cover more advanced spreadsheet and charting operations.

System Requirements

This book is written for iWork '09. You must install the iWork '09 software before copying the lesson files to your computer or beginning the lessons.

Because iWork '09 is designed to work with Apple's iLife suite (which comes free with any new Macintosh computer), several of the lessons dip into iPhoto or other iLife applications, especially when you use photos or publish to the web. If you have an older version of iLife, certain exercises will not work exactly as written, but you will still be able to use this book and learn how to use the iWork '09 suite. You will need to upgrade to the current iLife '09 version to follow along with every exercise in every lesson. The upgrade can be purchased online at www.apple.com and is available from any store that sells Apple software.

Before you begin the lessons in this book, you should have a working knowledge of your Mac and its operating system. You don't need to be an expert, but you do need to know how to use the mouse and standard menus and commands, and how to open, save, and close files. You should have a working understanding of how Mac OS X helps organize files on your computer, and you should also be comfortable opening applications (from the Dock or the Applications folder). If you need to review any of these techniques, see the printed or online documentation that came with your computer.

For a list of the minimum system requirements for iWork, refer to the Apple website at www.apple.com/iwork/systemrequirements.html.

Copying the Lesson Files

This book includes a DVD-ROM, which contains all the files you'll need to complete the lessons. You must install the iWork '09 application before copying the lesson files to your computer.

Installing the iWork Lesson Files

1   Insert the DVD-ROM into your computer's DVD drive.

2   Double-click to open the DVD-ROM.

3   Drag the iWork09_Book_Files folder from the DVD to your computer's desktop. The files will be copied to your computer.

The iWork09_Book_Files folder contains the lesson files used in this course. Each lesson has its own folder.

About Apple Training and Certification

Apple Training Series: iWork '09 is part of the official training series for Apple applications, developed by experts in the field and certified by Apple. The lessons are designed to let you learn at your own pace. If you follow the book from start to finish, or at least complete the lessons in each section consecutively, you will build on what you learned in previous lessons.

Apple offers Associate-level certification for the iWork '09 product suite. Professionals, educators, and students can earn Apple Certified Associate status to validate entry-level skills in our digital lifestyle and productivity applications. As a special offer, this Apple Training Series book includes a discount code that lets you take the certification exam online for $45 (a $65 value). Details appear on the DVD.

For those who prefer to learn in an instructor-led setting, Apple also offers training courses that lead to certification at Apple Authorized Training Centers worldwide in iLife, iWork, Mac OS X, Mac OS X Server, and Apple's Pro applications. These courses are taught by Apple Certified Trainers. They balance concepts and lectures with hands-on labs and exercises.

To learn more about Apple Training and Certification, or to find an Authorized Training Center near you, go to www.apple.com/training.

Resources

Apple Training Series: iWork '09 is not a comprehensive reference manual, nor does it replace the documentation that comes with the application. For more information about program features, refer to these resources:

▶ Companion Peachpit Press website: As iWork '09 is updated, Peachpit may choose to update lessons as necessary. Visit www.peachpit.com /ats.iwork09.

▶ *The iWork '09 Reference Guide*: Accessed through the Keynote, Pages, and Numbers Help menus, this contains a complete description of all features.

▶ Apple's website: www.apple.com.

Keynote: Making
Great Presentations

1

Lesson Files	Lessons > Lesson_01 > 01Presentation1_Stage3.key
	Lessons > Lesson_01 > 01Sustainability_Stage2.key
	Lessons > Lesson_01 > Sustainability Outline.pages
Time	This lesson takes approximately 60 minutes to complete.
Goals	Build a basic presentation using outline view
	Choose a theme and master slides
	Modify text in the Fonts window, format bar, and Text inspector
	Work with the Inspector window
	Add a shape to contain text
	Add a table and perform data calculations
	Check for spelling errors

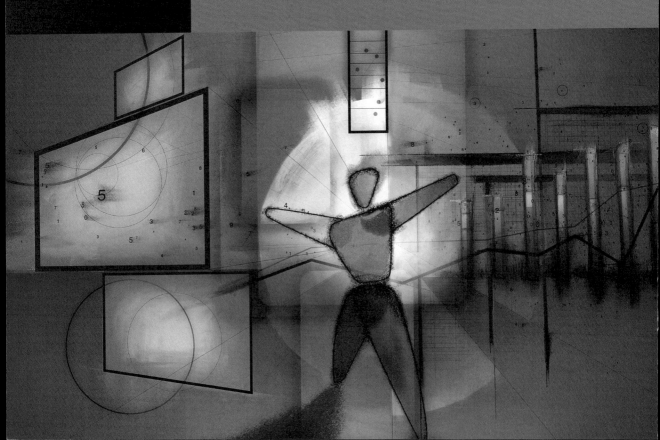

Creating a Presentation

These days, presentations are a part of life. No longer relegated to just the world of business reports, presentations are used to share everything from photography slideshows and school projects to product information in a self-playing retail kiosk.

Keynote '09 lets you create truly dynamic presentations. The application makes it easy not just to arrange text, images, and charts, but also to add audio and video, customize professionally designed backgrounds, and insert cool transitions between slides. It also lets you animate elements so that, for example, your bullet points can sashay jauntily onscreen one by one. Learning to integrate a variety of elements is essential to building a captivating, coherent presentation that informs and entertains your audience.

In this lesson, we'll start with the basics. We'll create a straightforward presentation for a fictitious firm that specializes in sustainable architecture. We'll start by choosing a theme for the presentation, and then add structure by outlining and adding text. Next, we'll format the text using the format bar, Inspector window, and other tools. Finally, we'll use Keynote to catch spelling errors before giving the presentation in front of an (equally fictitious) audience.

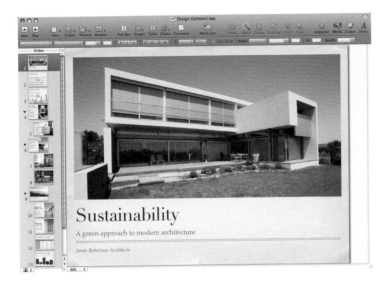

Before You Start

The exercises in this lesson require that you have both the iWork '09 suite installed on your computer and the lesson files copied to your hard drive from the DVD included with this book. You'll find instructions for copying the lesson files in "Getting Started," the introduction to this book.

Opening Keynote

You can open Keynote in three ways:

▶ Open the iWork '09 folder in your Applications folder and then double-click the Keynote application file.

▶ Click the Keynote icon in the Dock (if it's not there, you can drag the icon to your Dock from the Applications folder).

▶ Double-click any Keynote project file.

Choosing a Theme and Slide Size

Keynote ships with 44 Apple-designed themes that contain coordinated fonts, colors, textures, and styles. You're not limited to using the built-in themes; you can customize themes, create your own, or acquire others from online vendors.

When you first open Keynote, you'll see the Theme Chooser, where you can browse the available themes. Let's start by choosing a theme and a slide size for our Sustainability presentation.

> **TIP** ▶ Before you select a theme, decide on a size for your slides based on the resolution of the projector or display you'll use during the presentation. Some Keynote themes have only two resolutions available: 800 × 600 or 1024 × 768. These are the two most common resolution settings for projectors and presentations.
>
> Newer Keynote themes offer three additional sizes. The 1280 × 720 and 1920 × 1080 resolutions match the two most common sizes for HD displays. The other option, 1680 × 1050, is a common resolution setting for Apple Cinema displays.

1   If necessary, open Keynote by clicking the Keynote application icon in the Dock.

2   If the Theme Chooser is not visible, choose File > New from Theme Chooser.

The Theme Chooser opens, displaying the themes included with Keynote.

3 Browse the available themes by scrolling through the Theme Chooser.

Themes contain multiple master slides that serve special purposes such as displaying bulleted text or photos. A representative thumbnail is displayed for each theme (generally of a title slide).

TIP ▶ If you'd like a better preview of a theme's appearance, skim your pointer over a theme. You'll see several representative slides filled with sample content that give you a good idea what the theme can do.

4 Click the thumbnail for the Editorial theme to select it.

5 Make sure the Slide Size pop-up menu is set to 1024 × 768.

This is the size you'll use for this presentation. You can always modify the slide size in the Document inspector if you have to reformat a presentation.

6 Click Choose to select the theme and create a new document.

7 Choose File > Save. Name your file *Sustainability.key* and save it to your computer's hard drive.

Selecting a Master Slide

Each theme includes several *master slides*. A master slide is a preset layout for your slide. You can select a master slide based on personal preference and a slide's intended content. For instance, a slide that includes photos or a chart will likely require a layout different from a slide that contains bullet points of information.

1   In the toolbar, click the Masters button to see a list of master slides.

2   Choose the Photo – Horizontal master.

The slide layout changes to the new master. You will use this layout for your first slide.

NOTE ▶ Don't worry about the placeholder photos for now. You'll replace all of the photos in the next lesson.

Now that you've picked the theme and your first slide is ready, let's add some text.

TIP ▶ You can click the Masters button at any time to choose a new layout. Examine the themes closely and look at the available master slides. This approach will help you choose a theme for your layout based on both style and function.

Outlining a Presentation

When building a presentation, many users jump right in and start creating slides. They add text, artwork, and animation one slide at a time. Although this approach is valid, it usually works better to start by creating an outline.

TIP ▶ Pages offers several useful templates for organizing your thoughts. Be sure to explore the Outlines templates for outlining a presentation.

A presentation is often more coherent when you build it in stages. Think of the process as being similar to that of building a house. You could build and finish one room at a time, but most contractors like to start with blueprints, lay a foundation, build a frame, and move forward from there.

Keynote has a robust outline view that is an excellent tool for setting up your presentation's content. In this exercise, you will create a multislide presentation using outline view.

1　In the toolbar, click the View button and choose Outline.

As you work with a presentation, you will often change your view to better suit specific tasks. To make more room for typing in your current view, you can expand the slide navigator.

2　Move your pointer over the resize handle at the bottom of the slide navigator.

The pointer changes to a resize pointer to indicate that you can drag to resize the navigator.

3　Drag to the right to expand the viewable area for the slide navigator.

Creating the First Slide

Now it's time to begin structuring the order of the slides. We'll add some text to the first slide to accomplish two things: create a detailed outline that's easy to modify and share, and learn to quickly build slides with text content.

1   In the Outline pane, click to the right of the slide thumbnail (slide 1). The area turns light blue, and the insertion point blinks.

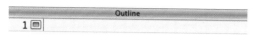

2   Type the following title into the slide: *Sustainability*.

3   Press Return. A new slide is created.

This quick shortcut adds a new slide. However, you really want a subpoint for slide 1 in this position. You can easily turn the new slide into that subpoint.

4   Press Tab to indicate that there should be secondary information for the previous slide.

NOTE ▶ If you change your mind about making a subpoint or text bullets, you can press Shift-Tab to "outdent" your text.

The insertion point moves to an indented location underneath the *Sustainability* title. The next text you type will become additional text for slide 1.

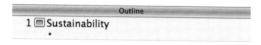

NOTE ▶ While the slide outline shows a subpoint as bulleted text, this doesn't mean that the selected slide will display the text in a bulleted list (the slide formatting depends on which slide master you've applied).

5   Type the following text into the outline: *A green approach to modern architecture.*

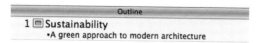

A third text box is present on the slide. Only the first two levels of text appear in outline view, so let's manually modify this text.

6   Click the third text box on the slide (currently labeled *Date*) and type *Jamie Robertson Architects.*

7   Choose File > Save to capture your progress so far. You've successfully built your first slide. Let's add several more slides to the presentation.

Adding More Slides

For the following slides, we'll use a different master because we want to present a bulleted list. Keynote provides master slides specifically for that purpose.

1   In the toolbar, click the New button to add a new slide.

The number 2 appears next to your new slide.

2   In the toolbar, click Masters, and choose the Title & Bullets layout.

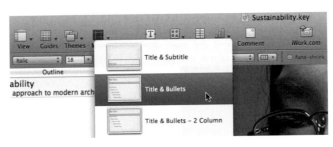

The layout of the slide changes to accommodate a title and bulleted text.

Pasting Text into an Outline

Now let's add some text. In the real world, it's not uncommon to pull text for a slideshow from another file, such as an email or a Pages document. Keynote makes it easy to paste that text into your slides.

In this exercise, instead of typing text into the presentation, we'll paste an outline from Pages.

1   In the Finder, open the Lesson_01 folder on your computer's hard drive.

2   Double-click the file **Sustainability Outline.pages**. The file opens in Pages.

This document contains the remaining text for the presentation. We'll copy it to the Clipboard to use it in Keynote.

3   Choose Edit > Select All to select all the text in the document; then choose Edit > Copy to copy the text to the Clipboard.

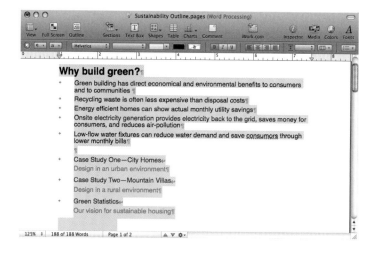

4   Close Pages (without saving changes) and return to Keynote.

> **TIP**   To quickly switch between open applications, press and hold Command-Tab to display the Application Switcher (a bar showing all open applications). Click the Keynote icon to switch to Keynote.

5 In outline view, click the empty area next to slide 2. Then choose Edit > Paste and Match Style.

The copied text is pasted into the Keynote presentation and matches the formatting of the current theme. (Keynote discards the original text formatting.)

When you add the text, a new slide is created for each paragraph. This presentation requires several styles of slides to present information. Let's adjust the master layout for some of the slides.

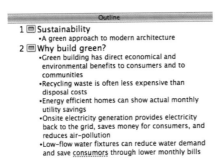

NOTE ▶ The pasted text intentionally contains spelling errors. We'll learn to fix them later in the lesson.

6 Click slide 3. This slide lacks a title for its bullet points, so let's change its layout.

7 In the toolbar, click the Masters button, and choose Bullets.

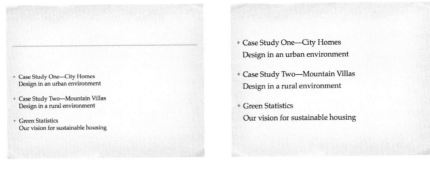

Before   After

The layout changes to better match the slide content. The next three slides are similar in structure and can use the same master slide.

8   Click slide 4 to select it; then Shift-click slide 6 to select three slides.

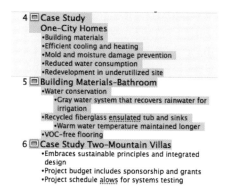

You have selected slides 4, 5, and 6 and can apply a slide master to all three slides with one click.

9   In the toolbar, click the Masters button and choose Title, Bullets & Photo.

All three slides update to the same layout.

NOTE ▸ The next two slides use photo layouts that you will work with in Lesson 2.

10   Click slide 10 to select it. This slide includes secondary information for slide 9.

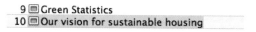

11   Press Tab to indent the slide and convert it to a bullet point on slide 9. When text is joined to slide 9, slide 9 is selected.

12   Click the Masters button and choose Photo – Horizontal.

13   Click slide 11 to select it.

This slide includes secondary information for slide 10.

14   Press Tab to indent the slide and convert it to a slide 10 bullet point.

15 Click the Masters button and choose Photo – Vertical.

This layout will work well as you enter a new section of the presentation. It has room for a very large photo as well as a large title.

16 Repeat the slide formatting for the next two slides (11 and 12) using the technique you just learned.

17 Select slide 12 and choose the Title – Top master. This layout works well, as you will add a chart later in this lesson.

> 9 ▣ Green Statistics
>   •Our vision for sustainable housing
> 10 ▣ 85%
>   •Recycled construction materials
> 11 ▣ 75%
>   •Eco-friendly supply chain
> 12 ▣ The worldwide wood supply

18 When you're done, save your work by choosing File > Save. Then check your work by comparing it with **01Sustainability_Stage2.key**.

Formatting Text

Now that we've got the outline and text into the slides, it's time to format the text. It's always a good idea to start with clean, good-looking text—the bones of your presentation—before you dress it up with photos and animations. Good presentations start with good text.

About the Format Bar

The format bar —located at the top of your document window just below the toolbar— is a handy tool that lets you quickly format all content within a presentation. You can use it to format text, tables, charts, and images.

Keynote '09 has a contextual format bar that displays various tools based on the task you're working on and the objects you've selected. For example, if you select text, you'll see controls for changing its font and formatting; but if you select a table, you'll see controls for rows and columns.

If the format bar isn't visible, choose View > Show Format Bar.

TIP ▶ You can learn what a particular button does by holding the pointer over it until a help tag appears.

About the Inspector Window

The Inspector window contains inspectors with many of the advanced controls you will use to stylize and animate your presentation.

You may find the format bar more convenient for making most formatting changes, but the inspectors offer an additional level of control.

If the Inspector window is closed, click the Inspector button on the toolbar. To switch between inspectors for particular tasks, click the appropriate button at the top of the Inspector window.

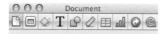

The Inspector window gives you access to these inspectors and their functions:

▶ Document—Set your slideshow properties as well as Spotlight comments.

▶ Slide—Create transitions between slides and control a slide's appearance.

▶ Build—Animate the text and other slide elements.

▶ Text—Format the layout of text and bullets on the slide canvas.

▶ Graphic—Control the properties and appearance of graphics.

▶ Metrics—Size and position elements.

▶ Table—Create and format tables to hold data.

▶ Chart—Control the properties of charts and graphs.

▶ Hyperlink—Add web links, links to slides, and webpages to your presentation.

▶ QuickTime—Control the properties of QuickTime files in your document.

In this lesson, we start off by using the format bar. We'll use some of the inspectors as we refine the presentation project in Lesson 2, and we'll be working with all of the inspectors throughout this book.

▶ Designing Great Slideshows

Great presentations start with strong ideas, creative writing, and thorough outlines. The rule of thumb is: Think first, design second, and then present. With
that in mind, follow these presentation dos and don'ts:

Keep It Simple

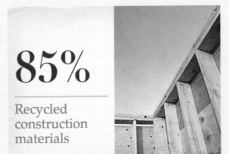 

▶   Clear, simple slides lead your audience through your presentation like wel-
    come signs on an unfamiliar highway. The messages should be brief. Don't
    distract your viewers with several images that compete for their attention.
    Next time you are on a highway, notice that the simplest billboards are often
    the most effective.

Be Consistent

▶   A consistent look and feel helps your audience focus on your content and
    not its changing background color. Font colors, sizes, and styles should
    remain uniform throughout your presentation. If you customize Keynote
    themes as you build your show, use a consistent design. You can quickly
    check that your presentation has a uniform design by reviewing your slides
    using the light table view.

Your Slides Are *Not* Your Presentation

▶   Think of yourself as the anchorperson on the evening news: you're delivering
    the story, and the slides behind you provide "speaker support," reinforcing
    your key points.

▶ Designing Great Slideshows *(continued)*

Don't Use Too Many Elements on a Slide

▶ A good presenter breaks down complex ideas to their simplest elements. Charts with tons of arrows pointing in all directions will confuse your audience. Lengthy paragraphs of text on a slide will tempt people to read the slide instead of listening to you. If you can't avoid long text, break it up between several slides.

▶ If you can't avoid a complex slide, pause your slideshow and give your audience a silent moment to read the slide without your commentary. You can then resume presenting and you'll have their attention.

▶ A picture can be a much more effective way of communicating complex information than too much text. Every Keynote theme offers multiple slide masters with places for images.

TIP ▶ Slides with less content can be easier for an audience to understand. In advertising, the use of white space (empty areas surrounding the text and images) is a classic technique for improving the comprehension and retention of important information.

Keep Bullet Points Short and Clear

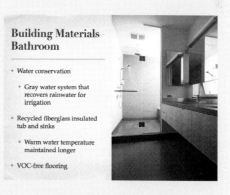

Case Study
One–City Homes

+ Building materials

+ Efficient cooling and heating

+ Mold and moisture
   damage prevention

+ Reduced water consumption

+ Redevelopment in
   underutilized site

Building Materials
Bathroom

+ Water conservation

+ Gray water system that
   recovers rainwater for
   irrigation

+ Recycled fiberglass insulated
   tub and sinks

+ Warm water temperature
   maintained longer

+ VOC-free flooring

▶ Even the best presenters come across audience members who zone out or become distracted. You can help avoid that by keeping your messages brief and punchy. Make sure your audience can quickly grasp your bullet points and instantly understand where your presentation is headed. Use just a few words to convey a clear, complete thought.

Making Text Bold

Not all fonts include a bold style, but the Keynote themes tend to use fonts that offer both bold and italic styles. Let's emphasize some text by making it bold.

1   Choose View > Navigator.

Navigator view is useful for browsing and modifying your presentation. In navigator view, the slide navigator appears to the left of the document window, and the slide canvas is displayed to the right.

2   Click the thumbnail for slide 1 to select it.

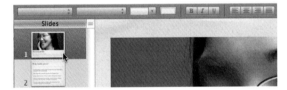

Let's make the presentation title stand out more clearly.

3   On the slide canvas, double-click the slide's title to select it. The text is highlighted in light blue, indicating that it is active and ready for modification.

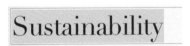

4   In the format bar, click the Bold button.

NOTE ▶ This shortcut works only if the font chosen has a bold typeface available.

Shrinking Text

Sometimes you'll have too much text to fit into a selected slide layout. You can fix this problem by reducing the amount of text, reducing the point size of the text, or doing both.

Let's quickly format some text to fit a slide layout.

1   In the slide navigator, click the thumbnail for slide 4 to select it.

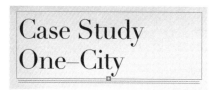

The text in the title is too big, so at least one word is not visible. The + (plus sign) at the bottom of the box indicates this.

2   Click the text box to select it; then Control-click or right-click the title text box and choose Auto-shrink Text.

> **TIP**   You can also select the Auto-shrink checkbox in the format bar to reduce the size of text to fit it in a box.

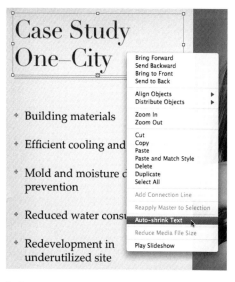

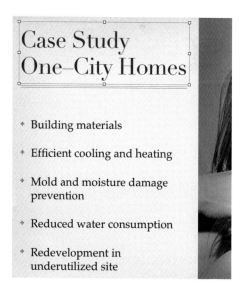

Before   After

The text sizes down to fit the text box.

3   Apply the Auto-shrink Text command to slides 5 and 6 to fit their titles.

Enlarging Text to Improve Readability

If a slide doesn't have a lot of information on it, you may choose to make its text larger to fill up the slide and visually balance the information. Using a larger point size is also useful if you want to add emphasis.

Let's adjust the font size on two slides where the text is too small.

1   In the slide navigator, click the slide 10 thumbnail to select it.

2   Select the top text box (85%).

3   In the format bar, enter a point size of *200* and press Return.

4   Click the Bold button.

Now we'll reuse this formatting on the next slide.

5   Triple-click to highlight the entire paragraph of text and choose Format > Copy Style.

6   In the slide navigator, click the slide 11 thumbnail to select it.

7   Triple-click to select the text in the top text box (75%).

8   Choose Format > Paste Style.

The text is resized to match the text box in slide 10.

9   Return to slide 10.

10 Triple-click the text *Recycled construction materials* to select it.

11 Change the font size to 64 points. The text grows larger but is cut off because the text box is too small.

12 In the format bar, click the Line Spacing button and choose 0.8.

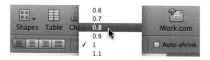

13 Press Command-Return to stop editing the text box, then resize the text box to accommodate the text by dragging the bottom selection handle.

14 Highlight the text in the second text box, and choose Format > Copy Style.

15 Switch to slide 11.

16 Click in the second text box, then drag to select the text and choose Format > Paste Style.

17 In the format bar, click the Line Spacing button and choose 0.8.

18 Resize the text box to accommodate the text by dragging the bottom selection handle.

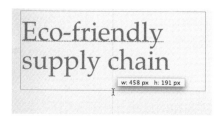

19 Choose File > Save to store your work.

Customizing a Slide Layout

So far, you've modified text within existing slide layouts. However, Keynote lets you add as many text boxes to a slide as you need. You can add text by inserting a new text box or by inserting a shape.

Adding a Shape for Text

Putting text inside a shape is a great way to make it stand out. Let's create a new slide and add a shape to contain text.

1   In the slide navigator, select slide 12.

2   In the toolbar, click the New button to add another slide to your presentation.

3   Click the Masters button and choose Blank.

   NOTE ▶ The Blank master still contains the default formatting of other slide masters; however, it does not include placeholder photos or text.

4   In the toolbar, click the Shapes button and choose the rounded rectangle.

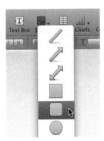

The rectangle is added to the center of the slide, in a color dictated by the theme you have chosen. Let's make it larger so that it can hold text.

5   Option-drag a corner selection handle until the shape is 800 px (pixels) wide and 152 px tall.

   TIP ▶ Holding down the Option key while dragging scales the shape outward from the center.

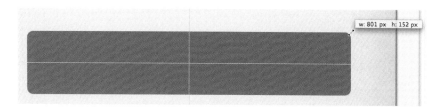

Now that the shape is sized, you can adjust the roundness of the corners.

6   Drag the blue editing point to the right to round the shape's corners.

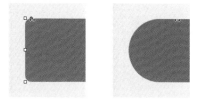

You have successfully added a shape to the slide.

Placing Text Inside a Shape

Now that we've created the rounded rectangle, let's place some text inside it.

1   Double-click inside the shape.

2   Type *Thank you.*

3   Highlight the text and press Command-B to format it as bold.

Let's size the text so that it fills the shape.

4   In the format bar, locate the Font Size field, enter *100,* and press Return.

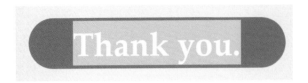

5   With the text selected, select the Shadow checkbox in the format bar. This helps the text stand out a bit.

6   Press Command-Return to apply the text, then choose Edit > Deselect All.

This deselects any object you have selected on your slide and exits the formatting of the shape.

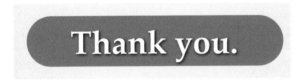

Stylizing a Shape with the Format Bar

If you want to further enhance a shape, you can use the format bar to add a drop shadow or a reflection.

> **TIP** ▶ It is generally considered bad taste to apply both a drop shadow and a reflection. For an attractive look, you should use only one or the other on an object.

1   If the change is not made to step 6 above, you will have to insert to click on the background then click the blue shape to select it.

The format bar offers another effect to enhance the shape.

NOTE ▶ You may need to enlarge your window to see all of the format bar's controls.

2   In the format bar, select the Reflection checkbox.

A reflection is added to the rounded rectangle.

TIP You can customize the appearance of a reflection using the Graphic inspector.

3   Press Command-S to save your work.

Adding a Table

Slide 12 is intended to contain information comparing the worldwide wood supplies in the years 2000 and 2010. A table is a good way to present data in a clear, precise manner.

1   In the slide navigator, select slide 12.

2   In the toolbar, click the Table button.

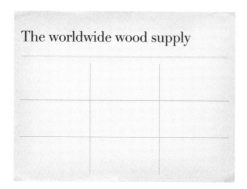

Keynote automatically opens the Table inspector and adds a 3-by-3 table to your slide.

TIP ▶ If you want to manually specify the size and location of a table, chart, text box, or shape, Option-click the object in the toolbar. You can then drag to define its size on the slide canvas.

3   In the format bar, click the Header Row button.

A new row is added to the top of the table. Header row cells contain labels for columns. The header column is also formatted to help the labels stand out and be easily read.

4   In the format bar, click the Header Column button.

A new column is added to the side of the table. A header column contains the labels for the table.

5   In the format bar, change the number of rows to 6 (5 rows and 1 header row).

The table is now set to compare the performance of five countries over two decades and show the change in value.

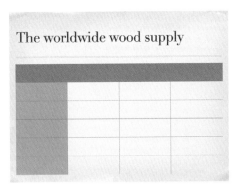

Filling the Header Row and Header Column

A table header row identifies the contents of a table, helping viewers to quickly understand the data.

1 Click in the second cell of the header row.

2 Type *2000.*

3 Press Tab to move to the next cell.

4 Type *2010,* and press Tab to apply the text and move to the next cell.

5 Type *Change* to label the final column.

The header row is filled in. Now let's adjust the header column.

6 Click in the second cell of the header column.

7 Type *Canada* and press the Down Arrow key.

8 Enter the following text into the next four cells, one country per cell.

India

China

Norway

US

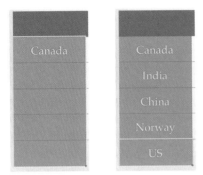

9   Choose File > Save.

You've successfully labeled the table. Now let's insert some numerical values.

Filling and Formatting Table Cells

Now that the table is properly set up, you can populate it with data to communicate information to your audience. Additionally, you can insert calculations to perform mathematical operations on the contents of the table.

1   Enter the information from the following figure into your table.

	2000	2010	Change
Canada	75,000,000	91,000,000	
India	45,000,000	25,000,000	
China	103,000,000	120,000,000	
Norway	55,000,000	45,000,000	
US	90,000,000	75,000,000	

NOTE ▶ These values are millions. Enter six zeros after the initial number. For simplicity, the numbers have been rounded to the nearest million-dollar amount.

Let's format the cells to display the dollar amounts more clearly.

2 Drag to select all the numbers in the table.

3 In the Table inspector, click the Format button.

You can now create a number format to adjust the data display.

4 From the Cell Format pop-up menu, choose Custom.

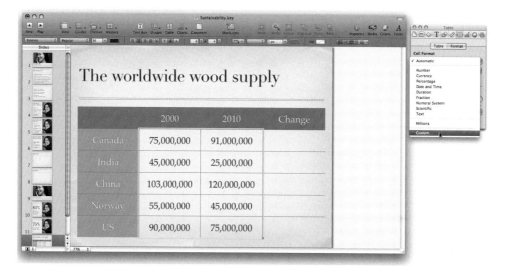

The custom format dialog opens.

5 In the Name field, enter *Millions*.

6 Make sure that Number & Text is chosen in the Type pop-up menu.

7 Drag the currency symbol (the dollar-sign icon) into the first position of the format field.

The second element, integers (#,###), is already in place. This determines how many digits are shown.

8 Drag the scale element (the K icon, representing thousands) into the third position.

Use this element to size the display value of a number. In this case, setting the scale to millions will simplify 123,000,000 to 123.

9   Click the scale element disclosure triangle and choose Millions (M).

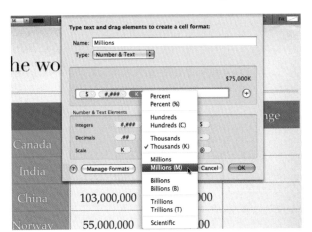

TIP ▶ You can type any custom text into the custom format field if you don't find an element to serve your needs.

10 Click OK to store the custom number format.

The formatting is applied, and the custom number format is stored for later use.

NOTE ▶ Any custom format names that you create are listed in the Cell Formats pop-up menu in the Format pane of the Table inspector.

Calculating the Value of Table Cells

iWork '09 can perform calculations within tables. In the current table, you can tell iWork to calculate the change in value between the years 2000 and 2010, and you don't need to leave Keynote to perform a calculation.

1   Click the table to select it; then click the second cell in the fourth column (just below the word *Change*).

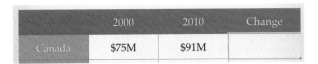

	2000	2010	Change
Canada	$75M	$91M	

NOTE ▶ Be sure to click only once each time! Otherwise, you'll modify the contents of the cell.

2   Type = (the equal sign).

The Formula Editor opens. Along the top and left sides of the table, you can see the *reference tabs* (the letters and numbers that identify the columns and rows of the table). You are going to enter a formula so that Keynote will automatically calculate the difference between the years 2010 and 2000.

3   Click the cell for the 2010 Canada value (this is cell C2, which is the intersection of column C and row 2).

4   Press the – (minus sign) key to subtract the next value.

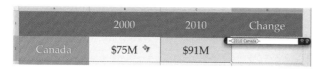

5   Click cell B2 to select the 2000 Canada value.

The Formula Editor displays = *2010 Canada – 2000 Canada*. It will subtract the numbers in column B from column C and place the result in column D.

6   Press Return to apply the formula.

The formula does its work and correctly calculates values for the first cell in column D. The formula can now be applied to the remaining cells.

7   Click to select the first cell containing the formula.

8 Drag the blue Fill handle to the bottom of the table.

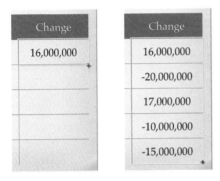

The values in all five cells are calculated.

9 In the Table inspector, from the Cell Format pop-up menu, choose Millions.

The worldwide wood supply

	2000	2010	Change
Canada	$75M	$91M	$16M
India	$45M	$25M	-$20M
China	$103M	$120M	$17M
Norway	$55M	$45M	-$10M
US	$90M	$75M	-$15M

The custom format you created is now applied to these new cells.

10 Choose File > Save to save your work.

Fixing Spelling Errors

Spelling errors are common when creating any text-based document, and Keynote makes it easy to fix them in your presentation before it goes in front of an audience.

The text you copied earlier has a few spelling errors to work with.

1   In the slide navigator, click slide 1.

    Let's use the Spelling window to correct those spelling errors.

    TIP ▶ If you want to quickly fix a word right on the canvas, Control-click or right-click an underlined word. Keynote will suggest possible replacements.

2   Choose Edit > Spelling > Spelling.

    The Spelling window opens. It allows you to browse spelling errors and choose a suggested replacement word.

3   The first spelling error on slide 2 is *consumors*. To fix the error, select *consumers* from the Guess list and click Change.

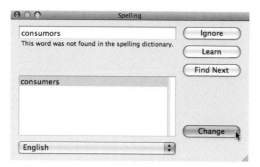

4   The next spelling error is *ensulated*. From the Guess list, select *insulated* and click Change.

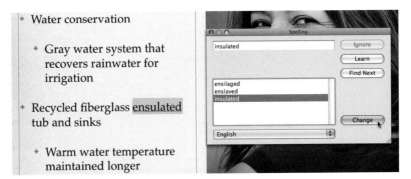

5   The next spelling error is *alows*. From the Guess list, select *allows* and click Change.

6   The next word is *Eco-friendly*. Because it is spelled correctly, click Ignore.

Clicking Ignore tells Keynote to skip the word in this document (but not add it to the dictionary on your computer).

TIP   Click Learn to add a word to your dictionary. This command is useful when text includes jargon and technology words that aren't in your Mac's dictionary.

7   There are no additional errors in this document, so you can close the Spelling window.

8   Choose File > Save to store your work.

You can check your work by comparing it with **01Presentation1_Stage3.key** in the Lesson_01 folder on your computer.

Lesson Review

1.   How do you choose a theme?

2.   How do you change which master slide is used?

3.   How can you paste text into a presentation and apply the theme's formatting?

4.   How do you switch to a different Inspector window?

5.   How do you open the Spelling window?

Answers

1. Choose themes from the Theme Chooser. This window opens automatically when you open Keynote or when you choose File > New from Theme Chooser.

2. You can access master slides by clicking the Masters button in the toolbar. The available master slides will be shown in the list.

3. Choose Edit > Paste and Match Style.

4. At the top of the Inspector window, click one of the available buttons to switch from one inspector to another.

5. Choose Edit > Spelling > Spelling.

2

Lesson Files   Lessons > Lesson_02 > 02Presentation1_Stage1.key

Lessons > Lesson_02 > Sustainability Photos

Lessons > Lesson_02 > Sustainability.mp3

Time   This lesson takes approximately 60 minutes to complete.

Goals   Understand supported media types

Create an album in iPhoto

Optimize images using iPhoto and Keynote

Add transparency to a photo using Instant Alpha

Add music to a slideshow

Place a basic chart in a presentation

Insert a webpage and hyperlinks

Reduce the size of image files in a presentation

Keep media files with the presentation

Lesson **2**

Adding Photos, Charts, and Sound

While text is often the most important part of a presentation, a picture is worth the proverbial thousand words.

Keynote supports a wide variety of media formats—including graphics, sound, and video file formats—that are easy to pull into your presentation. The heart of this graphic support is QuickTime Player, the Mac's versatile media player. In fact, if you can open a file in QuickTime Player, you can use it in Keynote to enhance your presentations.

You can also jazz up your presentation with embedded web links. And there's a whole world of beautifully designed and animated charts waiting to be discovered.

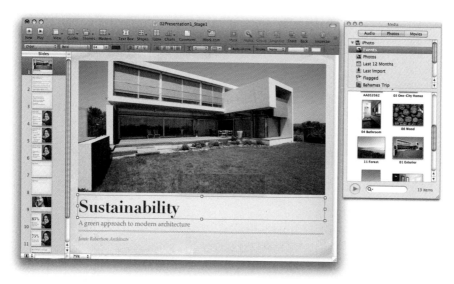

In this lesson, we'll create a photo album–type presentation that includes music, a basic chart, a webpage, and live links. Along the way, we'll learn how enhancing a presentation with interesting, dynamic media content gives you greater flexibility and influence in addressing your audience.

Adding Photos

There are four ways to add images to a Keynote presentation:

▶ Drag the image directly into the Keynote document.

▶ Choose Insert > Choose and navigate to the image file.

▶ Drag a folder of images into Keynote's Media Browser.

▶ Use Keynote's Media Browser to choose images from your iPhoto library.

In this exercise, you'll use the Media Browser to access images that are located in your iPhoto library. (We'll use all of these methods later in these lessons.)

> **NOTE** ▶ You can use the Media Browser to access any media files stored in systemwide default locations, such as your iPhoto or iTunes library, or your Movies folder.

Adding Images from iPhoto

iPhoto library is the place you're most likely to keep your images, so you may frequently use iPhoto, an application in the iLife '09 suite. iPhoto makes it easy to manage and adjust your photos—which can come in handy when you need to organize your images for a slideshow or presentation.

Of course, you can't pull images *from* your iPhoto library until you've put them *into* that library in the first place. So we'll start off by adding six images to iPhoto.

1   Open the Lesson_02 folder.

2   Select the Sustainability Photos folder.

The folder contains 13 photos for use in your presentation.

3 Drag the folder to the iPhoto icon in your Dock; then release the mouse button to begin importing the images.

iPhoto opens and becomes the active application.

When the spinning progress indicator stops, the photos are available in your iPhoto library. iPhoto '09 uses Events to organize your photos. The newly imported photos are associated with an Event called Sustainability Photos.

4 Click Events to view the Events in your library.

5 Locate the Event you just created, and double-click to open it.

Let's sort the photos so that they're in the right order for the presentation. The filenames contain numbers to indicate the order in which the photos will appear in your slideshow. The sorting order of your pictures in iPhoto affects their order in the Media Browser.

6 Choose View > Sort Photos > By Title.

The pictures are reordered to match their numbered filenames.

7   Close iPhoto.

Adding Photos to Slides

Your photos are ready to be added to the green building presentation you started in Lesson 1. The first step is to replace the placeholder images in your presentation with real photos.

1   In the Lesson_02 folder, open **02Presentation1_Stage1.key**.

> **NOTE** ▸ The file is set to 100% magnification. If your display is cutting off part of the image, click the View pop-up menu along the bottom edge of the window and choose a lower magnification percentage.

2   In the toolbar, click the Media button to open the Media Browser.

3   Click the Photos button in the Media Browser. From the list beneath the iPhoto icon, choose the Events category.

> **NOTE** ▸ If you don't see a list of items below the iPhoto icon, be sure to click the disclosure triangle next to the word *iPhoto* in the Media Browser. If you have several items in your library, you may need to scroll down to view them all.

The Media Browser displays a thumbnail for each Event.

4   Double-click the Sustainability Photos Event to open it.

5   In the slide navigator, click slide 1. The title slide is selected.

6   Drag **01 Exterior.jpg** onto the media placeholder in the slide canvas.

The photo is added to the page and replaces the existing image in the frame.

NOTE ▶ Most themes include slide masters with placeholder photos in their lay-outs. When you create your own slide layout, you can define any image or movie as a media placeholder. Select the object and choose Format > Advanced > Define as Media Placeholder.

7   Double-click the image so that you can edit it. Resize the image within its frame using the mask controls that appear when the image is selected. Drag the image within the picture frame to adjust its position to match the figure below.

Any portion of the image that extends beyond the mask will be hidden during your Keynote presentation.

NOTE ▶ You may want to zoom out from your slide to see the edges of your photo. To do so, choose a lower slide magnification (such as 50%) and enlarge your document window until you see the edges of the photo.

8   Switch to slide 3. In the Media Browser, find the photo **02 Grass.jpg**.

9   Drag the photo until the image is centered on the canvas. Yellow pop-up alignment guides will help you position the image.

You'll further modify this slide in a moment.

10   Select slide 4 and add the image **03 One-City Homes.jpg**.

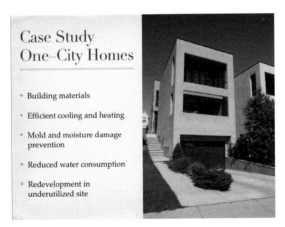

11   Select slide 5 and add the image **04 Bathroom.jpg**.

12   Select slide 6 and add the image **05 Mountain Villa.jpg**.

Let's skip slides 7 and 8 for now, as we'll customize these layouts later in this lesson.

TIP ▶ By default, Keynote automatically reduces the size of images to better fit your slides. If you want to change this behavior, choose Keynote > Preferences and deselect the "Reduce placed images to fit on slides" checkbox.

Enhancing Photos in Keynote

In a perfect world, photos would never need retouching. But most images can usually benefit from a little digital attention.

You can easily fix common image problems, such as exposure and color balance, within Keynote. The application includes a standard toolset for adjusting an image and improving its appearance. This toolset is similar to the image editing tools in iPhoto, but it's often more convenient to adjust your images within Keynote than to leave that application and open the image in iPhoto.

1   Select slide 9 and add the image **11 Forest.jpg**.

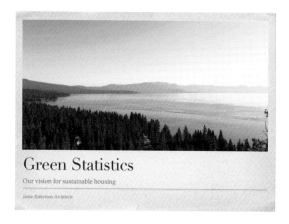

The image is overexposed and lacks detail.

2   Select the image and choose View > Show Adjust Image.

3   Click the Enhance button to improve the image's contrast.

The image looks better but is still overexposed. Keynote is trying to brighten the trees in the image, but the sky is now too bright. Sometimes it takes human intervention to fully fix your photos.

4   Experiment with adjusting the Saturation, Temperature, and Exposure sliders. Notice how the image changes as you drag the sliders. Finish your experiments with values close to these:

▶   Saturation—60

▶   Temperature—10

▶   Exposure— –15

The image is now better exposed and color balanced.

5   Examine the other photos in your presentation. Make any adjustments that you think are necessary. Close the Adjust Image window when you are finished.

Straightening a Photo

The photo you want to use for slide 10 is a little skewed in its frame. Because this is a construction photo, you'll want to level the walls with a little digital adjustment.

1   Select slide 10, which discusses 85% recycled construction materials.

2   Add **12 Frame.jpg** to the slide. The photo is crooked and needs to be straightened.

3   Choose View > Show Rulers to display the rulers.

4 Drag a guide from the ruler at the top of the photo to a location near the edge of the wall.

5 Double-click the image in the slide canvas to select it. Double-clicking an image lets you edit it within its mask.

6 Choose the Metrics inspector to access the image properties.

Determining the right adjustment in this case is a matter of trial and error. You can use alignment guides to assist you.

7 To adjust the image, you can click and turn the Rotate wheel, click the Angle steppers to incrementally increase and decrease the rotation, or enter a value directly in the field. In this case, an angle of 12 degrees effectively straightens the photo.

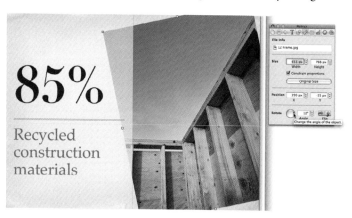

The image is now level. Although this was a minor adjustment, it was an important one. Crooked images can distract your audience and diminish the overall appearance of your presentation.

NOTE ▶ You could also open the image in iPhoto and use the Straighten tool to accomplish the same result and then bring the straightened image into Keynote.

8   If necessary, adjust the Scale slider to better fit the image on the slide.

9   Select slide 11, which discusses a 75% eco-friendly supply chain.

10   Add **13 Interior.jpg** to the slide.

11   Using the techniques you just learned, adjust the image to suit yourself and your slide. Use your creative judgment in positioning the photo.

12   Choose File > Save to save your work.

▶ Enhancing Photos in iPhoto

If you want to take your image adjusting a little further, iPhoto offers some image editing tools that you won't find in Keynote, Pages, or Numbers. Note that you need to make any iPhoto adjustments to an image before you bring a copy of an image from your iPhoto library into Keynote. Here's a look at a few useful adjustments you'll find in iPhoto.

1   Open iPhoto. In the Sustainability Photos Event, select **03 One-City Homes**.

2   At the bottom of the iPhoto window, click the Edit button.

iPhoto switches to Edit mode. This mode allows you to adjust the image as well as enhance or crop it.

3   Click the Enhance button to automatically adjust the photo's color and contrast. Notice that the image looks brighter and sharper after iPhoto has adjusted it.

Before   After

The photo looks better but still needs work.

continues on next page

▶ Enhancing Photos in iPhoto *(continued)*

4   Click the Adjust button to open the Adjust pane. Make the following changes to the image:

- ▶ Highlights—35 (increases detail by darkening highlights)

- ▶ Saturation—60 (increases the vibrancy of the colors)

- ▶ Temperature—6 (makes colors warmer)

- ▶ Definition—50 (improves details and local contrast in the image)

- ▶ Sharpness—30 (improves focus in the picture)

TIP ▶ When adjusting Definition and Sharpness, it's a good idea to view your image at 100 percent; this makes it easier to see subtle changes. Press the 1 key to zoom in on the image and view a higher degree of detail. When you're finished making changes, press the 0 key to zoom out and view the whole picture.

5   If you want additional practice, you can use iPhoto to improve the overall look of the remaining images.

6   When you're finished, click Done to accept the changes to the most recently edited photo. Close iPhoto. You can now bring your corrected images into Keynote, whenever you like.

Customizing Photo Layouts

So far, you've used only a single photo on a slide, but Keynote is excellent at handling multiple photos on a single slide.

Let's create two slides that contain a total of five photos.

1   In the slide navigator, click slide 7 to select it.

Let's select one additional slide and change both of their layouts at the same time.

► **Improving the Readability of Your Slideshow**

Here are a few tips for using images and textures in your slides, but still making the words easy to read.

► **Watch text over images**—It has become quite popular to use a photograph as a background for slides. The key to pulling this off successfully is to make sure that there is a high level of contrast between your image or texture and your text. Don't put black text on a brown cow; don't put white text on a yellow chicken.

► **Tone down background textures**—If you intend to use a texture of any kind for a slide or shape background, make sure that the color or contrast does not compete with the text or images on your page.

► **Spread out your content**—When it's important to have a large amount of text in a presentation, it's better to spread the text out over several slides than to cram it all into one slide.

► **Use text alignment**—Hands down, left-aligned text is the easiest to read. However, when using less text with larger typefaces, alignment is less of an issue.

► **Create a hierarchy**—Take a step back and look at your slide. Do any of the graphical elements compete with one another or overwhelm the type? It's important to visually guide your audience through your layout by attributing a hierarchy of importance using size, color, and contrast.

► **Group and align**—Avoid randomly placing items on a slide. If you have a series of photos, try aligning them consistently with each other as well as distributing them evenly, vertically or horizontally, across the slide.

2   Shift-click the thumbnail for slide 8.

Slides 7 and 8 are both selected.

3   Click the Masters button and choose Photo – 2 Up.

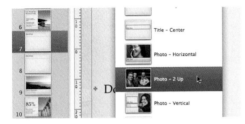

The layouts of both slides change.

4   Drag **06 Bathroom.jpg** to the left placeholder on slide 7.

5   Drag **07 Porch.jpg** to the right placeholder on slide 7.

6   Adjust the images to closely match the following figure.

You have successfully updated slide 7. You have three photos left to use, and two of them have definite landscape aspect ratios (meaning that the photos are very horizontal in their composition). Let's customize the slide 8 layout to accommodate them.

7 In the slide navigator, select slide 8.

You can adjust the mask to orient the photo horizontally.

8 Select the right media placeholder and click the Edit Mask button.

9 Slowly drag the bottom edge of the mask upward until the yellow alignment guides indicate that you have reached the halfway point. The approximate height of the box will be 345 pixels.

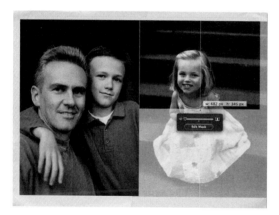

You now can duplicate the box directly below this image to fill out the slide.

10 Press Return to apply the mask.

11 Option-drag the smaller masked media placeholder downward.

Keynote creates a copy of the photo.

12 Align the top of the duplicated photo with the bottom edge of the larger photo. Use the yellow alignment guides for assistance.

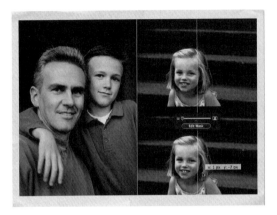

13 Replace the media placeholders using the remaining three images (**08 Wood.jpg**, **09 Tub.jpg**, **10 Stone.jpg**).

14 Using the figure below for guidance, adjust the images within their masks using the techniques you've learned.

15 Choose File > Save to save your work.

Making Part of a Photo Transparent

Sometimes your photos include undesired elements or areas (such as in the grass photo on slide 3). The Instant Alpha tool allows you to make parts of an image transparent, effectively removing them.

1 In the slide navigator, select slide 3.

2 Select the photo of the grass.

3 In the toolbar, click Alpha, or choose Format > Instant Alpha.

4 Drag slowly over the white area near the top of the photo, which is the area that you want to make transparent.

TIP ▶ For best results, try to remove areas with clear boundaries. The areas removed must be contiguous (touching).

As you drag, the selected area grows to add areas of similar colors. You can control how much is selected by dragging over more or less of the area.

The command worked well but didn't get the noncontiguous areas of color in the image. The Instant Alpha command offers an important modifier key to solve this very problem.

5   Option-click to select another area of white.

The grass photo looks good, but it could be better integrated into the layout of the slide so as not to obscure the bulleted text.

6   Choose Arrange > Send to Back to place the photo behind the text layer.

Let's blend the photo into the background a little more.

7   In the format bar, click the Opacity pop-up menu and lower the grass opacity to 40%.

The grass looks better, but it could be repositioned on the slide for a cleaner layout.

8   Press Shift–Down Arrow ten times to move the image down 100 pixels.

The layout is almost complete; let's adjust the text box to finish it.

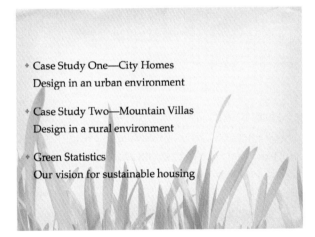

9   Select the text box that contains the three bullets.

10   Open the Text inspector.

11   Click the Align Top button to align the text with the top of the text box.

12   Click the Bold button to make the selected text bold.

13 Change the text size to 48 pt to make it easier to read.

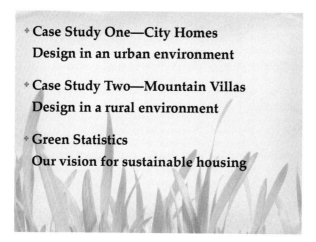

14 Choose File > Save to save your work.

You can compare your results with the version in **02Presentation1_Stage2.key**.

Adding Hyperlinks and Navigation

Keynote lets you add controls to navigate between slides. By adding hyperlinks, you can create a link to a specific part of your presentation. Additionally, you can embed links to point to webpages that you may want to access during a presentation. Let's explore both techniques.

Adding a Menu

As your presentation begins, a title slide displays its title and introduces you as the presenter. The second slide includes important reasons why building green is so important. The third slide identifies the three sections of your presentation.

These slides represent a perfect opportunity to use hyperlinks. By linking each bullet to its respective section, you can have greater flexibility as a presenter. The links will take you and your presentation to whichever of the three sections seems most relevant to your current audience.

NOTE ▶ Hyperlinks that you add to a presentation don't have to be used. If you do not click a hyperlink, slides will naturally advance to the next slide in the presentation.

1   In the slide navigator, select slide 3.

2   Select the first bullet group.

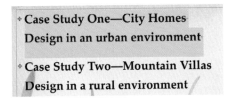

3   In the Hyperlink inspector, select the "Enable as a hyperlink" checkbox.

You can now identify and set up your link destination.

4   From the Link To pop-up menu, choose Slide. Then select the Slide button and set its pop-up menu to 4.

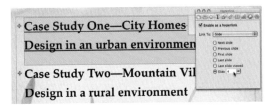

You have linked the first bullet to the first section of your presentation (slide 4).

NOTE ▶ If you reorder slides or add more slides to your presentation, Keynote will make sure that the links correctly reference your original destination slide.

5   Select the second bullet and link to slide 6.

6   Select the third bullet and link to slide 9.

Let's remove the underlined hyperlink formatting so that the slide's appearance is more subtle.

7   Choose Edit > Select All to highlight all the text in the box.

8   In the format bar, click the Underline button.

The underline is removed.

You now have links that jump from the main menu page to each section of your presentation. This is useful when you want to change the order of your presentation based on audience input. Links can also be useful at the end of a presentation to provide a way to quickly return to your opening.

1   Select slide 13.

2   Select the rounded blue rectangle.

3   In the Hyperlink inspector, link back to slide 3.

A small hyperlink icon is added to the rounded rectangle. This icon will not display while you are giving the slideshow.

You have just created an easy way to return to the opening menu and select a case study. This is extremely useful if your audience has questions at the end of your presentation.

4   Choose File > Save to save your work.

Embedding a Webpage

Sometimes, you will want to place a snapshot of a webpage into your presentation, either as a link to the actual webpage or as a still image. Your Mac has all the tools it needs to capture snapshots of webpages (or any computer screen).

Let's embed a webpage image and attach a link so that you can visit it during the presentation.

1   In the slide navigator, select slide 12.

2   Click the New button to add a slide to your presentation.

3   Click the Masters button and choose Blank.

The canvas is ready, so let's capture a screen shot of the webpage.

4   Open Safari by clicking its icon in your Dock.

Let's visit the Green Building page for the U.S. Environmental Protection Agency. This page contains relevant information about our presentation's topic.

5   In the address bar in Safari, enter *http://www.epa.gov/greenbuilding* and press Return.

When the page loads, you'll want to capture an image of it.

6   Press Shift-Command-4 to select an area to capture.

By default, this mode allows you to drag to define a capture area. It also can be modified to capture an individual window.

7   Press the Spacebar.

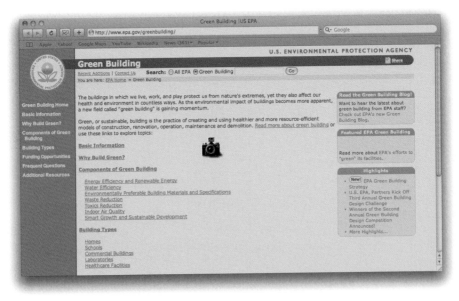

The pointer turns into a camera icon, and you are ready to capture the Safari window as an image file and save it to your hard drive or copy it to the Clipboard.

8 To copy an image of the page to your Clipboard, Control-click the active Safari window.

> **NOTE ▸** To save an image to your Desktop, click the Safari window. (Do not hold down Control.)

9 Return to Keynote and choose Edit > Paste.

The screen shot is pasted onto your slide.

10 Size the image to a width of 1000 pixels; then center it on your canvas.

11 With the image selected, open the Hyperlink inspector.

12 Select the "Enable as a hyperlink" checkbox.

13 From the Link To pop-up menu, choose Webpage.

14 In the URL field, enter *http://www.epa.gov/greenbuilding* and press Return.

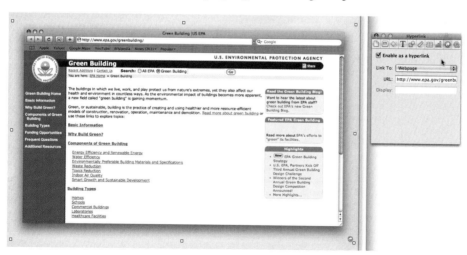

You have successfully added a screen shot to a slide and linked it to the original webpage.

15 Choose File > Save to save your work.

Adding a Chart

In addition to enabling you to add photos and images to a presentation, Keynote offers rich support for easy-to-read charts. A chart is a visually effective way to show trends or to display relationships between sets of data. Keynote includes 19 chart types.

> **NOTE** ▶ You'll further explore charting in iWork in Lesson 5, "Importing from PowerPoint and Working with Charts" and Lesson 16, "Advanced Charting Operations."

Let's add a basic chart to show some of the data from the table on slide 12.

1   In the navigator, select slide 12.

Let's show the results for the year 2010 as a column chart.

2   Press Command-D to duplicate the slide.

A copy of the slide is added to your presentation. Let's copy the data to the Clipboard to use for the chart.

3   Select the table on slide 13 and choose Edit > Cut.

The data is removed from the page and stored on the Clipboard.

4   In the toolbar, click the Charts button and choose the 3D Column Chart.

When you create a chart, Keynote fills it with placeholder data in the Chart Data Editor. Let's replace this with the data that you copied to your Clipboard. First, remove the placeholder data.

5   Click the first column (2007); then Shift-click the last column (2010). All four columns are selected and highlighted in blue.

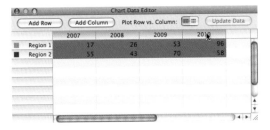

6   Press Delete to remove all but the first row of data.

Let's add the data currently on your Clipboard.

7   Choose Edit > Paste to insert the information from the table.

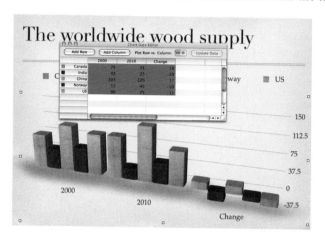

Keynote draws the chart, but it has too much information and might be unclear. Let's refine what is shown.

8   Click the column for the year 2000 and press Delete. Do the same for the Change column. Close the Chart Data Editor.

The chart updates and now shows just the 2010 data for a one-year comparison between countries. Let's format the chart to improve its readability and to match the subject of your presentation.

9   Select the Chart inspector.

Keynote lets you change the shapes and colors of columns. Let's make them look more like wooden pillars.

10   Click the Bar Shape pop-up menu and choose Cylinder.

11 Increase the setting in the "Gap between bars" field to 25% to provide a little separation between the cylinders.

12 Click the Chart Colors button, and from the pop-up menus, choose the 3D Texture Fills fill type and the Wood fill collection .

13 Click Apply All to update the chart.

The chart now matches the subject matter of the presentation. Let's change its viewing angle slightly for a more distinctive appearance.

14 Select the Axis tab of the Chart inspector. In the Max field, enter *125*, and in the Steps field, enter *5*.

The y-axis is now numbered 0 to 125 with gridlines every 25 units.

15 Select the chart on the canvas, then drag the four-way arrowhead to experiment with different viewing angles.

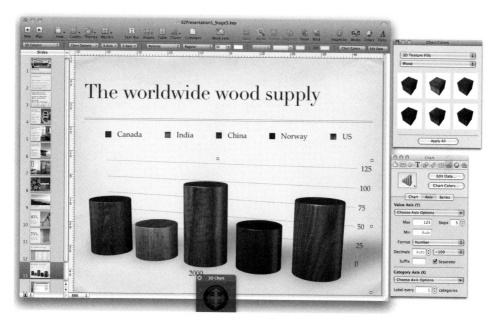

16 Choose File > Save to save your work.

Adding Audio

Keynote presentations support an *audio bed*—music or narration that plays along with your slideshow. You may want to add narration or sound effects to individual slides if you are preparing a kiosk or developing a self-running presentation(you'll learn more about this in Lesson 6). You also can add *underscore* music that plays throughout your slideshow.

> **NOTE ▶** Some audio files are protected by copyright law. Be sure to secure the necessary rights for any audio file you use in a presentation. If you use audio purchased from the iTunes Store, remember that the playback computer must be authorized for the files.

1 Open the Document inspector and click Audio.

2   Switch to the Finder. Open the Lesson_02 folder and locate **Sustainability.mp3**.

> **TIP** ▶ Keynote opens all QuickTime-compatible file types, including MP3, AIFF, and AAC.

3   Drag the **Sustainability.mp3** audio file from the Finder into the Audio well.

> **NOTE** ▶ The current Soundtrack playback option is Play Once, which means that the song will play through one time and stop. This works well for playing background music to set the mood at the start of your presentation. If you want the audio file to play continuously throughout the presentation, choose Loop in the Soundtrack pop-up menu. If needed, you can adjust the volume of the song with the Volume slider.

4   Choose File > Save to save your work.

You can compare your results with the file **02Presentation1_Stage3.key**.

Adding a Global Transition

Now that we've populated the slideshow, let's add a simple transition between the slides for a little more continuity and smoothness. For this presentation, we'll add the same dissolve transition to every slide. In the next lesson, we'll explore transitions in depth.

1   Click slide 1 in the Navigator.

2   Choose Edit > Select All to choose all your slides.

3   Open the Slide inspector and click Transition.

4   Click the Effect pop-up menu and choose Dissolve.

The default values for the effect is fine.

5   Click the Play button in the toolbar to view the slideshow.

6   Press the Spacebar to navigate your slides.

7   When finished, press Escape to exit the slideshow.

8   Choose File > Save to save your work.

Reducing the Presentation File Size

As you add images and sounds to a presentation, its file size will increase. Larger Keynote files use more storage space on your hard drive; they also take longer to load (when you open the file and when animations are cached).

One inadvisable but common practice is to add large images to a presentation and then eventually scale them down or mask unwanted portions of them. While the images appear smaller in the presentation, they actually retain their full file size. Keynote can help keep your presentation document size at a minimum by saving only the smaller versions of the images in your presentation.

NOTE ▶ There are several good reasons to shrink your files, but chief among them is that smaller files are easier to transport or email. Keep in mind, though, that reducing images is something you do at the very end of the process. Once you reduce the size of a masked or shrunken image file, you won't be able to restore it to its original size. If you want to resize the image or restore masked portions, you will have to replace the original image files in the document.

1   Before you reduce the size of an image or media file, save your document. Choose File > Save to write the latest version to your hard drive, or choose File > Save As to save a copy of the presentation.

There are three methods for reducing file size:

▶   To reduce the file size of an individual image that you've masked or scaled down, select the image and choose Format > Image > Reduce Image File Size. You can also Control-click (or right-click) the image and choose Reduce Image File Size from the shortcut menu.

▶   To reduce the size of an individual media file, select a sound or movie file. If you've set the Start and Stop sliders in the QuickTime inspector to trim the media, you can discard those unused portions by choosing Format > Image > Reduce Media File Size.

▶   To reduce the sizes of all masked and resized images and all trimmed video and audio files, choose File > Reduce File Size.

2   For this exercise, we'll choose File > Reduce File Size.

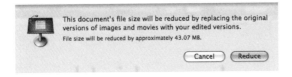

Keynote calculates the amount of storage space that will be saved.

3   Click Reduce to process the media in the slideshow. A warning dialog will open.

The dialog usually states that some template images or files are used at their original sizes and were not further optimized. In this case, that will not significantly affect the look or size of the document.

4   Click Clear All and close the Document Warnings.

NOTE ▶ Some image and movie file formats may not be reducible with this method.

Saving Media with Your Presentation

Keynote (by default) copies all of the media used in your presentation into the Keynote file, which simplifies the process of transporting your presentation to another Mac. So, when you take your Keynote presentation on the road, you have to take only one Keynote file.

Before we save our media, let's verify that all of the elements made it into your presentation file.

NOTE ▶ Fonts are not saved in a Keynote document. Fonts used in a presentation must also be installed on the computer running the presentation. If you use fonts that are not installed with iWork '09 or that are not Mac OS X system fonts, be sure to install the necessary fonts on the presentation computer.

1   In Keynote, choose Keynote > Preferences.

2   Click the General button, and in the Saving area, make sure that checkboxes are selected as shown in the following figure.

The Saving area includes a number of options:

▶   **Back up previous version**—A backup file is created each time you save. The backup is stored in the same folder as the original, which is helpful in the rare event that your project file is corrupted. It can also come in handy if you close your document and make some changes, but then have second thoughts and want to revert.

▶   **Include preview in document by default**—Allows you to use the Quick Look feature of your Mac running OS X 10.5 Leopard. This lets you browse a high-quality preview of your presentation without opening it in Keynote.

▶   **Copy audio and movies into document**—All media files are stored within the document and not linked. This may increase the file size but makes it easier to transport a presentation and guard against accidental deletions.

▶   **Copy theme images into document**—All template images are saved in the Keynote document, so the file has no dependent links for backgrounds or custom fills.

3   Close the Preferences window to store your preferences.

TIP If you ever need to access an element from a presentation and don't have access to the original files, you can borrow it from the Keynote document. You'll need to first save a copy of the presentation as an iWork '08 document with the File > Save As command. Then Control-click (or right-click) the Keynote document and choose Show Package Contents from the shortcut menu. The folder contains all the elements of your presentation. You can Option-drag any of the elements to a new folder to copy them. Be careful when modifying your presentation. If you remove the wrong element, you could damage the file. Be sure to use the Save As command to create a new copy of your presentation before modifying it.

Lesson Review

1. What engine drives media playback in Keynote?

2. Which window allows you easy access to movies, audio files, and photos?

3. Which command in both iPhoto and Keynote allows you to fix common image problems with one click?

4. Where do you modify the data for a chart?

5. How can you reduce the file size for all scaled images in a presentation?

Answers

1. QuickTime allows you to play back a wide variety of image types, audio formats, and movie files.

2. The Media Browser gives you quick access to the content you created using the iLife and Aperture applications.

3. Clicking the Enhance button will automatically fix brightness and contrast issues in most images.

4. Adjust the data in the Chart Data Editor.

5. Choose File > Reduce File Size to have Keynote optimize scaled, masked, or trimmed media in your presentation.

3

Lesson Files
Lessons > Lesson_03 > 03_Superbike_Start.key
Lessons > Lesson_03 > 03_Superbike_End.key
Lessons > Lesson_03 > Apparel_Photos
Lessons > Lesson_03 > Ducati_Evolution.mov

Time
This lesson takes approximately 75 minutes to complete.

Goals
Create builds to reveal text or objects on a slide
Create interleaved builds to reveal slide elements concurrently
Create a Smart Build to add animation to a slide
Add transitions between slides
Configure preferences for smooth playback of a presentation
Run a presentation

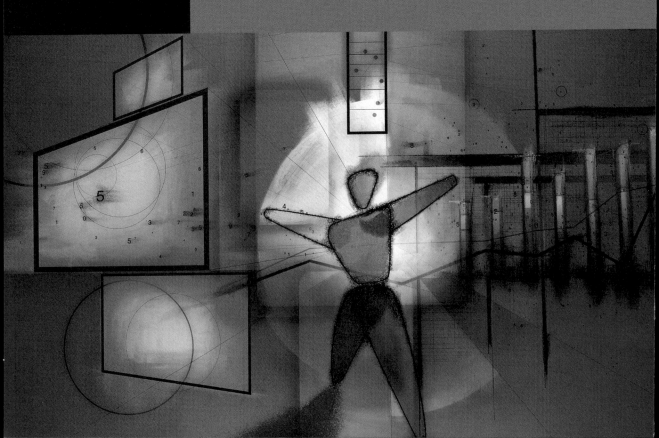

Lesson 3
Adding Video and Animation

Now that we've built a presentation, the next step is to add some motion—namely, video and animation. Adding movement to your slides doesn't just keep your audience's attention, it transforms a static presentation into a compelling and persuasive display piece.

Keynote offers a robust engine for playing video within slides. And it lets you create several types of slide animation, including *builds*—elements that animate one at a time onto a slide—and cool *transitions* between slides that go far beyond the simple transition we just used in Lesson 2.

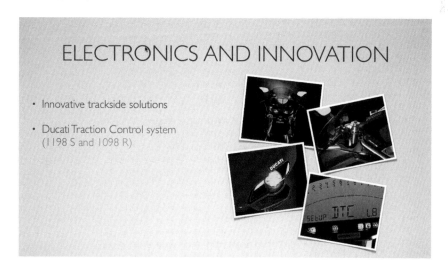

In this lesson, you'll enhance a marketing presentation for Ducati, an Italian motorcycle manufacturer, by adding video, builds, and transitions. The subject matter is dynamic, and your slides should be, too. So let's add some motion to accelerate the show!

Creating Builds to Reveal Text

The most common style of animation on a slide is a *build*, an animation that sequentially reveals the slide content.

When used appropriately, builds can focus your audience's attention on the current topic. Objects that zoom into place or change position when selected attract much more attention than items that sit motionless on a slide.

Builds are often used to reveal lines of text as you click. Some effects animate the entire text box at once; others break up the text by word or character before animating. All text animation is controlled within the Inspector window.

In this exercise, we'll animate a set of bullet points so they are revealed one at a time. This helps control the flow of information by preventing your audience from reading ahead. It also adds visual pop to reinforce each bullet point.

1   From the Lesson_03 folder, open the file **03_Superbike_Start.key**.

   NOTE ▶ Most of content has already been added to these slides for your convenience, but nothing is animated yet.

2   In the slide navigator, click slide 7 to select it.

   This slide contains a text box with several bullets; let's animate those bullet points to reveal them one at a time.

3   Open the Build inspector.

4 Click the box of bulleted text to select it.

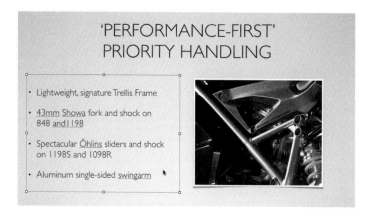

5 In the Build inspector, click Build In. Then configure the following options:

▶ Effect—Dissolve by Word

▶ Direction—Forward

▶ Add slow fade

▶ Delivery—By Bullet

▶ Duration—1.00 s

TIP To preview the animation, click the thumbnail image in the inspector. As you change each option, the thumbnail will reflect the new animation.

Let's adjust the timing so that the first bullet automatically animates when the slide initially appears.

6 Near the bottom of the Build inspector, click the More Options button. The Build Order drawer opens. You'll adjust the animation timings here.

7 Click object 1, First Bullet.

8 Set the Start Build pop-up menu to "Automatically after transition." The animation will now occur immediately after the slide appears.

9 In the Build inspector, click the thumbnail and preview the build animation.

This style of animation is clean and professional; let's copy and apply it to the bullet points in your next two slides.

10 Choose Format > Copy Animation to copy the animation in the selected text box.

11 Switch to slide 8 and select the bulleted text box.

12 Choose Format > Paste Animation to add the same animation to the bulleted text.

13 Repeat steps 11 and 12 for slide 9.

14 Press Command-S to save your work. You now have animated bullet points on your slides.

Creating a Build to Reveal a Table

Beyond text, Keynote offers flexible build options for other elements in your presentation. For example, applying a build to a table can help make your data more accessible for an audience. By revealing table information in stages—as you previously did with slide bullet points—you can guide viewers through your data.

1   In the slide navigator, click slide 11 to select it.

   This slide contains a table.

2   On the slide canvas, click the table.

3   In the Build inspector, click Build In. Then choose the following options:

   ▶   Effect—Dissolve

   ▶   Delivery—By Row (to reveal information one row at a time)

   ▶   Duration—1.00 s

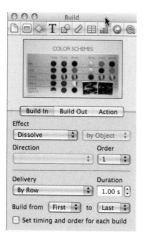

TIP   To animate objects entering the slide, choose Build In. To animate objects leaving the screen, choose Build Out.

Let's animate both of the photos in the lower right corner so they zoom into place.

4   Click the first photo; then Command-click the second to select both.

5   In the Build inspector, choose the following options:

▶   Effect—Scale

▶   Direction—Down

▶   Duration—1.00 s

6   Choose File > Save to save your work.

Creating Interleaved Builds

The photos in your slide animate nicely, but they do so after the text has appeared, which diminishes the slide's impact. The slide would be clearer if the text and related photo animations occurred at the same time. In Keynote, you can interleave animation elements, so that multiple events take place concurrently.

In this exercise, you have a table about color choices for motorcycles and two photos that relate to the contents of that table. By creating an interleaved build, you can reveal a bullet point and animate your photos at the same time.

1   Verify that slide 11 is selected.

2   Open the Build inspector, if necessary.

NOTE ▶ The Build Order drawer should still be visible. If it is not, click the More Options button.

To create the interleaved builds, you'll need precise control over each individual build.

3   In the Build inspector locate the Build Order drawer and select object 1, which is Table First Row.

4   Select the box next to "Set timing and order for each build."

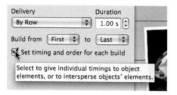

You can now precisely control every build for the text box. Let's integrate the photo animation so that it occurs during the text animation.

5   At the lower right of the slide, select the photo of two motorcycles. Its name is high-lighted in the Build Order drawer.

6   Drag item 8 so that it is placed immediately after item 5 (Row 5).

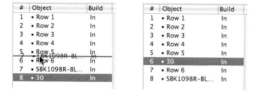

The photo now animates after row 5 of the table and before row 6.

7   From the Start Build pop-up menu, choose "Automatically with build 5."

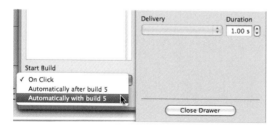

The two objects will appear at the same time. If you want a small delay to occur between the objects' appearances, specify the length of time in the Delay field. The two builds must occur consecutively in the Build Order list.

8   In the Build Order drawer, select object 8. In the Start Build pop-up menu, choose "Automatically with build 7."

> NOTE ▶ The On Click option in the Start Build menu tells Keynote to initiate the build when you advance the presentation. Choosing "Automatically after build" initiates the build after the previous build). You can also specify a delay for these options.

9   Choose File > Save to save your work.

Revealing Graphics and Charts

You can use builds for much more than text or tables. Let's take a moment to apply builds to several other types of graphic objects.

1   In the slide navigator, click slide 1 to select it.

This slide contains a Ducati logo. Let's reveal it in a dramatic fashion at the start of the presentation.

2   On the canvas, select the logo.

3   In the Build inspector, choose Build In. Then set the following options to make the slide appear as it does in the following figure:

   ▶   Effect—Lens Flare

   ▶   Direction—Left to Right

   ▶   Duration—2.00 s

4   Click the thumbnail to preview the animation.

Charts can be animated like any other element in Keynote. For example, you can make charts appear or disappear one bar or wedge at a time. Additionally, six special builds specifically designed for 3D charts are quite impressive. Preview the builds in slides 17 and 18 to see two of these chart animations at work.

NOTE ▶ You'll work with charts more extensively in Lesson 5.

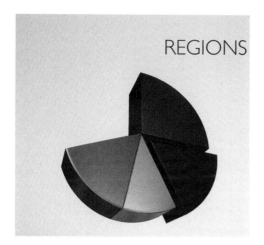

Rotate & Grow

Z Axis

Creating a Smart Build

If you want to show several images within one slide—a sort of "in-slide slideshow"—that's the time to use Smart Builds, which let you animate multiple images with drag-and-drop ease. It's a huge space-saver, because you can show multiple images without having to add a slide for each image.

In this exercise, we'll add a Smart Build to one of the slides to show off several items of motorcycle clothing and gear.

1   In the slide navigator, select slide 13.

2   Choose Insert > Smart Build > Revolve.

An empty Smart Build is added to the slide, and the Smart Build editor opens to control the effect. Let's scale up the Smart Build.

3   Option-drag a selection handle and resize the Smart Build to 1280 px (pixels) wide (the width of the slide) by 480 px tall.

The images will display larger. Let's add some photos.

4   Switch to the Finder and navigate to the Lesson_03 > Apparel_Photos folder.

5   Select all of the photos in the folder.

6   Drag the seven photos onto the Smart Build to add them to the build.

The seven photos become an animated presentation within the slide. If you'd like to preview the effect, click the thumbnail image in the Build inspector. While in the inspector, you can modify the Smart Build animation.

7   In the Build inspector, click Action and change Duration to 1.50 s.

8   From the Direction pop-up menu, choose Alternating Horizontal to add a little variety to the animation.

TIP You can change the order in which your images appear by dragging them left or right in the Smart Build editor. If you want to remove an image from the Smart Build, select it and press Delete.

9   Choose File > Save to save your work.

To check your work, you can compare your presentation with the file **03_Superbike_ Stage2.key** in the Lesson_03 folder.

TIP You can easily change the style of the Smart Build animation by choosing another animation type in the Build inspector.

Creating Custom Animations

So far, we've used animated builds that are included with Keynote. These preset options are easy to use and create compelling animation.

But if you want more control, Keynote also lets you make custom animations by creating action builds. These let you take precise control over the way objects rotate, change opacity, move position, and scale in size. Let's create a custom action build to reveal the logo on the final slide.

1   In the slide navigator, click slide 20 to select it.

This slide contains a Ducati logo and a motorcycle. Let's animate the motorcycle "changing lanes" to reveal the logo, then have it drive off the screen. The logo already has a vertical wipe applied to it, so let's animate the motorcycle moving from left to right to coincide with that wipe.

2 On the canvas, select the motorcycle.

3 Open the Build inspector.

4 In the Build inspector, click Action.

5 From the Effect pop-up menu, choose Move.

On the slide canvas, Keynote shows a red line connected to a "ghosted" image of the object. This transparent image shows the object's destination.

6 Drag the ghosted object to the right until it just covers part of the letter *E* in the logo. You can use the following figure for guidance.

As the bike moves, let's bank it in the direction in which it's moving (just as a real rider would steer the bike).

7 Move the pointer to the upper left selection handle. Hold down the Command key and the pointer turns into a curved-arrow cursor to indicate that you can rotate the object.

8 Drag the cursor to rotate the bike to approximately 12 degrees using the following figure as a guide.

The ghosted image updates to show its final position.

9 In the inspector, click the thumbnail image to see the animation.

It looks good, but let's set the two animations so that they start at the same time.

10 In the Build inspector, click the Start Build pop-up menu and choose "Automatically with prior build."

11 In the inspector, click the thumbnail image to see the animation.

The two animations start at the same time but have different durations. The wipe on the logo is 1.50 s, while the action build is only 1.00 s.

12 Change the Duration for the action build to 1.60 s and preview the animation.

You're just about there. By moving the bike a little more slowly, you make sure that it doesn't drift ahead of the logo wipe. Let's have the motorcycle get larger so that it appears to approach us and drive off the screen. First, you'll want to see some additional empty area around the canvas.

13 Resize your canvas window so that it fills your entire computer screen.

14 From the View pop-up menu, choose 75% or 50% magnification so that you can see some of the empty area around the slide canvas. Now you're ready to add another move.

15 Click the + (plus sign) in the red diamond to add another action build. Press Tab to switch to the new action build.

16 Drag the corner selection handle to make the bike bigger. A height of 1000 px should work well.

17 Command-drag to rotate the bike so that it leans slightly back toward the left.

18 Drag the bike so that it moves completely off the canvas.

19 In the Build Order list, select only object 4 and choose "Automatically after build 3."

20 In the inspector, click the thumbnail image to see the animation.

Adding Sound to a Build

Your action build looks great, but you can also make it sound great. Let's add some audio to amp up your big finish.

You may have noticed a speaker icon on the page. This is a sound file that was added to the canvas by the original slide designer.

MORE INFO ▶ This sound effect was made using GarageBand. To read more about GarageBand, see *Apple Training Series: iLife '09* (Peachpit Press, 2009).

1   Click the speaker icon to select it.

Let's configure the sound so that it will start with a mouse click.

2   In the Build inspector, choose Build In. Then, from the Effect pop-up menu, choose Start Audio.

Now, let's choose when the audio will play.

3   Drag the Cycle Pull object to the top of the Build Order list.

4   Click the second item (Group) and from Start Build pop-up menu, choose "Automatically with build 1."

5   In the toolbar, click the Play button.

Keynote plays your presentation at the current slide.

6   Press the Spacebar to trigger all of the animation.

You should hear the roar of the engine and see the motorcycle animate across the screen, then pull away and out of the slide.

7   Press Esc to exit full-screen playback.

8   Choose File > Save to save your work.

Creating Transitions Between Slides

Up to this point, we've used builds to control animation on a slide. Keynote offers another category of animations called *transitions*, such as the simple transition we added between our slides in Lesson 2.

Transitions are meant to signify a change in topic for your audience. Although Keynote offers several transition options, good design practices call for using the right transition mix in a presentation. Learning how (and when) to add transitions can liven up and clarify your presentation.

Keynote includes some great 2D and 3D effects that can add cinema-quality pizzazz to your presentation. Keynote '09 also adds new transition options that work with the text or objects on two slides.

It's easiest to set transitions when you can see all your slides, so we'll start by switching to light table view.

1   In the toolbar, click the View button and choose Light Table.

2   In the lower left corner of the light table view, click the Thumbnail button and choose Medium or Large (whichever allows you to see all the slides at once).

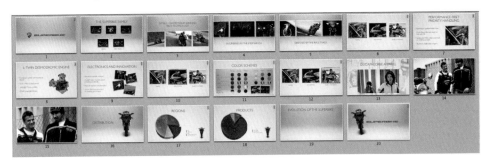

NOTE ▶ You can add transitions by using any view. However, light table view is an easy way to view your presentation globally.

Creating 2D and 3D Transitions

The most common transitions you'll use on slides are the 2D and 3D effects. These are used to move one slide off the screen as the next slide moves on.

> **NOTE** ▶ 3D transitions may require that your Mac have an advanced graphics card to play smoothly.

1 In the slide navigator, select slide 7.

2 Select the Slide inspector and click Transition. Then set the following options:

  ▶ Effect—3D Effects > Swap

  ▶ Duration—1.50 s

  ▶ Direction—Right

> **NOTE** ▶ The appearance of a triangle in the lower right corner of a slide's thumbnail in the slide navigator indicates that you have added a transition to that slide.

Let's add a lightly modified version of the same transition to slide 8.

3 In the slide navigator, select slide 8.

4 In the Slide inspector, set the following options:

  ▶ Effect—3D Effects > Swap

  ▶ Duration—1.50 s

  ▶ Direction—Left

You can simultaneously add transitions to multiple slides to speed up the process.

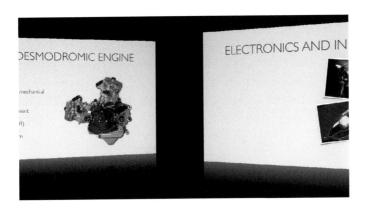

5   In the slide navigator, select slide 13. Command-click slides 15, 18, and 19 to select all four slides.

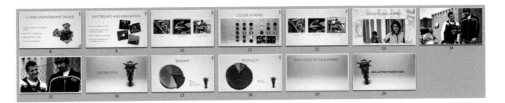

Slides 13, 15, 18, and 19 are highlighted in yellow to show that they are selected.

6   In the Slide inspector, set the following options:

▶   Effect—3D Effects > Reflection

▶   Duration—2.00 s

▶   Direction—Left

TIP▶   To keep the build and transition choices from becoming unwieldy, Keynote '09 has pruned some lesser-used effects from its interface. These effects are still available, however, if you'd like to use them. Choose Keynote > Preferences and select the "Include obsolete animations in choices" checkbox.

7   Choose File > Save to save your work.

Now let's explore some transition types that create animation based on slide content.

Creating Object Effects Transitions

If your slides have a lot of content, such as photos or text, Keynote offers a specialized transition category called *object effects*. These effects are best used between two slides with very prominent graphic elements. When used at the right time, object effects provide visually dramatic 3D transitions that can capture the audience's attention.

Let's try out a few object effects transitions.

1   In the slide navigator, select slide 1.

2   In the Slide inspector, click Transition. Then choose the following options:

   ▶   Effect—Object Effects > Object Zoom

   ▶   Duration—1.50 s

3   In the inspector, click the thumbnail image to see the animation.

   Each individual object between the two slides zooms independently as part of the transition. This is different from the 3D Effect Zoom, which zooms the entire slide at once.

4   In the slide navigator, select slide 2.

5   In the Slide inspector, click Transition. Then choose the following options:

   ▶   Effect—Object Effects > Perspective

   ▶   Duration—1.50 s

The objects on the slide rotate and move in 3D space.

6   In the slide navigator, select slide 3.

7   In the Slide inspector, click Transition. Then choose the following options:

▶   Effect—Object Effects > Object Push

▶   Duration—1.50 s

▶   Direction—Right to Left

8   In the slide navigator, select slide 4.

9   In the Slide inspector, click Transition. Then choose the following options:

▶   Effect—Object Effects > Object Push

▶   Duration—1.50 s

▶   Direction—Left to Right

The individual objects are pushed between slides during the transition.

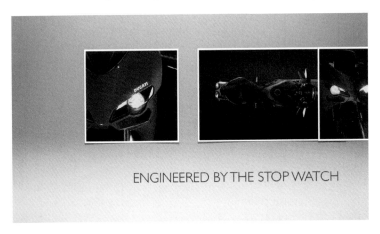

There's one object effects transition that you haven't tried; let's apply it to a few other slides in the presentation.

10 In the slide navigator, select slide 6, and then Command-click slides 10 and 12.

> **NOTE** ▶ You've selected the section-title graphics that are similar in style. Applying matched transitions to similar slides helps make a slideshow feel more cohesive.

11 In the Slide inspector, choose the following options:

▶ Effect—Object Effects > Revolve

▶ Duration—1.50 s

▶ Direction—Simultaneous

12 In the inspector, click the thumbnail image to see the animation.

Let's apply another transition effect to more slides that are similarly designed.

13 In the slide navigator, select slide 5, and then Command-click slides 9 and 11.

14 In the Slide inspector, choose the following options:

▶ Effect—Object Effects > Perspective

▶ Duration—1.50 s

15 Click the thumbnail image in the inspector to see the animation.

16 Choose File > Save to save your work.

Using Text Effects Transitions

The text effects transitions in Keynote are similar to object effects in that they create animation between two slides based upon their contents. Text effects work best when used for transitioning between two slides with prominent text.

Let's give text effects a try between two slides with similar layouts.

1 In the slide navigator, select slide 17.

2   In the Slide inspector, choose the following options:

▶   Effect—Text Effects > Anagram

▶   Duration—2.00 s

▶   Direction—Straight Across

NOTE ▶ The text effects work best when text has the same position, font, and size on both slides.

3   Click OK to accept the instructions for using the Anagram transition.

The Anagram transition retains letters that are identical between the two slides and moves them into their new positions while dissolving in the new letters and elements.

TIP ▶ The other text effects transitions work well when you have just a few large words on the canvas.

Using Magic Move

The Magic Move transition is a unique animation tool that essentially creates an automated transition between objects that appear on two consecutive slides. You can move, scale, rotate, and fade the object with Magic Move.

NOTE ▶ The Magic Move transition works only when you use an identical image, shape, or text box at a different location or size on the second slide. Magic Move will not work with tables, charts, or movies.

The easiest way to understand the Magic Move effect is to try it out. Slide pairs 14 and 15, and 16 and 17, are ready for the Magic Move transition.

1   In the slide navigator, select slide 14 and double-click to edit it.

   This slide contains a photo in the apparel section of the presentation. Let's perform a slow zoom and pan on the photo. The photo was copied from slide 14 and pasted into 15. It has already been sized to save you time.

2   In the Slide inspector, choose the following options:

   ▶   Effect—Magic Move

   ▶   Duration—10.00 s

   Click OK to accept the tip on using Magic Move. Let's see the animation full screen.

3   Click the Play button, wait a few seconds for the animation to cache, and then press the Spacebar.

   You've created a move on the photo that is similar to the Ken Burns effect in iMovie.

You can create zooms and pans with photos using Magic Move.

4   If you want to review the animation a second time, press the Left Arrow key followed by the Spacebar.

5   Press Esc to return to the presentation.

   You have one more opportunity to use Magic Move. Let's animate the motorcycle between slides.

6   In the slide navigator, select slide 16.

7   In the Slide inspector, choose the following options:

   ▶   Effect—Magic Move

   ▶   Duration—2.00 s

8   In the toolbar, click the Play button.

Magic Move automates animation tasks and saves you time.

9   Choose File > Save to save your work.

You can compare your presentation with the file **03_Superbike_Stage3.key** in the Lesson_03 folder.

Your entire presentation is now enhanced with animated builds and transitions. You are almost done with your presentation. To wrap up, you'll add some video and tweak the playback settings to realize the smoothest animation and video.

Using Video in a Slideshow

Integrating video is a powerful way to communicate your ideas to the audience. Video can both educate and entertain your audience, and express a lot of information in a short period of time.

In this presentation, let's add a Ducati promo video that showcases the new motorcycle.

Adding Video to a Slide

Placing video on a slide is similar to adding a photo. You just navigate to the file and drag the video onto a slide.

1   Select slide 19 in your presentation.

2   Choose Insert > Choose.

3   Navigate to the Lesson_03 folder and choose **Ducati_Evolution.mov**.

4   Click Insert to add the movie.

Keynote centers the movie on your slide. The video fades up from black, so the first frame looks pretty empty at present. In the next exercise, you'll adjust the QuickTime settings to change that.

Choosing QuickTime Settings

Keynote gives you precise control over audio and video files in the QuickTime inspector. You can make important changes to the way content plays without ever leaving Keynote.

1   Open the QuickTime inspector.

2   Drag the Poster Frame slider to choose which image is displayed before the movie plays. Choose a shot that clearly shows the motorcycle.

Let's lower the clip volume a bit so that the presenter can be heard over the movie soundtrack.

3   Drag the Volume slider a little to the left to lower the volume.

4   Select the "Start movie on click" checkbox to enable the presenter to control when the movie plays.

> **TIP** During your presentation, you can control movie playback from the key-board. Press K to toggle between Pause and Play. Hold down J to rewind the movie. Hold down L to fast-forward through the movie.

5 Choose File > Save to save your work.

NOTE ▶ In Keynote preferences, "Show playback controls when pointer is over a movie" is selected by default. This useful option gives you playback and volume controls for the movie when you use your trackpad or mouse.

▶ Optimizing a Video for Playback

Video files can be quite large. To ensure smooth video performance during your presentation, the video should be optimized. The key is to create a high-quality, compressed video file that your Mac can play without skipping frames.

The best way to achieve this is to create an H.264 file. If the video is correctly optimized, Keynote can play HD video files in full screen. Here's how to encode video in iMovie and iTunes.

iMovie '09

After you've edited your movie in iMovie, you can choose to publish it to your Media Browser, which makes it easy to access in Keynote.

1 Choose Share > Media Browser to create a movie file.

The Publish pane opens.

2 Select the checkbox for "Medium for Standard Definition video" or "Large for High Definition video," depending on the resolution you desire.

3 Click Publish.

The movie file is published to your Media Browser. Depending upon your machine speed, the process may take a few minutes to finish encoding the file.

4 When it's finished, choose iMovie > Quit iMovie to close the application.

▶ **Optimizing a Video for Playback** (continued)

iTunes

In iTunes, it's easy to build a media library of video podcasts and movies, including your own movie content. One benefit of using iTunes with Keynote is that its playlist makes it easy to organize presentation content. You have all your videos on one list, so you can manage them easily in the Media Browser.

Another, lesser-known benefit is that iTunes can encode and optimize video files.

1   Select a movie in your iTunes library.

2   Choose Advanced > Create Apple TV Version.

iTunes encodes the video as an H.264 compressed file according to the Apple TV specifications.

TIP ▶ You can Command-click multiple clips and choose Advanced > Create Apple TV Version to encode them all at once.

3   You should add the newly compressed file to a playlist so it is easier to find in the Media Browser.

4   When finished, choose iTunes > Quit iTunes to close the application.

Configuring Preferences for Smooth Playback

Factors such as the quality of your graphics card and display (or projector) resolution can greatly affect the playback quality of your presentation. Before running your presentation, you may want to tweak a few preferences to optimize its playback.

Freeing Up RAM

Before giving a presentation, close any applications that are not necessary to your presentation. Doing so will make most of your computer's RAM available to Keynote and reduce playback hiccups.

Scaling Up Slides

Often, your slideshow resolution does not match your playback device's resolution, result-
ing in a black border surrounding your presentation (because not enough slide information exists to fill the screen).

To solve this problem, you can temporarily fit the presentation to the display during playback.

1   Choose Keynote > Preferences.

2   Click the Slideshow button.

3   Select the "Scale slides up to fit display" checkbox.

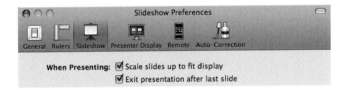

This option does not change the slide size of your Keynote document; it simply scales
up the slides during playback to fill the display.

4   Close the Preferences window to apply the change.

> **NOTE ►** If your presentation is larger than the playback screen, Keynote automati-
> cally scales down your presentation regardless of the state of the "Scale slides up to fit
> display" checkbox.

Changing the Pointer Behavior

Generally, your pointer shouldn't appear onscreen during a presentation, except when
you're clicking a hyperlink or controlling a movie. In Keynote '09 you can set preferences
to display the pointer only when slides contain hyperlinks or when the mouse is moved.

1   Choose Keynote > Preferences.

2   Click the Slideshow button.

3   Select one of the "Show pointer" options:

▶   Show pointer only on slides with hyperlinks or movies—A good choice if you are using a mouse to advance your slides and you don't want to accidentally activate the pointer.

▶   Show pointer when the mouse moves—Gives you maximum control and makes the pointer visible when it is needed.

4   Make sure the "Show playback controls when pointer is over a movie" checkbox is selected.

> ⦿ Show pointer only on slides with hyperlinks or movies
> ◯ Show pointer when the mouse moves
> ☑ Show playback controls when pointer is over a movie

5   Close the Slideshow Preferences window to apply the change.

TIP ▶ While presenting a slideshow, you can show or hide the pointer by pressing the C key.

Turning Off Exposé and Dashboard

In Mac OS X, Exposé allows you to quickly view all open windows, and Dashboard provides widgets that you can customize for specialty tasks and desktop activities. Some users decide to turn these off so they don't trigger them unintentionally during a slideshow.

1   Choose Keynote > Preferences.

2   Click the Slideshow button.

3   Make sure that the "Allow Exposé, Dashboard and others to use screen" checkbox is not selected.

> ☐ Allow Exposé, Dashboard and others to use screen
> Caution: Can reduce animation performance on some hardware.

4   Close the Slideshow Preferences window to apply the change.

Running Your Presentation

Now that your system is configured, it's time to test-run your presentation. This will give you a chance to see all of your work in action.

If you followed all the exercises in this lesson, your presentation is ready to go. If you skipped some steps, open **03_Superbike_End.key** from the Lesson_03 folder to access a completed version of the slideshow.

In Lesson 7, we'll explore the use of a second display or a projector in your presentation. For this exercise, we'll focus on playback commands that work regardless of your display devices.

1   In the toolbar, Option-click the Play button.

    This plays the presentation from the first slide.

2   Press the Spacebar or click your mouse to advance slides.

3   Along the way, try out the following keyboard shortcuts:

    ▶   To advance a slide, you can press either Return, N, Down Arrow, Page Down, or Right Arrow.

    ▶   To advance to the next slide (regardless of whether stages remain to be seen in the build), press either] (right bracket), Shift–Page Down, or Shift–Down Arrow.

    ▶   To back up one slide, press either P, Left Arrow, Up Arrow, Shift–Up Arrow, Page Up, or Delete.

    After testing a few slides, let's skip forward in the presentation.

4   Press the = (equal sign) key on your keyboard to open the slide switcher.

You can use several keyboard shortcuts to interact with the slide switcher:

▶   You can scroll left or right or click a desired slide to go directly to that slide.

▶   To go to the next slide in the slide switcher, press + (plus sign) or = (equal sign).

▶   To return to the previous slide, press – (minus sign).

▶   To go to a selected slide and close the slide switcher, press either Return or Enter.

▶   Close the slide switcher (without changing slides) by pressing Esc.

TIP ▶ Keep a printout of your slide outline (with slide numbers) handy while presenting. You may need to jump around during a presentation, especially if your allotted time for the presentation changes, and the printout will help you navigate through your slide sequence.

5   Press Esc to return to the current slide.

6   Continue advancing through your remaining slides and builds until you reach the end of your presentation.

7   To exit the slideshow, press Esc.

TIP ▶ You can also exit a slideshow by pressing Q, or . (period), or Command-. (period).

You did it! You've created and viewed an elaborate presentation with audio and video. You've also created builds and transitions to control the flow of information.

TIP ▶ To see a list of keyboard shortcuts you can use while giving a presentation, press Help, or ? (question mark), or / (forward slash).

Pausing and Resuming a Slideshow

You'll often want to switch gears during a presentation. For instance, you may want to switch to another application to show off a document or to access a file with the Finder. Keynote offers several ways to pause a presentation:

▶   To pause a presentation and display the current slide, press F (as in *freeze*). To resume the presentation, press F or the Spacebar.

▶   To pause a presentation and display a black screen, press B. To resume the presentation, press B or the Spacebar.

▶   To pause a presentation and display a white screen, press W. To resume the presentation, press W or the Spacebar.

▶   To pause the presentation and hide Keynote, press H. To resume the presentation, click the Keynote icon in the Dock. This works very well if you want to switch to Safari to open a web link or show material in another application.

Troubleshooting Your Presentation

Most likely, the presentation ran perfectly on your computer—the video played back smoothly and all builds worked properly. The following information is offered in case you hit a snag or if you are presenting on a different machine from the one you used to build the presentation. We hope you won't need this information, but it's still good to have it.

If your slideshow stutters or if artifacts appear, be sure that all media is running from a hard drive and is not located on removable media such as a DVD or USB thumb drive. If media access speed is not the issue, the problem could be insufficient VRAM (video RAM), projector setup issues, or an improper screen refresh rate.

If your computer has less than 32 MB of VRAM and your slideshow has a playback issue, you may be able to improve performance by modifying your computer's display settings. From the Apple menu, choose System Preferences, click the Displays button, and try the following:

▶ Turn on video mirroring.

▶ Set your displays to a lower resolution. Lower screen resolutions use less VRAM.

▶ Set your displays to use fewer colors. You can use Thousands instead of Millions as a last-effort solution.

Lesson Review

1. Where can you modify build options?
2. To make two builds occur simultaneously, which button do you click first?
3. True or false: Keynote offers both 2D and 3D slide transitions.
4. How can you access the slide switcher during your presentation?
5. Which keys do you press to pause a presentation and hide Keynote?

Answers

1. The Build inspector offers complete control over build options.
2. Click the More Options button to access timing controls.
3. True. Keynote offers more than 40 advanced slide transitions.
4. Press the = (equal sign) key to open the slide switcher.
5. Pressing H will hide the presentation. Clicking the Keynote icon in the Dock will resume the presentation.

4

Lesson Files Lessons > Lesson_04 > 04_Desert_Theme.key

Lessons > Lesson_04 > 04_Desert_Content.key

Lessons > Lesson_04 > 04_Desert_End.key

Lessons > Lesson_04 > Backgrounds

Lessons > Lesson_04 > Theme Images

Time This lesson takes approximately 60 minutes to complete.

Goals Create a custom theme

Create a slide with a media placeholder

Save and share a theme

Apply a new theme to an existing presentation

Lesson 4
Creating a Custom Theme

Keynote '09 includes more than 40 Apple-designed themes, but it also lets you customize existing themes or design a new one.

With a custom theme, you can combine a unique set of background images, fonts, colors, shapes, and table and chart styles to create a distinctive look for your slideshow. Whether you're a company looking to reinforce its brand or a teacher reinforcing your students' learning, a custom theme can strengthen your presentation.

What's more, custom themes are easy to recycle. If you build a theme with customization in mind, you can update the look of an entire presentation with just a few mouse clicks. This makes it easy to personalize your presentation for each new audience and thereby improve the overall impact of your slideshow.

Keynote provides the tools to create uniquely themed presentations, whether you just want to tweak an existing theme's colors and add a logo, or design one from scratch.

In this lesson, we'll create our own custom theme from start to finish for a presentation about the deserts in the southwestern United States. Customizing a theme can be a bit intimidating at first, because Keynote offers lots of modification options and a wealth of components to use. However, the result is very rewarding and can become a big time-saver for your future projects.

Creating an Empty Theme

Keynote never faces you with a completely blank canvas, because you choose a theme from the Theme Chooser whenever you open the application or create a new document (choose File > New in Theme Chooser).

To create a custom theme, we'll begin by creating as blank a canvas as we can: a starter file. You can use any theme as a starting point; simply choose the theme that most closely matches the style you'd like to use, and delete the parts of the theme you don't want.

We'll use the Kyoto theme as the starting point for this exercise. This theme has a gently organic feel that suits our Southwest subject matter and includes several layouts with prominent photos.

1   Open Keynote; or, if Keynote is already open, choose File > New from Theme Chooser.

2   Choose the Kyoto theme. Set the size to 1280 × 720 pixels, and click Choose.

    A new document is created based on the theme.

3   Choose View > Show Master Slides to see the master slides for this theme.

    Master slides contain all of the layout options for a slide that you can use in a presentation.

4   In the master slide navigator, drag the resize handle down to see more of the slide masters.

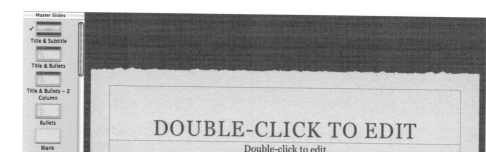

You will remove a few masters from the theme to simplify it.

5   Select the Photo – Horizontal master and press Delete.

6   Repeat the selection and deletion commands for the following master slide types:

▶   Title, Bullets & Photo

▶   Title & Bullets – Left

▶   Title & Bullets – Right

7   Choose File > Save. Name the file *Desert Theme.key* and save it to the Lesson_04 folder.

Creating a Title Slide

Now that we've got our blank Desert theme, the first step is to create a theme for our title slides. Opening each section of your presentation with a title slide helps your audience to follow your organization and signifies when you're about to address a new topic.

1   In the master slide navigator, select the Title & Subtitle slide.

2   Open the Master Slide inspector and click Appearance.

3   Click Choose to select a file for the slide background.

> **TIP** ▶ You can design your own slide backgrounds by opening a blank slide master, then combine images and shapes within Keynote. You can then export a flattened graphic by choosing Share > Export and choosing the Image option.

4   Navigate to Lesson_04 > Backgrounds > **BG_1.jpg**, and click Open.

> **MORE INFO** ▶ This new background was created using Adobe Photoshop Elements. The existing background from the Kyoto theme was exported as a visual reference, and then a photo of desert rock was added. You can use the graphics tool of your choice to create backgrounds.

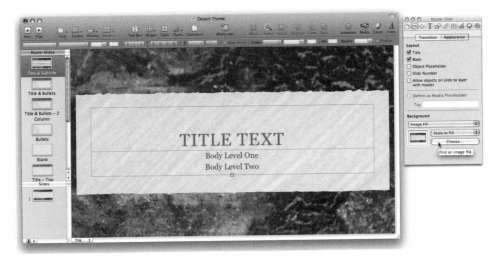

Now that the background is updated, let's tweak the text so that it better matches the color and style of the background.

5   Select the title text box.

Let's change the text from all capitals to upper- and lowercase.

6 Choose Format > Font > Capitalization > None to remove any automated capitalization from the text.

Let's change the text so that it is larger and easier to read.

7 In the format bar, set the font to Georgia, Bold, 90 pt.

The text looks good, but the text box is not large enough to contain a two-line title.

8 Drag up the center selection handle at the top edge of the text box until the box is big enough to include two lines of text (a height of 200 px works well).

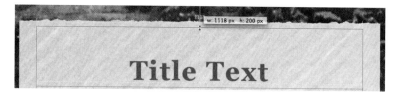

You may want to change the body text so that it is a better match for the title text.

9 Select the entire body level text box and change the font to Gill Sans, Regular, 36 pt.

10 Drag down the center selection handle at the bottom edge of the text box until the box is big enough for two lines of text (around 100 px in height).

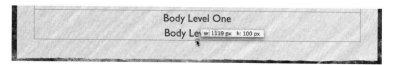

The text is easier to read and a good match for the background. However, the text color could be a better match. Let's change both text boxes at once.

11 Click the title text box. Shift-click the body text box to add this text to the selection.

12 In the format bar, click the Text Color well and choose Show Colors.

The Colors window opens; here you can specify a color. Let's select a dark red from the background.

13 In the Colors window, click the magnifying glass icon and then select a dark red from the upper right corner of the slide.

The text color updates. You can store the color for reuse later.

14 Drag the color into an empty square in the color palette at the bottom of the Colors window.

To complete this set of adjustments, center the text and review the slide.

15 Drag the two text boxes down at the same time until the alignment guides pop up to indicate vertical and horizontal alignment on the slide.

Because the two text boxes are both active, Keynote shows alignment guides based on both objects and their relationship to the entire layout.

16 Choose File > Save to save your work.

For more practice, you could update the next six master slides with the following changes:

Element	Background	Title	Body
Title & Bullets	BG_2.jpg	Georgia Bold, cream color, 96 pt	Gill Sans, dark red color, 36 pt
Title & Bullets – 2 Column	BG_2.jpg	Georgia Bold, cream color, 96 pt	Gill Sans, dark red color, 36 pt
Bullets	BG_3.jpg		Gill Sans, dark red color, 36 pt
Blank	BG_4.jpg		
Title – Top	BG_2.jpg	Georgia Bold, cream color, 96 pt	
Title – Center	BG_1.jpg	Georgia Bold, dark red color, 90 pt	

NOTE ▶ For comparison, a finished version of the theme, **04_Desert_Theme.key**, can be found in the Lesson_04 folder.

Creating a Photo Master

Another important slide master that you'll frequently use is the Photo – Vertical master slide, which prominently features a single photo next to descriptive text. In this case, we'll customize the Photo – Vertical master slide to display bullet points of information next to that same strong visual.

1   In the master slide navigator, select the Photo – Vertical master.

2   Open the Master Slide inspector and click Appearance.

3   Click Choose to select a file for the slide background. Navigate to Lesson_04 > Backgrounds > **BG_3.jpg**, and click Open.

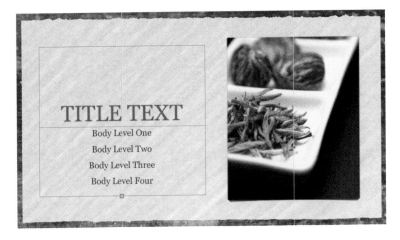

You can format the photo on the slide with something related to the theme.

4   On the canvas, select the photo and choose Insert > Choose.

5   Navigate to Lesson_04 > Theme Images > **Rocks.jpg**. Click Insert.

The image is added to the slide, but it needs to be resized and reformatted.

NOTE ▶ The image on this master was defined as an image placeholder. If you add photos to a slide master that previously didn't have placeholders, select the slide master and open the Master Slide inspector. (The Master Slide inspector will not open unless a master is selected.) Then choose the placeholder object and select the Define as Media Placeholder checkbox.

6 Open the Graphic inspector.

7 From the Stroke pop-up menu, choose Line.

8 From the Line Style pop-up menu, choose the rough line, located at the bottom of the menu.

9 Set the line's color to the same dark red you stored earlier in the Colors window.

10 Choose a width of 15 px (pixels).

   The picture is attractively formatted, but let's make it a little larger.

11 Click the Edit Mask button.

12 Resize the mask to a width of approximately 450 px and a height of 625 px; then press Return.

13 Drag the photo so that it is centered vertically on the slide.

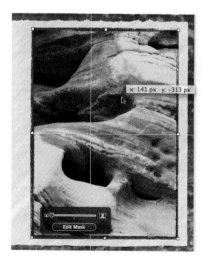

Formatting Text

The picture is now sized correctly; next, let's format the text to match the style we created earlier in the lesson.

1   Return to the Title & Subtitle master slide.

2   Click in the title text box.

3   Choose Format > Copy Style.

4   Return to the Photo – Vertical master slide and select the title text.

5   Choose Format > Paste Style.

    The text updates to match the previously used formatting.

6   Resize the title text box to a height of 250 px.

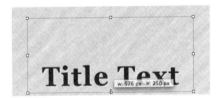

7   Drag the text box until it's aligned with the top of the photo.

    TIP ▶ If you don't see alignment guides while lining up the top edges, choose Keynote > Preferences. Select the "Show guides at object edges" checkbox.

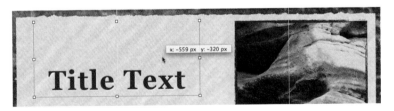

    Now let's format the bullet text on the slide.

8   Select the entire body level text box and change the font to Gill Sans, Regular, 36 pt. Make the font color the same dark red that you stored earlier.

9 In the format bar, click the Align Left button.

Let's add bullets to the text and indent them.

10 Open the Text inspector and click Bullets.

11 From the Bullets & Numbering pop-up menu, choose Text Bullets and choose the first bullet from the pop-up list. Leave the Size field set to 125% so that the bullets are slightly larger than the text.

12 Set Bullet Indent to 15 px and Text Indent to 25 px so that a separation exists between the edge of the text box, the bullet, and the first character of text.

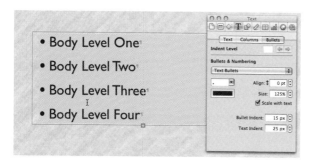

13 Select Body Level Two and enter a value of 40 px for Bullet Indent. Select Body Level Three and set Bullet Indent to 65 px. Then select Body Level Four and set Bullet Indent to 90 px.

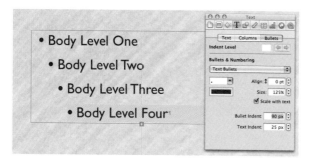

The indentation is now very clearly presented, but let's add some extra space between the bullet lines.

14 Choose Edit > Select All to select all of the text, then in the Text inspector, click the Text button to change the space between lines.

15 In both the Before Paragraph and After Paragraph fields, enter a value of 16 pt.

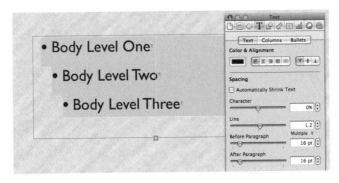

16 Resize the body text box so that the top edge touches the title text box.

17 Resize the body text box so that the bottom edge touches the bottom of the photo.

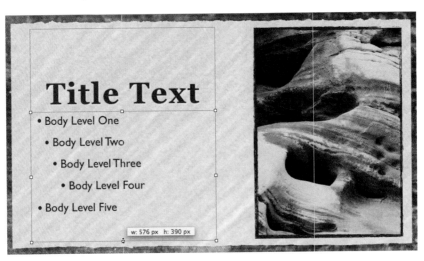

18 Choose File > Save to save your work.

Congratulations! You've formatted the background, a media placeholder, title text, and bullets for your custom theme. The skills you've used in this lesson can be applied to any master slides.

▶ ## Adding Default Transitions, Shapes, Tables, and More

To take your custom theme even further, try these modifications on your own time:

Add Default Transitions
Select the master slide and apply a transition from the Master Slide inspector.

Add Default Builds
Select the master slide and apply a build from the Build inspector. These animations will be applied by default when the master slide is chosen, but you can override them by choosing a new animation in the Inspector window.

Add Default Shapes
Insert a shape, and change its fill, stroke, and font to suit your tastes. Then choose Format > Advanced > Define Shape for All Masters (or Current Master).

Add Default Tables
Insert a table and format its style and appearance. Choose Format > Advanced > Define Table for All Masters (or Current Master).

Add Default Charts
Charts have to be captured individually (each chart type, more or less), so just do the ones you use most often. Insert a chart and format its style and appearance. Choose Format > Advanced and choose the appropriate "Define for All Masters" command.

Saving and Sharing Themes

Thus far while building the custom theme, we've been saving it as a presentation file. Now it's time to save the modifications we've made as a new custom theme.

Saving a theme allows you to apply your unique formatting to an existing presentation or to create an entirely new presentation based on that theme.

To save time, we'll work with a fully designed version of the custom theme, which has been completed for you.

1   Close all Keynote documents (save your changes).

2   Choose File > Open, and navigate to the Lesson_04 folder.

3   Open **04_Desert_Theme.key**.

This file contains final versions of all the master slides, along with a few sample slides.

TIP ▶ When creating a custom theme, it's a good idea to build a few sample slides that include content. When you save a theme, those sample slides become part of the preview in the Theme Chooser. Additionally, be sure to create a title slide with a descriptive name for your theme.

4   Choose File > Save Theme.

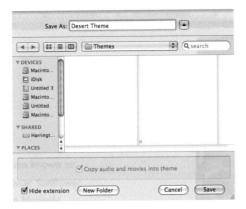

A sheet opens with the default Themes folder selected to store custom themes.

5   Name your theme *Desert Theme*. Click Save to save the theme.

The theme file is saved in your Themes folder and will appear near the bottom of the Theme Chooser when you first open Keynote or when you open the Theme Chooser.

Backing Up a Theme

After you've created a theme, be sure to back it up. Not only will you have a backup copy, but you can also share your theme more easily with other Keynote users.

1   In the Finder, locate your custom theme in Macintosh HD > Users > [*your home folder*] > Library > Application Support > iWork > Keynote > Themes.

2   Select **Desert Theme.kth**, and then drag the file to a removable device such as a hard drive or USB thumb drive , or to a connccted server such as your iDisk. When your pointer turns into a + (plus sign), release the mouse button to copy the file to the backup drive.

The file is now backed up. You can also share it with other users by attaching it to an email or by lending them the drive.

3   Return to Keynote, save your work, and close all open Keynote files.

Applying a Custom Theme

The customized theme file is ready and can be applied to an existing presentation. The text for this exercise has already been entered on slides. However, the slides are generic and require styling and images.

1   Choose File > Open, navigate to the Lesson_04 folder, and open **04_Desert_ Content.key**.

You can now apply a theme to this presentation.

2   Choose File > Choose Theme to open the Theme Chooser. Select the newly created Desert Theme and click Choose.

Custom themes appear near the bottom of the Theme Chooser.

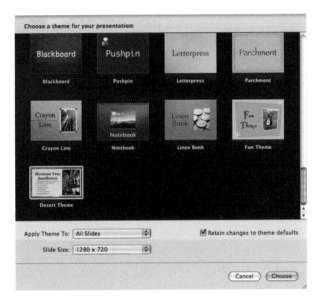

The Desert Theme is applied to your presentation. Because the slide masters of both presentations used the same names (Bullets, Blank, and so on), Keynote matches the new formatting to the appropriate slide.

NOTE ▶ If you want to force an update to an individual slide, select the slide and choose Format > Reapply Master to Slide.

3   The slides now match the template. You may want to further customize the slides to complete your presentation. Here are a few suggested areas to tweak.

▶   If text is too big to fit in a text box, select the text box, and in the format bar, select the Auto-shrink checkbox.

▶ You can adjust the size of photos by dragging the selection handle above the Edit Mask button.

▶ If you'd like to adjust which part of a photo is showing in the slide, double-click any masked image and drag the image to relocate it within its mask.

4 Choose File > Save to save your reformatted, custom presentation.

Lesson Review

1. How can you take precise control over master slide properties?

2. How can you view master slides?

3. If you want the Theme Chooser to display a preview of a slide theme, how do you create it?

4. How can you control the spacing around a bullet?

5. How do you apply a new theme to an existing presentation?

Answers

1. Select a slide master, then select the Master Slide inspector. The inspector gives you control over master slide properties.

2. Choose View > Show Master Slides to see their thumbnails in the slide navigator.

3. Add a few slides to the Keynote document you are using to build the theme. These slides become visible when you skim the pointer over the theme in the Theme Chooser.

4. Open the Text inspector and choose Bullet. The two primary controls are Bullet Indent and Text Indent.

5. Open the presentation and choose File > Choose Theme. Choose the new theme you want to apply.

5

Time   This lesson takes approximately 90 minutes to complete.

Goals   Open a PowerPoint presentation with Keynote

Use Pages to change a Word document into an iWork-compatible format
and add its content to a Keynote presentation

Modify and enhance imported content

Enhance and animate chart graphics

Export a Keynote presentation to PowerPoint and PDF files

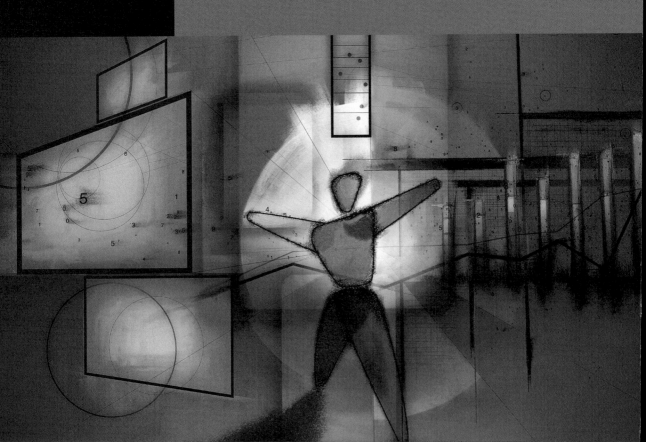

Lesson **5**

Importing from PowerPoint and Working with Charts

Because Keynote was built from the ground up to take advantage of the powerful graphics features in Mac OS X, one of its big strengths is its rich media playback capability and expert handling of text, animation, and charts.

Another of Keynote's strengths is how well it handles Microsoft PowerPoint files. PowerPoint is a common format, and on any given project chances are good that some of your collaborators used PowerPoint to create and distribute their presentations.

Fortunately, Keynote imports and exports Microsoft PowerPoint files effortlessly, which makes it easy to use Keynote's expanded graphics features to enhance PowerPoint charts, tables, and other visual elements.

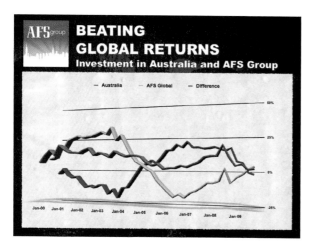

In this lesson, we'll import and modify an existing PowerPoint presentation about the global performance of a fictitious Australian investment company. We'll enhance slides and content to improve the overall appearance of the presentation and work more extensively with charts and animation.

The goal in this lesson is to improve the appearance of charts and data, making them clearer and more interesting to the audience. You'll also learn how to animate charts, so you can control how the information is presented to the audience.

Importing a PowerPoint Presentation

Importing a PowerPoint presentation into Keynote allows you to modify and edit the content. The conversion process is as easy as opening a file.

1   If necessary, open Keynote.

2   Choose File > Open.

3   Navigate to the file **05_AFS Group Presentation.ppt**.

> **NOTE ▶** Newer Microsoft Office Open XML formats found in PowerPoint 2007 and 2008 use the .pptx extension. Keynote can also import these files.

4   Click Open.

Keynote imports the PowerPoint file and gives it a name identical to the original but with the *.key* extension. The original PowerPoint document remains unmodified on your hard drive.

5   A warning dialog may appear to inform you of any conversion errors.

Depending upon the fonts installed on your system and a few other factors, you may see two error warnings. These errors are minor and will result in slight cosmetic changes to some of the charts. You'll be changing the appearance of the charts in this exercise, so the error warnings don't present a problem.

6   If necessary, close the warnings window by clicking the red close button.

7   Choose File > Save As. Name the file *05_Presentation Stage 01.key*, and save it to your hard drive.

Resizing a Document

A PowerPoint file is usually imported into Keynote at 720 × 540 pixels. This is an uncommon size for Macs, and it's always a good idea to choose a resolution that's supported by your video projector or computer display. Let's resize the new presentation to optimize it for the Mac screen.

1   Open the Document inspector.

2   From the Slide Size pop-up menu, choose 1024 × 768.

Your slides and all their contents scale up to match the new size.

3   Choose View > Zoom > Fit in Window.

4   Press Command-S to save your document.

> **NOTE ▶** On the DVD included with this book, you'll find a PDF file called **05_AFS Group Presentation_PPT.pdf**. This document shows how the slides in this exercise looked when originally created in PowerPoint.

Animating a Title Slide

The first slide in your financial presentation could benefit from animation to immediately capture your audience's attention. Let's apply some built-in animations to enhance your slide.

Adding Multiple Builds

A build can animate an individual element on a slide, but you can choose to synchronize or interleave builds, so that multiple animations occur simultaneously. In the Build inspector, you can activate multiple movements that bring a presentation to animated life.

1   In the slide navigator, choose slide 1.

2   Select the Build inspector and click the Build In button.

3   Select the logo on the canvas.

4   From the Effect pop-up menu, choose Scale. From the Direction pop-up menu, choose Down.

5   On the canvas, select the white box.

6   From the Effect menu, choose Convergence.

The logo shrinks, and then the white box appears over the background. This creates a dramatic way to reveal the company's logo and can add some excitement to the start of the presentation.

Setting Simultaneous Builds

Currently, the two animations happen sequentially when you click. Sometimes this is desirable, such as when revealing lines of text on a slide. In this example, you are animating the logo to reveal it on the slide. However, in this example, it is desirable to have the animations occur simultaneously to create a highly customized and attractive introduction to the corporate logo.

1   At the bottom of the Build inspector, click More Options.

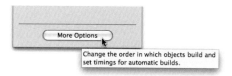

The Build Order drawer allows you to adjust the timing of build animations.

2   From the Build Order list, select Item #1.

3   From the Start Build menu, choose "Automatically after transition."

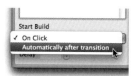

4   From the Build Order list, select Item #2.

5   From the Start Build menu, choose "Automatically with build 1."

6 Click the slide thumbnail in the inspector to preview the animation.

Because you synchronized your animations, they happen concurrently. Now, let's create a transition to the next slide.

7 Click the Slide Inspector button and then click Transition.

8 From the Effect menu, choose 3D Effects: Doorway and set Duration to 1.50 s.

9 To preview the animation, in the Inspector, click the slide thumbnail.

The logo is dramatically revealed on the slide.

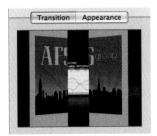

10 Press Command-S to save your document.

Cleaning Up a Chart

Now that we've successfully animated the first slide, let's enhance the remaining charts. The skills you'll acquire will be useful for more than just financial presentations, because charts are commonly used to represent all types of data.

Updating Data

Whether you import a chart or create a new one, the chart's data is always editable. This allows you to make changes or updates as new information becomes available.

1   In the slide navigator, choose slide 2.

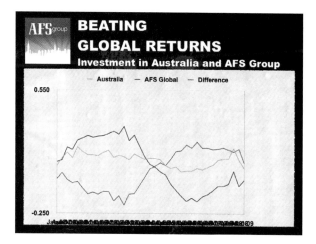

2   On the canvas, select the chart.

3   Select the Chart inspector and click Edit Data.

The Chart Data Editor opens. The information is partially cut off, so let's resize the window.

4   Drag the control at the lower-right corner of the Chart Data Editor to enlarge the window. You can now view all of the financial data, and you're ready to modify it.

5   Click the Add Row button eight times to add rows for two years of quarterly financial data.

6   Drag the vertical scroll bar so that you see the last row of empty data.

7   Enter data for the Australia and AFS Global columns as shown in the following figure. (While you're typing, notice how easy it is to update the data in this chart you imported from another application. It'll make it go faster.)

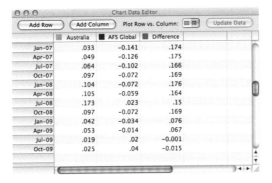

8   Close the Chart Data Editor.

Formatting Labels and Legends

Charts are intended to make data more comprehensible; but when a chart has a lot of information, it can easily become cluttered. When that happens, you may want to reduce the number of labels on a chart to simplify it.

1   In the Chart inspector, click the Axis tab, and from the Format pop-up menu, choose Percentage.

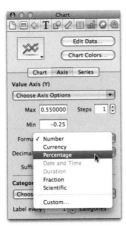

2   In the Value Axis fields, enter the data values shown in the following figure to give the y-axis of the chart a more legible range of values:

3   In the Category Axis (X) area of the Chart inspector, set the "Label every" value to 4 categories.

This reduces the number of labels on the x-axis so that only the first month of each year is labeled.

4   Click the text box in the x-axis to select it.

5   In the format bar, change the font size to 14 points.

6   Click the legend near the top of the slide, and drag it so that it is horizontally centered on the slide canvas.

Yellow alignment guides will appear when the text is centered.

Now that the text on the slide looks better, let's enhance the data.

Enhancing a Chart

Keynote offers several 3D chart styles and options in the Graphic inspector that can be applied to improve the readability of a chart. To help the viewer better understand the data, you will change your chart to 3D. You will also enhance its appearance to more closely match your slides.

Creating a 3D Line Chart

Keynote allows you to display most charts using two- or three-dimensional perspective. Which one you choose is really a matter of personal taste. In some cases, 3D charts are clearer because the illusion of depth can increase the viewer's understanding of the relationships between data values. Fortunately, Keynote quickly changes charts from one chart type to another.

1   On the canvas, click the chart to select it.

2   Select the Chart inspector. Click the Chart Type icon to open a pop-up menu.

3   Choose a 3D line chart (the fifth icon in the second column).

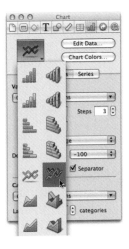

The conversion may take a few seconds. When finished, let's enhance the chart to make it more readable and match your other slides.

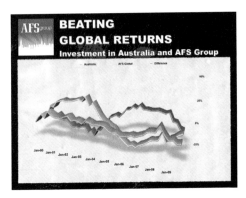

4 In the Chart inspector, click the Chart button.

The 3D Scene pane of the Chart inspector lets you adjust the graphic 3D properties of the chart, such as depth, angle, and shadows.

TIP ▶ If you want to adjust only the angle of the chart, select the chart and change the angle using the four-way arrowhead that appears on the canvas. This is a fast way to tweak the chart position without opening the Inspector window.

5 Modify the lighting style, chart depth, and viewing angle of the chart by using the 3D scene controls. You can adjust the size of the chart by pulling the selection handles at the chart border. Adjust them to suit yourself.

Examine the viewing angle, as well as depth and shadow settings. Be sure you haven't accidentally changed the meaning of the chart with a perspective error (see sidebar).

▶ **A Matter of Perspective**

One of the most common ways to affect the perception of data in a chart is to change the viewing angle and 3D scene settings. You can use the four-way arrowhead that appears when the chart is selected to adjust the viewing angle, and the complete controls in the Chart inspector to control depth and lighting. Notice how the two charts here present the same information in very different lights. In the chart on the right, the altered viewing angle makes the chart more truthful as it is easier to tell which line indicates higher performance. The angle of the chart on the left makes the value of the purple line seem much lower than it actually is.

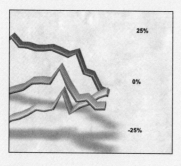

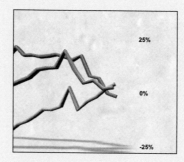

Before   After

Showing Gridlines

Adding gridlines to a chart makes it easier to quantify changes in data values at a glance.

1   In the Chart inspector, click the Axis button.

2   From the Value Axis (Y) pop-up menu, choose Show Major Gridlines.

3   Double-click a gridline to select all of the gridlines in the chart.

4   In the format bar, change the line width to 2 px to improve its readability.

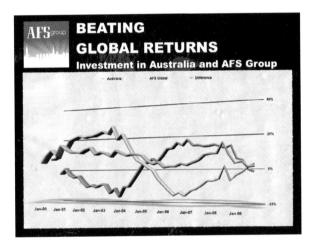

Changing Chart Colors

Now that we've made the chart easier to understand, let's improve its appearance. By matching the colors of your chart to the colors in the logo and slide background, we'll get a more unified design.

1   In the chart, double-click the purple line.

2   Select the Graphic inspector.

Notice that the Fill color well matches the purple in the chart.

3   Click the color well to open the Colors window.

4   Click the magnifying glass icon to activate the color sampler. Click a reddish-orange area in the logo to match the bar color.

5   Change the other two lines of the chart to match the gold in the logo and the bright blue in the background, as in the following figure:

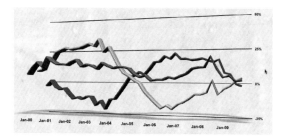

6   Check the chart to make sure it's clear and easy to read; then close the Colors window.

7   Press Command-S to save your work.

You can compare your presentation with the file **05_Presentation Stage 02.key** in the Lesson_05 folder.

Animating a Chart

Adding movement to a slide can be an effective way to grab your audience's attention and control the flow of information. Now that the chart is built, let's animate it to reveal the slide data one series at a time.

1   Select the chart on slide 2. Then select the Build inspector.

2   From the Effect pop-up menu, choose Grow.

3   From the Delivery menu, choose By Series. This option will animate each element in the chart, first the gridlines and then each data series.

4   Set the Duration to 2.00 s.

5   To preview the animation, in the Inspector, click the slide thumbnail.

Notice how the background and grid wipes onto the screen first. Generally, you'll want this part of the chart already on the page, so you'll remove it from the animation.

6   Choose 2 from the "Build from" menu. This starts the animation with the second element on the slide, your first data series.

Leave the "Build to" pop-up menu set to Last. The animation will continue through the last data series.

7   Select the Slide inspector and click Transition. Then choose the following options:

▶   Transition Effect—3D Effects: Twist

▶   Direction—Left to Right

▶   Duration—2.00 s

▶   Twistiness—1.0

You've now created a gentle but dynamic slide transition. You can click the slide thumbnail in the Inspector to show the preview again.

TIP ▶ As we saw in Lesson 3, Keynote offers an extensive library of slide transitions. Take some time experimenting with different transitions until you find ones that you prefer.

Slide transitions help signify a change of information. Use them tastefully, and try to limit yourself to only a few styles of transitions in a presentation.

8   Press Command-S to save your document.

Improving Title Text

The title text on all of your slides should be adjusted slightly to improve its appearance. When you adjust the line spacing, the text boxes will be more aesthetically pleasing, as they will match the height of the logo. Many viewers find slides easier to comprehend when you use alignment to visually balance the information.

1 At the top of the slide, select the text box.

2 In the format bar, click the "Choose the line spacing" button and choose 0.9.

3 Examine the text at the top of the slide. You'll notice that the height of the text box now more closely matches the height of the logo.

4 Repeat the formatting for slides 3 through 7 using the method described in steps 1 and 2.

Animating a Table

A chart is not the only object that can be animated in Keynote. In this exercise, we'll use a build animation to reveal the contents of a table.

1 In the slide navigator, choose slide 3.

The row heights in the table are all slightly different, but you can easily fix them.

2 Click the table to select it.

3 Select the Table inspector and click Table.

4   Set the Row Height value to 120 px.

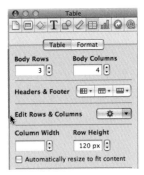

Let's change the font to match the one used in the rest of your presentation.

5   Command-click the cells that contain dollar values and percentages.

A yellow border indicates the selected cells.

6   In the toolbar, from the Font Family pop-up menu, choose Arial.

7   Select the Build inspector and then choose the following options from the Build In tab:

▶   Effect—Flip

▶   Direction—Top to Bottom

▶   Delivery—By Row

▶   Duration—1.00 s

The table is animated. You can click the slide thumbnail in the Inspector window to preview it again.

Next, let's add a transition to the following slide.

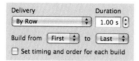

8   Select the Slide inspector and click Transition. Then choose the following options:

▶   Transition Effect—3D Effects: Twist

▶   Direction—Left to Right

▶   Duration—2.00 s

▶   Twistiness—1.0

You can click the slide thumbnail in the Inspector window to preview the 3D transition again.

9   Press Command-S to save your document.

You have successfully animated information on the table using a build and created a transition to the next slide. Next, let's use a build to reveal information in a bar chart.

Animating a Column Chart

You can set up a column chart so that one data series is revealed at a time. You also can use 3D perspective to improve your profit chart's readability.

1   In the slide navigator, choose slide 4.

2   Select the chart on the canvas. Then select the Chart inspector.

3   From the Chart Type pop-up menu, choose the first 3D Column chart.

The chart is rendered in 3D, but in a flat red color, which you will change later in this exercise.

4   Select the Build inspector and click Build In. Then choose the following options:

▶   Effect—Rotate & Grow

▶   Delivery—Cascade

▶   Duration—2.00 s

The Rotate & Grow effect is designed to dramatically reveal information in a chart. By setting the delivery to Cascade, the information will be revealed progressively when you click or press a key.

5   Choose More Options.

6   In the Start Build pop-up menu, choose "Automatically after prior build."

7   Select the Slide inspector and click Transition. Then choose the following options:

▶   Transition Effect—3D Effects: Twist

▶   Direction—Left to Right

▶   Duration—2.00 s

▶   Twistiness—1.0

8   To change the dull red bars back to your eye-catching red, click a series in the chart to select it. All of the columns are selected.

9   Select the Graphic inspector; then click the Fill color well to open the Colors window.

10 With the magnifying glass, select the reddish-orange in the logo to color the chart.

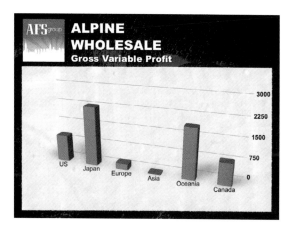

The chart now has a more unified look as its color and style matches other elements in your presentation. You can click the slide thumbnail in the Inspector window to preview the transition again.

11 Press Command-S to save your document.

Animating a Pie Chart

Your next slide breaks out investment percentages, so it's best displayed as a pie chart. You can make this information appear more dynamic by revealing one slice of the pie at a time. Before you animate the chart on slide 5, let's give it some 3D pizazz.

Creating a 3D Pie Chart

Pie charts displayed in 3D are more dynamic than those presented in 2D.

1 In the slide navigator, choose slide 5.

2 Select the chart on the canvas. Then select the Chart inspector.

3 From the Chart Type pop-up menu, choose the 3D Pie chart.

The chart is rendered in 3D, but it is small and its colors ought to be more harmonious. First, let's resize and position the chart.

4   Option-drag the resize handle in the upper-right corner of the pie chart toward the upper-right corner of your screen. Release the mouse button when the pie chart fills the empty area at the bottom of the slide.

> **TIP** ▶ Holding down the Option key while dragging scales the image equally from its center point. You can also press the arrow keys on your keyboard to nudge the pie chart into the desired position.

5   Select the chart legend and drag it to the right of the chart. Next, select the pie chart and position it near the left edge of the slide.

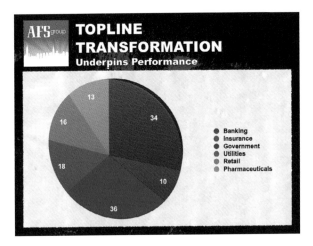

6   With the chart still selected, drag the four-way arrowhead to adjust the viewing angle as desired.

7   Increase the 3D depth of the chart by dragging the Chart Depth slider to the right.

8   In the Chart inspector, select the Show Bevel Edges checkbox.

This makes the individual pie wedges easier to see.

9   Shift-click the legend.

Both the chart and the legend are now selected.

10 In the format bar, change the font to Arial Narrow, change the style to Bold, and set the point size to 24.

Because the size and style of the text changed, the chart layout requires readjustment.

11 Now that the chart is further extruded and angled, reposition the chart and legend on the slide to improve the composition. You can use the following figure for reference:

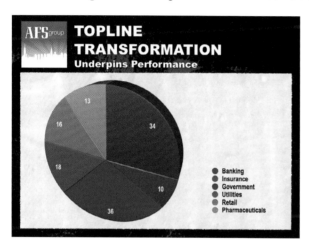

Adding Chart Colors

The current pie chart uses a lot of similar colors (notice how often blue or purple is used). Let's add more colors to differentiate the pie wedges.

1 Select the chart.

2 In the format bar, click the Chart Colors button. The Chart Colors window opens.

3 From the "Series fill type" pop-up menu, choose 2D Image Fills.

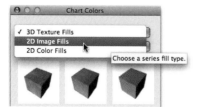

The next menu offers several fill types that you can explore later on your own. For this chart, leave it set to Bright.

NOTE ▸ Keynote offers several fill types for charts. You used a 3D texture in Lesson 2 and will explore other options throughout these lessons. While you'll usually apply 3D texture fills to a 3D chart, you are free to use fill types in any combination.

4   Click the Apply All button to use the chosen color palette.

TIP ▸ You can drag colors or textures directly onto a data series in any chart to change its color.

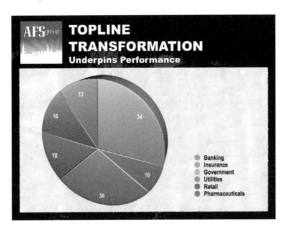

5   Close the Chart Colors window when you're finished changing colors.

Animating Individual Wedges

Now that the pie chart looks good, you can animate it to slowly reveal each piece of the pie.

1   Select the chart; then, in the Build inspector, click Build In. Choose the following options to create a build animation for the pie chart:

▸   Effect—Z Axis

▸   Delivery—Cascade

▸   Duration—2.00 s

The Z-axis effect reveals information with a zoom. By choosing Cascade, all of the pie wedges will be revealed sequentially when the build is triggered.

2   Click the More Options button.

3   From the Start Build menu, choose "Automatically after prior build."

4   For Delay, choose 0.5 s.

5   Select the Slide inspector and click the Transition button. Then choose the following options:

▶   Transition Effect—3D Effects: Twist

▶   Direction—Left to Right

▶   Duration—2.00 s

▶   Twistiness—1.0

You can click the slide thumbnail in the Inspector window to preview the animation again.

6   Press Command-S to save your document.

You can compare your presentation to the file **05_Presentation Stage 03.key** in the Lesson_05 folder.

Changing a Chart Style

Not only can you change the style of a chart to make it appear 3D, but you can also change the entire method of charting. By switching the manner in which your costs data is presented, you can increase the clarity and effectiveness of your presentation.

Cleaning Up a Restyled Chart

Because changing the charting method results in an entirely different look for a chart, you will often have to make many adjustments to improve its appearance.

1   In the slide navigator, choose slide 6.

2   Select the chart on the canvas.

3   Control-click (or right-click) the chart, and choose Chart Type > 3D Stacked Area.

    The chart should be reset to the default style because it appears cluttered.

4   Choose Format > Reapply Master to Selection.

    An area chart is designed to show information from left to right in chronological order, unlike your original chart, which was read from bottom to top. Because you are changing the type of chart, let's also reorder and format the chart data.

5   With the chart selected, in the format bar, click the Edit Data button.

    The Chart Data Editor opens.

6   Click the column data labels and drag them to change their positions so that they are ordered, from left to right, 2007, 2008, and 2009. Close the Chart Data Editor.

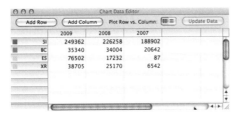 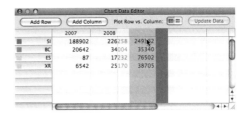

7   Open the Chart inspector and click Chart.

8   In the 3D Scene controls, increase the depth of the chart by dragging the Chart Depth slider to the right.

9   In the Format bar, click the Y Axis value menu and choose Show Axis on Right.

10   Select the chart and adjust the viewing angle of the chart as desired using the four-way arrowhead.

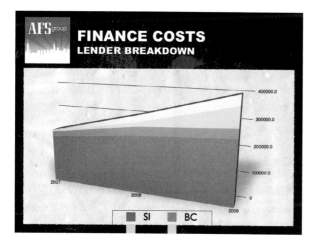

11   Shift-click the legend so that both the chart and legend are selected.

12   In the format bar, change the font to Arial Narrow, change the style to Bold, and set the point size to 24.

13   If necessary, adjust the borders of the legend so that it fits on a single line.

14   Drag the legend to center it on the page. Use the alignment guides as visual references.

15   Resize the chart so it fills up the slide's area.

To resize, drag the selection handles at the edges and corners of the chart.

3   Navigate to the project folder for the lesson and open **05_Table.doc**.

The file opens in Pages as an untitled document. The original Word document remains unaltered on your hard drive.

4   Click the table to select it, and copy it to the Clipboard by pressing Command-C.

	2009	2008	Better/ (Worse)
Turnover	$4,822	$4,602	$220
EBITDA (per leaver)	$1,385	$1,418	($33)
Leaver costs	($37)	($8)	($29)
Depreciation and other	($692)	($704)	$12
Operating profit post leavers	656	706	(50)
Associates and other	3	(3)	6
Finance costs (net)	(100)	(154)	54
Profit before tax	599	549	50
Tax	(139)	(143)	4
Tax rate	24.9%	26.0%	1.1%
Profit for the period	420	406	14
Earning per share	5.0	4.8	0.2

5   Return to Keynote.

6   In the slide navigator, choose slide 7.

You're going to replace the table in the slide with the table you just copied in Pages.

7   Select the table in the current slide and press Delete.

8   Choose Edit > Paste (or press Command-V) to add the new table.

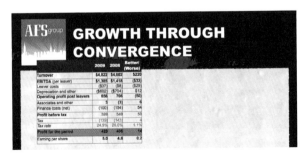

The new table should be resized and modified.

9   Drag the table to position it on the page. Drag the selection handles to adjust its size. Position the table in the slide using the pop-up alignment guides as a visual reference.

10   In the format bar, change the font to Arial Narrow and the point size to 24 points.

11   Select the Slide inspector and click Transition. Then choose the following options:

▶   Effect—3D Effects: Doorway

▶   Duration—1.50 s

12   Press Command-S to save your document.

You can compare your presentation to the file **05_Presentation Stage 04.key** from the lesson folder.

Saving a PowerPoint or PDF File

Not only is it easy to bring PowerPoint presentations into Keynote, it's just as easy to save presentations that you can share with PowerPoint users or others who don't have Keynote installed on their computers. Two common formats are a PDF file or a PowerPoint file—although it's important to note that neither the PDF nor the PowerPoint file format supports all of the animation and display features that Keynote offers.

NOTE ▶ We'll explore many other options for publishing and exporting a presentation in the next lesson. For example, one way to share an animated presentation with users who don't have Keynote is to create a QuickTime movie using the Manual Advance option.

Saving a PowerPoint File

To save a copy of your presentation as a PowerPoint (.ppt) file to share it with PowerPoint users, simply use the Save As dialog.

1   Choose File > Save As or press Command-Shift-S.

2   In the Save As field, modify the filename for the document (if desired).

3   In the Where pop-up menu, select the location where you want to save the PowerPoint file. Click the disclosure triangle to the right of the Save As field if the file browser isn't visible, and navigate to the desired folder.

4   Select the "Save a copy as" checkbox and choose PowerPoint Presentation.

   NOTE ▶ You can choose File > Save As, then select the checkbox next to "Save copy as." From the pop-up menu you can choose Keynote '08 to save a version of the presentation that is compatible with iWork '08. Some features of your presentation may be disabled if they are new to Keynote '09.

   MORE INFO ▶ You'll learn how to share your slides as PDF files in Lesson 6.

5   Click Save.

   A new PowerPoint file is created.

   NOTE ▶ If your presentation has video in it, Keynote creates a folder—which must always accompany your presentation file—that contains movie elements. Not all video formats play under all Windows configurations, so be sure to test your presentation on the Windows-based computer that you'll be using.

Sending a PDF or PowerPoint File with Mail

If you just want to quickly send a PDF or PowerPoint version of your presentation via email, Keynote gives you a shortcut. The revised file formats used in iWork '09 are ready for email with no additional preparation.

1 With your Keynote presentation open, choose Share > Send Via Mail > PDF or PowerPoint. Your computer will switch to Mail or open it and automatically attach the exported file.

2 Address the email message to the recipient.

3 Enter a subject and message for the email.

4 In the From menu, choose which account to use.

5 Click Send to deliver the message (you must be connected to the Internet).

Lesson Review

1. How do you import a PowerPoint presentation into Keynote?
2. How can you import a Microsoft Word document using the iWork suite?
3. What must you click first to add unique timings to a build animation?
4. How do you add animation to a slide?
5. How do you save a Keynote project as a PowerPoint presentation?

Answers

1. Choose File > Open; then navigate to the PowerPoint file and click Open.
2. Open Pages and then open a Microsoft Word document. You can copy material from Pages into Keynote or Numbers.
3. Click the More Options button to access timing controls.
4. Select the slide, then open the Build inspector and choose a build animation.
5. Choose File > Save As. Select the "Save a copy as" checkbox and choose PowerPoint Presentation.

6

Lesson Files Lessons > Lesson_06 > 06Photo Portfolio.key

Time This lesson takes approximately 45 minutes to complete.

Goals Add comments and presenter notes to a presentation

Index a presentation with Spotlight

Customize the presenter's view

Rehearse the presentation

Give a presentation with a portable computer

Control Keynote with an iPhone or iPod touch

Create a self-running slideshow

Run a presentation as a kiosk

Lesson 6

Rehearsing and Delivering Your Presentation

The whole point of building a presentation is to actually give it to a living, breathing, and sometimes stress-inducing audience. One of the best things you can do to improve a presentation is to rehearse it in advance.

A rehearsal is when the fine-tuning happens: you may decide to reorganize a section, move slides around, or skip slides to get your presentation audience-ready. You can insert notes about the presentation, adding comments to a slide to help remind yourself of changes or to flag points for other team members. You can also use speaker notes to help keep you on track during the presentation.

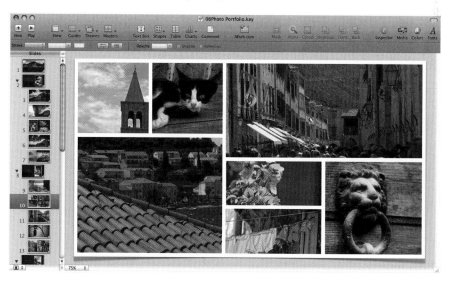

In this lesson, we'll use a photographer's portfolio to practice rehearsing, modifying, and delivering a presentation to suit our intended audience—in this case, a group of other photo enthusiasts.

Reviewing a Presentation with Light Table View

In earlier lessons, we used the navigator and outline views to build a presentation. For this exercise, we'll use a versatile view called *light table view*, which is great for organizing and reordering your slides—particularly if your show contains a lot of images, charts, or other graphical objects.

Because light table view displays thumbnails of your slides, you can usually see most of your presentation in one glance. This makes it easy to delete, skip, duplicate, or move slides, and get them into exactly the right order for a compelling presentation.

1   In the Lesson_06 folder, open **06Photo Portfolio.key**.

2   In the toolbar, click the View button and choose Light Table.

3   Click the button in the lower left corner, and from the thumbnails menu, choose Large to make it easier to see your slides.

Note that the slides are numbered to help you see the flow of the presentation.

Let's change the order of the slides to improve the presentation's flow. Slide 9 is a nice detail shot, but slide 10 would probably make a better introduction to this section, because showing multiple photos would allow you to talk about the country where the photos were taken. Let's reorder the two slides.

4   Click slide 10 to select it.

5   Drag slide 10 to go before slide 9.

> **TIP** ▶ To modify a slide, double-click it. This will return you to either outline or navigator view (whichever view you used last).

6   Press Command-S to save your document.

Adding Comments to a Presentation

To add notes or reminders to a presentation while you work on it, you can add comments, which look and act like sticky notes. Comments appear while you're editing your slides, but are invisible when you present the slideshow.

1   Double-click slide 7 to return to navigator view.

2   In the toolbar, click the Comment button to add a comment to the slide.

A virtual sticky note is added to the slide.

▶ Flight-Checking Your Presentation

Here's a checklist for reviewing your presentation.

Get an Overview

▶ Step back and look at your presentation in context, as a whole. Use the light table view.

▶ Make sure you have an overall balance of graphics throughout, rather than text-heavy sections and graphics-heavy sections.

▶ Check for repetitive chart types. If you have four bar charts in a row, is that really the most effective way to deliver the information?

▶ Check for repetitive images. If you use it once, don't use it again.

▶ Check for repetitive editorial. You shouldn't need to make a point more than once.

▶ Don't overuse flashy transitions between slides. Used sparingly, they're great. Too many, and they can become gimmicky.

Check Your Organization

▶ Does the order of your slides reflect the priorities of the presentation? If not, try dragging them into a new order and see if that works better.

▶ Have you made it easy to find the most important points?

▶ Try skipping less-critical slides by Control-clicking and choosing Skip Slide. This will drop a slide from the presentation, but not permanently delete it.

Check Your Colors and Type

▶ Not all color combinations work for presentations. Some, like yellow type on an orange background, lack adequate contrast. Printing your slides as grayscale images first is a great way to check for good contrast.

▶ Check for readability: is the type large enough, and is the font clean enough, to be easily read?

> ### Flight-Checking Your Presentation *(continued)*

▶ Check for type density: don't jam too many points onto one slide. Aim for a generous amount of white space.

▶ Use graphics, fonts, and transitions that are appropriate to the subject matter.

Proof Your Presentation

▶ Spell check one last time; choose Edit > Spelling > Spelling. Alternatively, you can Control-click an underlined word and pick a replacement from a list of suggestions.

▶ Print out a hard (paper) copy of your slides, then take a red pen to the pages. The traditional route is the best way to spot errors.

▶ Have a friend help you out. A co-worker can often find errors that you'll miss. You can use iWork.com to easily post a presentation for online review.

Take It to the Big Screen

▶ Run through your presentation on a large screen with a projector if you possibly can. This "tech rehearsal" is a great time to look for glitches, missing transitions, and readability issues, as well as checking for overall flow and timing.

3 Click inside the note and type: *Find a stronger image to use here.* Format the text using the format bar to make it larger.

4 Drag the note so it is located over the left photo.

To make the note stand out even more, you can change its color.

5   In the format bar, click the Fill color well.

6   Choose a red color for the note.

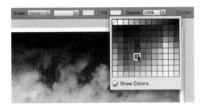

7   Press Command-S to save your presentation.

TIP To permanently remove a note, click the X in the upper right corner of the note.

Adding Presenter Notes

Keynote lets you include *presenter notes* (also called speaker notes) to prompt you as you speak. During your presentation, you can see the notes for each slide on your Mac's display; the audience won't be able to see your notes.

Presenter notes are incredibly handy. They can be used to jog your memory about an important talking point or to add that useful nugget that you want to mention but which would clutter up your slide with too much information.

You can also use notes to mark which member of your presentation team should speak when, or to add time-check markers so you stay within your speaking time. Well-planned presenter notes can add that extra bit of professionalism and confidence to your presentation.

Let's try adding a presenter note to a slide.

1   In the slide navigator, select slide 4.

2   Choose View > Show Presenter Notes.

3 Click in the area below the canvas and type *Discuss black and white conversion process and tinting with Aperture.*

Discuss black and white conversion process and tinting with Aperture.

4 Press Command-S to save your presentation.

Printing Presenter Notes

The presenter notes you've prepared are now part of your Keynote project. On some occasions you may want to create printed copies of your slides and presenter notes to refer to during your speech. Printed copies are also great to use for rehearsing if a portable computer is not available.

1 Choose File > Print. Open the Printer pop-up menu to display the Print options.

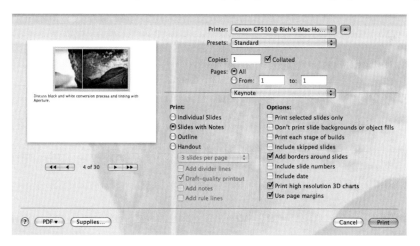

2 From the Print options, choose Slides with Notes. This option prints a single slide per page, with your speaker notes printed below each slide.

> **NOTE** ▶ To print multiple slides per page with notes, select Handout. (See "Printing Handouts," in Lesson 7 for more information.)

3 Click Print if you want to send the document to your printer, or press the Esc key to exit the window without printing.

Indexing Your Presentation with Spotlight

Starting with Mac OS X v10.4 Tiger, Apple has made it easier and more efficient to search the contents of your hard drive. Using Spotlight, you can enter keywords to search a constantly updated index of your system. The more metadata you add to a document, the more accurate your index will be.

Keynote lets you index your presentation files for easy searching later. You can add your name, the title of your presentation, keywords, and comments to a Keynote presentation.

1 Open the Document inspector.

2 Click the Spotlight button.

3   Enter the information you want to use for searches:

▶   Author—[*Your name*]

▶   Title—Photography Portfolio

▶   Keywords—Titles of slides or major topics

▶   Comments—A description of the presentation

4   Save your work.

The next time you search with Spotlight, your presentation will be easier to find.

Rehearsing Your Presentation

Practicing a presentation allows you to work out timing and flow issues, as well as grow more comfortable with your slides.

When giving a Keynote presentation, you have the option of using a *presenter display*. This is a specialized display that can include a timer, speaker notes, and other useful information, such as the next slide.

Many presenters choose to view the presenter display on a computer screen while they send the full slideshow to the connected projector. You can practice your presentation and simulate the presenter display even without a projector connected to your Mac.

1   Choose Keynote > Preferences to open the Preferences window.

2 Click the Presenter Display icon to open the Presenter Display pane.

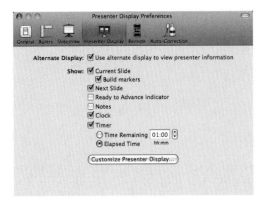

3 Choose any of the options that you find useful:

▶ Alternate Display—Show the presenter's view on a portable or second computer monitor (not the projector).

▶ Show: Current Slide—Display the active slide.

▶ Show: Next Slide—Show the next build or slide in the presentation.

▶ Show: Notes—Display any speaker notes that you may have added.

▶ Show: Clock—Show the current time.

▶ Show: Timer—Count down from a specific time (if you have a limit) or show how much time has passed since the start of your presentation.

▶ Show: Ready to Advance indicator— Show bar to indicate when you can continue to the next slide. A green bar means the next build or animation is loaded and ready for playback. A red bar means you should wait before clicking.

4 Close the Preferences window.

5 In the slide navigator, choose slide 1.

6   Choose Play > Rehearse Slideshow.

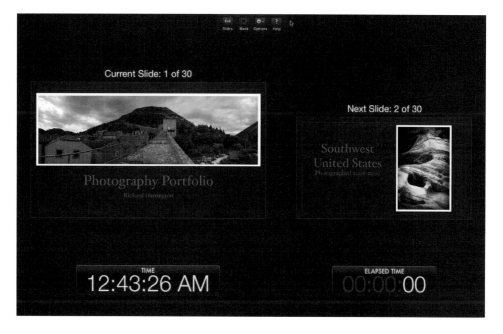

You can now rehearse your presentation with much more information at a glance: your notes, the time, the remaining time, and which slide comes next.

7   Press the Spacebar to advance the presentation from slide to slide.

NOTE ▶ In the presenter display, you cannot see animations such as transitions or builds. At least once, you should rehearse your slideshow by running it in normal mode to see exactly what the audience will see. To do so, choose Play > Play Slideshow.

8   When you're finished, press the Esc key to exit the rehearsal.

TIP ▶ In the presenter display, dots indicate how many builds you have on a slide. Initially, all of the dots are blue to indicate that the animation builds are present. As you click and animate each build, the blue dots become empty circles. Be sure to enable the Ready to Advance indicator so you'll know when an animation is ready for playback.

Giving Your Presentation with a Portable Computer

You will probably be giving your Keynote presentation using a portable computer. Using a portable, you can easily rehearse the presentation at home or elsewhere, as well as make last-minute changes.

Connecting a Portable Computer to a Projector

Depending on your Mac portable model, the steps for connecting an external monitor will vary. Here's a general guide to connecting a portable computer to a projector for your presentation.

1   Close your portable so that the Mac goes to sleep.

2   Determine whether the projector requires a VGA connector or a DVI connector.

VGA connector   DVI connector

> **NOTE** ▸ Different Mac portable computers have various connector options. You might have to use a video adapter to connect to your presentation display, so it's a good idea to carry a both a VGA and a DVI converter in your portable computer bag. You can pur-chase the correct adapter from an Apple Store or an authorized Mac reseller.

3   If necessary, connect the Mini DisplayPort, DVI to VGA, or Mini-DVI to DVI adapter to your portable.

4   Connect the display cable from the projector to your Mac portable.

5   Open your Mac portable and wait a moment to allow your Mac to detect the display. If your Mac desktop appears on the projector, you can skip to step 8.

   If the portable does not communicate with the projector (in other words, if your computer's desktop does not appear on the projector), you may have to manually configure your Mac to detect the display using the following steps:

6   To force the portable to detect the display, click the Apple menu and choose System Preferences. Then choose Displays.

7   Click the Detect Displays button.

   Your Mac should detect the display and choose the appropriate settings, and your Mac desktop should be displayed by the projector.

NOTE ▸ If your computer still fails to recognize the projector, check your cable connections, make sure the projector is powered on, and restart your computer.

8 Select the monitor resolution that matches your slideshow resolution.

You can check your slide size in the Document inspector.

If the exact resolution is not available, choose the closest size.

9 Return to Keynote.

10 Choose Keynote > Preferences.

11 Click Slideshow and select the "Present on secondary display" radio button.

NOTE ▶ If the presenter display shows up on the wrong screen during your presentation, simply click the Options button at the top of the presenter display window and choose Swap.

12 Select "Scale slides up to fit display."

Keynote scales the slides to automatically fill as much of the screen as possible on the target display.

TIP ▶ You can also choose to scale up slides during a presentation by clicking the Options button in the presenter display window.

13 Click Presenter Display and select the "Use alternate display to view presenter information" checkbox.

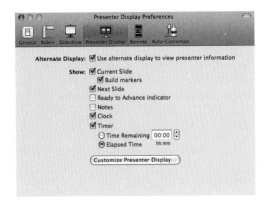

The presenter display will show useful information about your presentation that can be viewed on your portable computer screen while the audience sees the show on the projector or second monitor without that information.

14 Close the Preferences window.

15 Click Play and test your slideshow.

Pause, Skip, Resume

It's very common to switch gears during a presentation. For instance, you may want to switch to another application to show off a document or to access a file at the Finder level. Keynote offers several ways to pause or navigate a presentation:

▶   To pause a presentation and display the current slide, press the F key (as in *freeze*). To resume the presentation, press the F key or Spacebar.

▶   To pause the presentation and display a black screen, press the B key or click the Black button at the top of the presenter display.

▶   To resume the presentation, press the B key or Spacebar.

▶   To pause the presentation and display a white screen, press the W key. To resume the presentation, press the W key or Spacebar.

▶   To pause the presentation and hide Keynote, press the H key. To resume the presentation, click the Keynote icon in the Dock.

▶   To skip to a specific slide, you can either type its number or click the Slides button in the presenter display to display an interactive preview of all slides.

▶   To see a list of keyboard shortcuts you can use while you're giving a presentation, press the Help, ? (question mark), or / (forward slash) key during the presentation. Your audience may see your "cheat sheet" as well, so use this shortcut sparingly.

Using an iPhone or iPod as a Remote Control

Using a remote control to run your presentation lets you move away from the computer while you speak. This can make for a more dynamic presentation, as it allows you to interact with and engage your audience.

One way to take precise control of a presentation is by using the Keynote Remote application for iPhones and iPod touch devices.

> **NOTE ▶** Keynote fully supports several third-party remotes as well as the Apple Remote. A unique advantage of the Keynote Remote application is its significant range, because the application controls your computer over a Wi-Fi network. Additionally, you can see the upcoming slides on your iPod touch or iPhone screen.

Pairing Keynote Remote with Your Mac

Before you can control your computer, you will have to pair the remote with your computer. This requires that both your computer and iPod touch or iPhone are on the same network.

1   From the iTunes App Store, purchase, download, and install the Keynote Remote application.

2   To pair the remote with Keynote, choose Keynote > Preferences.

3   Click Remote.

4   Select "Enable iPhone and iPod touch Remotes."

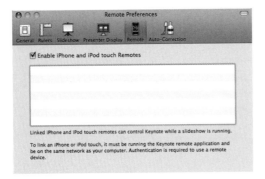

5   Make sure your iPhone or iPod touch is on the same Wi-Fi network as your computer.

   NOTE ▶ For information on joining Wi-Fi networks, see the documentation for your iPod touch or iPhone.

6   Open the Keynote Remote application on your iPod touch or iPhone.

7   Tap the Link to Keynote button.

8   Choose New Keynote Link.

   Keynote Remote displays a four-digit code that is required to link the devices.

9   Your remote device appears in the Remote Preferences window on your portable. Click the Link button.

10   Enter the four-digit code.

   Once the code is accepted, the window closes.

11   Close the Remote Preferences window.

Creating a Network

If no wireless network is available, you can create a computer-to-computer network to pair Keynote Remote with your portable computer.

1   On your Mac portable, open System Preferences.

2   Choose Network.

3   Choose AirPort. From the Network Name pop-up menu, choose Create Network.

4   Enter a name for the network and leave Channel set to Automatic.

5   Select the box next to Require Password and assign a password.

6   Re-enter the password in the Verify field.

7   Choose a Security method. (40-bit WEP is the most compatible choice.)

8   Click OK when you are ready to begin the network.

Your iPhone or iPod touch can join this new network like any other network.

9   When finished, choose to join the new AirPort network on your iPhone or iPod touch.

> **TIP** If you have the AirPort status shown in your menu bar, you can click it and choose Create Network. When finished, you can choose Disconnect from the AirPort menu.

Using Keynote Remote

When your portable and iPod or iPhone are on the same network, the Keynote Remote application offers two ways to control your presentation.

1   In the Keynote Remote settings window, choose from the Orientation options.

Portrait—The portrait view allows you to see presenter notes and view the current slide only.

Landscape—The landscape view shows you the current and next slides.

Portrait orientation   Landscape orientation

2   On your iPod touch or iPhone, tap Done to close the settings window.

3   Tap Play Slideshow to view the presentation.

> **NOTE ▶** Tilting the phone or iPod will not change the orientation. Tap the Options button and then Settings to make a change. You can change the Orientation setting in the middle of a slideshow without exiting.

4   To advance slides, swipe your finger across the screen from right to left (to go backward, swipe left to right). To scroll through lengthy presenter notes, flick up or down in the presenter notes portion of the display.

The spinning gear indicator means the slide is loading. If a slide has several graphics or complex animation, it may take a few seconds to load.

5   When finished with a presentation, you can press the Esc key on your computer.

You've unplugged yourself from the computer while presenting. Being free to move about the room makes it easier to connect with your audience and deliver a more dynamic presentation.

Creating a Self-Running Slideshow

Keynote '09 makes it easy to create a self-running slideshow with narration. This is great for making an auto-play presentation for an event, exhibition, classroom, or trade show kiosk.

It also works well if you want to record a presentation for later delivery. For example, some people prefer to record their timings for each slide, so they don't have to click to advance slides during the presentation. This type of presenting style works well for shorter presentations that are repeated multiple times, because it keeps your presentation consistently paced each time you give it.

Keynote can record not only your narration of each slide but also the duration of time each slide or animation is displayed as you give the presentation. To record your voice, you can use your Mac's built-in microphone or an external mic.

> **NOTE ▶** Not all Macs have built-in microphones. You'll find a microphone on any computer with a built-in iSight camera. To hook up an external audio source, see Apple's technical article 304741, "Mac 101: Audio Attachments" (http://support.apple .com/kb/HT2508).

1   Make sure the internal or external microphone is properly connected and functioning.

2   Open System Preferences.

3   Click the Sound button and then click the Input tab to configure settings as necessary.

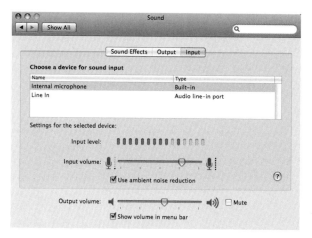

You can select a device and adjust the input volume.

TIP   If available, be sure to select the "Use ambient noise reduction" checkbox to reduce background noise in the recording.

4   Click slide 1 to choose it.

A recorded slideshow will always play back from the first slide that has audio.

5   When you are ready to begin, choose Play > Record Slideshow.

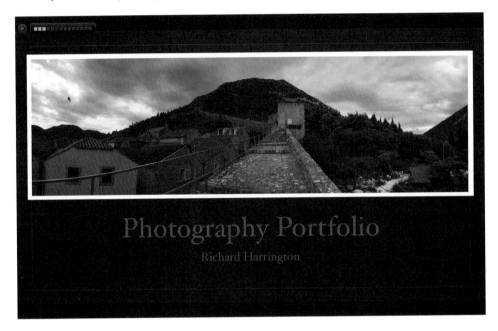

The presentation immediately goes into play mode and opens in full screen. All of the standard controls for navigating your slideshow are available.

6   Press the Spacebar to advance slides as necessary, and speak clearly into the microphone. Just talk about the slides—this is just for practice, so don't worry about what you're saying.

You'll notice a red light in the upper left corner of the screen, which indicates that recording is active. The levels meter helps you monitor the volume of your recording.

TIP ▶   If you see only a few bars, your audio level is probably too low. Try adjusting your recording volume in the Sound system preferences, speaking more loudly, or moving the mic closer to your mouth. However, if the bars consistently extend to the far right, your recording may be distorted.

7 Press the F key (freeze) to pause recording.

This is handy if you want to catch your breath, clear your throat, get a drink of water, or organize your thoughts for the next section of your show.

8 Press any key to resume recording. When you're finished, press the Esc key to stop playback.

Your recording is automatically stored as part of your presentation. Be sure to save the file to permanently capture the audio.

Your presentation is now ready to use. When you play the slideshow, it will automatically use your timing and recorded audio.

NOTE ▶ If you decide to permanently delete the audio recording and timing, choose File > Clear Recording.

Running a Presentation as a Kiosk

A kiosk-style presentation is designed for instances when you want a self-running slideshow that allows viewers to navigate and view slides, but doesn't let them exit the presentation. It usually runs on a computer without supervision—for example, in a museum, school, or retail environment.

You may want to make just a few modifications to control the kiosk presentation playback experience.

1 Open the Document inspector and click the Document button.

2 Select the "Restart show if idle for" checkbox and set the time to *5 m* (minutes).

3 If you want, select the "Require password to exit show" checkbox.

NOTE ▶ If you choose this option, you must know your system username and password to exit. If you do not, you'll have to power down the computer and reboot.

4   Choose Keynote > Preferences and click the General button. Ensure that both the "Copy audio and movies into document" and "Copy theme images into document" checkboxes are selected under Saving.

These selections store all of the required resources (other than fonts) in the project file, so it will work on another computer.

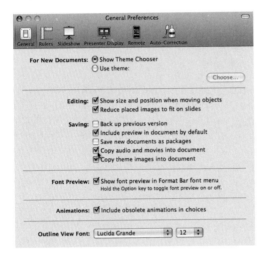

5   Close the Preferences window.

6   Choose File > Save to save your presentation.

7   Click the Play button to view your presentation. When you are done exploring, press the Esc key. (If you required a password, you must enter the username and password for the computer you are on.)

TIP You can also run any presentation as a kiosk. Just be sure to set the timing for each transition or build, then select the Document inspector and choose "Automatically play upon open" and "Loop Slideshow" from the Document inspector.

Your presentation is complete and you're now ready to play it on any system with Keynote installed.

Lesson Review

1. How do you add comments to your presentation?

2. How do you use the presenter display to rehearse your presentation?

3. If your computer can't communicate with a connected display, what can you do?

4. Can you control a Keynote presentation with an iPod touch or iPhone?

5. How do you create a self-running slideshow?

Answers

1. Click the Comment button to add a virtual sticky note.

2. Choose Play > Rehearse Slideshow.

3. Choose System Preferences and then Displays; then click the Detect Displays button. If that doesn't work, restart the computer with the projector connected and turned on.

4. Yes, by installing the Keynote Remote application from the iTunes Store, you can pair an iPhone or iPod touch with your Mac and use one of those devices as a remote control.

5. With a microphone attached to your Mac (or using the built-in mic) choose Play > Record Slideshow and record a narration track. When you are finished, press Esc and the narration and timing are automatically saved.

7

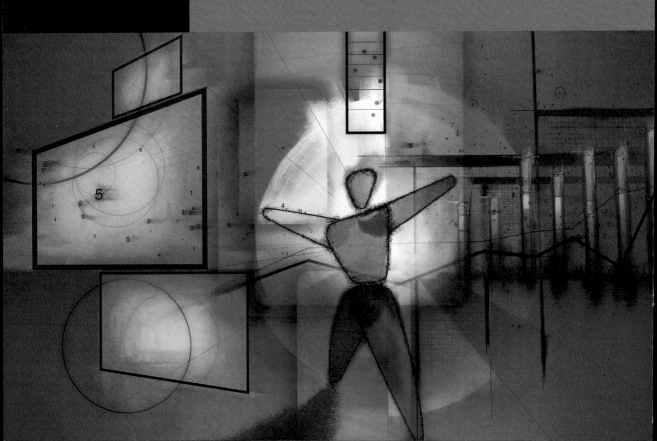

Lesson 7

Publishing Your Presentation

So you gave your presentation, and it was a hit, but not everyone could attend. Now you're being asked not only to send it, in various formats, to all those who missed it but also to share it with a wider audience on the web. Fortunately, Keynote is good at sharing.

The concept is essentially "Create once, publish many." By enabling you to export to a PDF file, a PowerPoint file, a DVD, the Internet, and even to an iPhone or iPod, Keynote ensures that you can distribute your good ideas and important information to the world.

In this lesson, we'll export the photographer's portfolio presentation in a variety of formats for easy publishing.

Printing Handouts

It's often useful to hand out printed copies of your slides so attendees can take notes or review the presentation after the meeting—a great takeaway for your audience. Keynote also lets you publish selected slides, slides with presenter notes, slides without backgrounds, just the outline, and much more.

> **TIP** In some situations, you may want to distribute handouts after your speech. That way, audience members won't skip ahead or browse the handouts during the presentation.

1   Open **07Photo Portfolio.key**, and choose File > Print (or press Command-P).

2   From the Print options, select Handout. Notice that you can select the number of slides per page as well as various display options, including the ability to print each stage of your builds on separate pages.

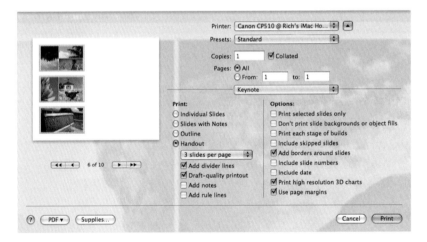

> **TIP** If you want to create a simpler handout, click Outline to omit the slide images and print a text-only version of your presentation. Keynote will use only the title and body text of each slide. Content in free text boxes will not print.

3   To preview printed pages, click the PDF button and choose Open PDF in Preview.

Keynote will generate a temporary PDF file from your document and display it in the Preview application.

NOTE ▸ If you want to save your notes as a PDF file, click the PDF button and choose Save as PDF.

4   Return to Keynote by clicking its icon in the Dock.

TIP To reduce printing costs (and speed up printing), choose the "Draft-quality printout" option in the Print section. It uses less ink, which saves time and money.

Exporting to PDF

The PDF file format has become the format of choice for creating and sharing documents. A PDF file retains its original appearance (including fonts and images) when viewed on computers running Mac OS X, Windows, or UNIX, as well as on mobile devices such as PDAs and cell phones.

Exporting your Keynote presentation as a PDF file is a versatile way to distribute your slides or speaker notes for onscreen viewing. In this exercise, we'll create a PDF and password-protect it.

1 With your presentation open, choose Share > Export. Click the PDF button.

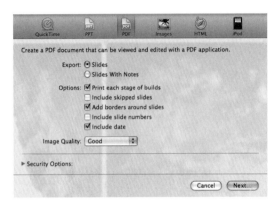

2 Select either Slides (to export slides only) or Slides With Notes. Then select any additional print options:

▶ Print each stage of builds—Creates a separate image for each stage of an object build.

▶ Include skipped slides—Includes skipped slides in the PDF file.

▶ Add borders around slides—Shows borders around slides.

▶ Include slide numbers—Shows a slide number next to each thumbnail.

▶ Include date—Adds the current date to your PDF file.

TIP Keynote does not give you precise control over the file size of the PDF. If you want to optimize the file for the Internet, you can use Automator, which is found in your Applications folder. Just open Automator and follow the guided steps to choose a file. You can then use Compress Images in PDF Document Workflow to shrink the file.

3 Specify an image quality of Good to create the smallest file.

4 Click the disclosure triangle next to Security Options.

5 In the area "Require a password to," select the checkbox next to open document.

6 Enter a password of your choice.

> **TIP** ▶ Using a password helps you protect sensitive information. You can give the recipient the password in a separate message or over the phone.

7 Click Next. Then give the PDF file a name and choose a location for the file.

8 Click Export.

> **NOTE** ▶ Most presentations exported as a PDF are intended to be viewed onscreen. If you want to create a PDF for printing, choose File > Print, and from the PDF pop-up menu, choose Save as PDF. You can also create PDFs when printing speaker notes. Just click the PDF button in the Print dialog and choose Save as PDF.

Exporting to PowerPoint

In Lesson 5, "Importing from PowerPoint and Working with Charts," you imported a Microsoft PowerPoint presentation and enhanced it. But you can also build a presentation in Keynote and then save it as a PowerPoint file, which can be useful when sharing presentations with Windows users.

1   With your presentation opened in Keynote, choose Share > Export. Click PPT.

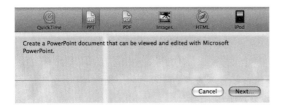

    NOTE ▶ You can also create a PowerPoint file by choosing File > Save As and choosing Save a Copy.

2   Click Next.

    Keynote opens a Save dialog.

3   Give the slideshow a name, and choose a location in which to save the file.

4   Click Export.

PowerPoint handles graphics differently than Keynote, so slight variations may exist between the original Keynote file and the exported PowerPoint slideshow (especially when presented on a Windows computer).

PowerPoint does not support some Keynote features:

▶   Be sure not to disable text by deselecting Body in the Slide inspector. Otherwise bulleted text will be lost when you export to PowerPoint.

▶   PowerPoint does not recognize features such as picture frames and Instant Alpha (transparent images). Alpha channel graphics may work on Macs running PowerPoint, but are less likely to function properly under Windows.

▶   Certain builds and transitions are unique to Keynote and will not export to PowerPoint. If a transition isn't supported, it will be replaced with the closest match or a dissolve.

Exporting Images

Keynote gives you flexible export options to save your slides as image files, which is very useful when preparing graphics for use with a page layout program such as Pages.

1   With your presentation open in Keynote, choose Share > Export. Click the Images button.

2   Select the images you want to export.

You can choose all the slides or specify a range of slides.

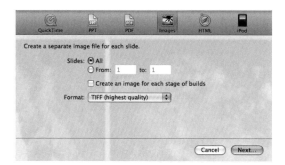

3   If you want to create a separate image for each stage of an object build, select "Create an image for each stage of builds."

4   From the Format pop-up menu, choose a file format suitable for your project and delivery platform:

▶ JPEG (variable quality)—JPEG files support variable compression rates that can be optimized for Internet delivery.

▶ PNG (high quality)—PNG files work well for multimedia use and support embedded transparency.

▶ TIFF (highest quality)—TIFF files work well for print projects.

5   Click Next. Give the file a name and choose a location in which to save the exported file.

It is a good idea to specify a folder that will contain the images.

6   Click Export.

Keynote exports each image and adds a sequential number to the filename you specified.

TIP ▶   To export images direct to your iPhoto library, choose Share > Send to iPhoto.

Making a Movie: Exporting to QuickTime

Making a QuickTime movie of your presentation makes sense for many reasons: to share it with others as a podcast, to edit it together with video footage, or to play it on a computer without Keynote.

In Lesson 3, "Adding Video and Animation" we imported and played back QuickTime movies in a presentation. The QuickTime exporting options in Keynote are just as powerful. Let's make a movie.

1   With the presentation open, choose Share > Export. The Export dialog opens.

2   Click QuickTime to access movie options.

The QuickTime options you choose will depend on the way you intend to use your QuickTime movie. For example, do you want to make a movie that runs interactively on a desktop computer, or do you want to convert your presentation to a video file and combine it with other video clips in iMovie?

For this exercise, let's assume you're creating a simple video of the presentation to put on a CD.

3   From the Playback Uses pop-up menu, choose Manual Advance.

The Playback Uses pop-up menu includes several choices that are suitable for a variety of presentation situations:

▶   Manual Advance—Gives viewers total control over the slideshow and requires them to manually click to advance slides. This is a good option to use for a self-paced viewing of slides or to create a QuickTime backup of your presentation. This method works well if you're creating a version to run from a CD or DVD-ROM, especially on a machine running Windows.

▶   Hyperlinks Only—Lets the movie run as an unattended kiosk presentation. The user can only click hyperlinks to navigate to other slides.

▶ Recorded Timing—Uses timings that you previously recorded into the slideshow by choosing File > Record Slideshow.

▶ Fixed Timing—Runs the slideshow with no user interaction. You must set slide duration and build options. If slides contain automatic build timings, those will be used.

NOTE ▶ You learned how to create hyperlink navigation in Lesson 2, "Adding Photos, Charts, and Sound."

4   Select the "Enter full screen mode when opened" checkbox.

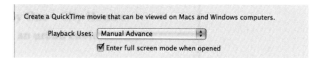

Now let's choose the playback quality settings for the movie.

Keynote offers three quality settings to choose from. The Small option is best for publishing to the Internet, because a smaller file size means a faster download. The Medium option provides more image quality at a larger file size, so use it in situations where downloading time is not an issue. The Large option works best when you want maximum image quality, such as when the movie will play from a hard drive.

5   From the Formats pop-up menu, choose CD-ROM Movie, Medium to set an appropriate playback quality for CD-ROM distribution.

6   This presentation has no audio, so deselect the "Include audio (sound files, movie audio)" checkbox, and click Next.

NOTE ▶ The "Include audio" checkbox is selected by default and can increase the file size of your movie. Even a silent soundtrack increases file size, so be sure to deselect "Include audio" if your presentation is silent.

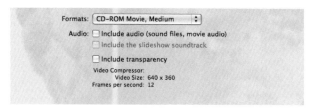

7 Give the movie a name, and choose the location where you want to save the exported file.

8 Click Export.

Depending on the number of slides and the speed of your Mac, the exporting process can take a few minutes. The preview window may distort wide-screen slide presentations, but they will play correctly in the final movie.

9 In the Finder, navigate to the file and double-click the file to open it.

The movie opens in the QuickTime Player application. It should fill your screen and loop indefinitely if you used the settings in this exercise. Because the movie was exported at CD-ROM quality, the image quality will be reduced (especially during animated transitions).

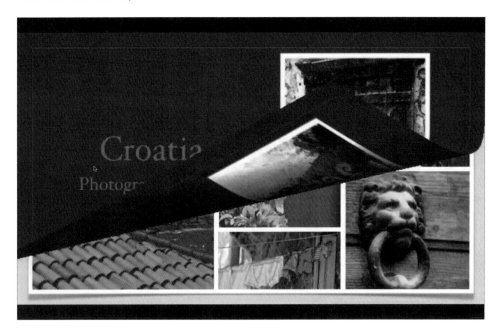

10 Press Esc to close the full-screen movie.

11 Close QuickTime Player and return to Keynote.

Exporting to iPod

The Export to iPod command automatically creates a movie properly sized and compressed for playback on an iPod or iPhone. Publishing your presentation in this format is a great way to take a presentation to a small group or a one-on-one setting.

The exporting process is nearly identical to the Export to QuickTime method, with the following exceptions:

▶ The movie is automatically added to your iTunes library.

▶ The movie is sized to 640 × 480 pixels (the maximum size for a video-capable iPod).

▶ The movie is compressed using the H.264 codec using iPod-compatible settings. (This is identical to the Share > Send to iTunes option.)

> **NOTE** ▶ If you want to include a voiceover narration with your presentation, see "Creating a Self-Running Slideshow" in Lesson 6, "Rehearsing and Delivering Your Presentation."

> **TIP** To publish a movie of your presentation as a podcast, you can use GarageBand. In Keynote, choose Share > Send To > GarageBand to create a movie file. You can use the podcasting tools in GarageBand to enhance the movie with music and then publish it as a podcast. For more information on podcasting, see *Apple Training Series: iLife '09* (Peachpit Press, 2009).

Exporting to HTML

Publishing a presentation on the Internet has several benefits. After a public presentation, the Internet is a great place for attendees to find your notes. Posting a presentation can also drive potential customers to your website. Keynote can build webpages from a presentation and place each slide as a graphic on a webpage.

> **TIP** Want to share the presentation with others during the construction stage? See "Sharing a Presentation on iWork.com" later in this lesson. Sharing a document on iWork.com can be helpful if you're developing a group presentation or creating one for a client.

Creating a webpage with Keynote is easy:

1   If necessary, in the Lesson_07 folder, open **07Photo Portfolio.key**.

2   Choose Share > Export; then click HTML.

3   In the Slides area, choose All.

    You're going to export all the slides to a website.

4   To include navigation controls (which is a good idea), select the "Include navigation controls" checkbox.

    This option adds Home, Previous, and Next navigation buttons.

5   For maximum compatibility with all web browsers, from the Format pop-up menu, choose JPEG.

6   Adjust the compression quality to suit your needs.

    A value between 50% and 80% is acceptable for most uses. Smaller numbers mean a quicker download, but also reduced image quality.

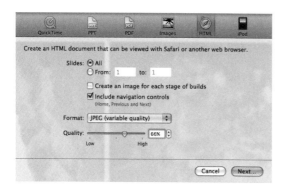

NOTE ▶ One drawback of the export module for the webpage is that many web browsers may cut off large slides. You can resize the image files in the folder Photo Portfolio by using an image editing application or Automator.

7   Click Next.

8   Name the webpage *Photo Portfolio*, and choose a location in which to save the exported file.

9   Click Export.

The webpage takes a moment to generate and then can be viewed by opening the HTML file that Keynote creates.

MORE INFO ▶ If you want more options for creating your webpage, send your slides to iPhoto and then create a MobileMe Gallery using the robust tools in iPhoto.

Sending to iWeb

Another way to share a presentation on the Internet is to create a website by using iWeb. This option is different from exporting HTML because you can share a video podcast. It also offers file-sharing capabilities for PDF and Keynote files.

1   With your presentation open, choose Share > Send To > iWeb.

2   From the File Type pop-up menu, choose PDF, and for this exercise, leave the default values unchanged.

The menu includes three file-type choices:

▶   PDF—Creates a PDF file for download and viewing.

▶   Keynote Document—Shares the Keynote file with others on your presentation team.

▶   Video Podcast—Converts the presentation to an iPod-compatible movie and offers a subscription option.

3   Click Send to export the presentation to iWeb.

iWeb opens as the active application.

NOTE ▶ If you don't have a MobileMe account active, iWeb presents a MobileMe signup dialog that you'll need to fill out before iWeb will display the template chooser. You can choose to register, sign up for a trial, or click Cancel.

In iWeb, you can specify a page type, as well as choose from several different themes.

4   For this exercise, choose the Darkroom theme and the Blog page type.

iWeb offers several themes to stylize the website. The Darkroom theme is designed for photography-oriented projects. Using a blog page allows you to describe the presentation and make the source file available for download.

5   Click Choose to create the webpage.

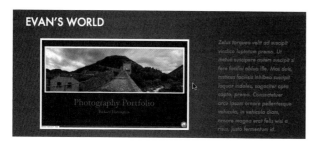

NOTE ▶ See the iWeb Help menu for more information on publishing web pages. Be sure to check out *Apple Training Series: iLife '09* for more on podcasting with iWeb and GarageBand.

Sending to YouTube

Keynote '09 allows you to publish your presentation to YouTube, the popular video-sharing website owned by Google. You can convert a Keynote presentation into a self-running movie configured for public or private viewing; and then, to share the presentation, you can distribute the link to potential viewers. This is an easy way to share a portfolio, a presentation, or other slides with a broader audience.

1   With your presentation open, choose Share > Send To > YouTube.

A dialog appears prompting you for additional input about your YouTube account.

NOTE ▶ You'll require a YouTube account to publish your video. You can set up a free YouTube account at www.youtube.com.

2   Enter your user name in the Account field.

3 Enter your password in the Password field.

4 From the Category pop-up menu, choose a category for your movie.

   Categories will help others find your content while browsing YouTube.

5 Enter whatever information you choose into the Title and Description fields.

6 Add keywords into the Tags field that will help people find your movie when
   searching for it on the YouTube website. Be sure to put a comma between each
   tag to separate them.

TIP If you don't want your movie to be available to the general public, select the
"Personal video" checkbox.

7 From the Size To Publish pop-up menu, choose a resolution to identify how large
   the movie should be. You can choose Mobile – 480 × 272 (which is good for mobile
   devices) or Medium – 640 × 360 (for use on a computer or Apple TV.)

8 Click Next.

   A new dialog opens with options to control the movie playback. The controls are
   similar to the iDVD export options discussed later in this lesson.

9   For this slideshow, let's have a slower-paced presentation that allows the viewer to enjoy the slides. Use the following options to set the pace of your show:

▶   Playback Uses—Fixed Timing

▶   Slide Duration—10 seconds

▶   Build Duration—2 seconds

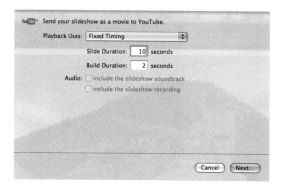

10 Click Next.

Read the YouTube Terms of Service, and be sure you have permission to upload the content.

NOTE ▶ For this exercise, you can publish this sample presentation. The rights to the photos still belong to the author, Richard Harrington.

11 Click Publish to create the movie.

Keynote prepares the slideshow and sends it to YouTube. Depending on the size of your presentation, as well as your Internet connection speed, this may take several minutes. When the export is complete, a new dialog appears.

12 Click the View button to see your movie on YouTube.

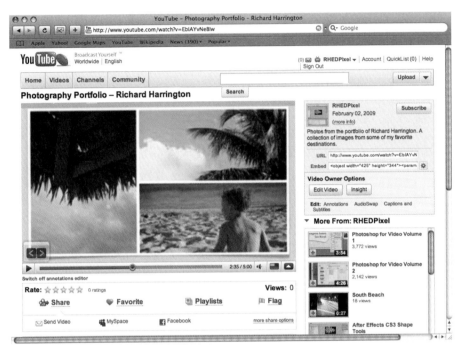

The video may not be immediately available after publishing. You can log in to your account later to see if it has been populated to the YouTube site. This process can take a while depending on how many videos have been published that day. If many new videos are submitted, yours may be queued for the server.

YouTube offers a special interactive controller for advancing slides. The YouTube player can also be embedded into blogs or websites. See the YouTube site for more information on sharing and playing YouTube files.

Sharing a Presentation with iWork.com

To more efficiently collaborate with others, you can post a document to iWork.com, a document-sharing service hosted by Apple. This service is currently in beta, which means it is open to public trial while still under development. The service is currently offered free of charge and allows others to view, comment on, or download presentations you have posted there.

1   Choose Share > Share via iWork.com.

   If this is your first time using the service on your current computer, you'll have to sign in.

   NOTE ▶ If you already have an Apple ID—from the iTunes store, MobileMe, or the Apple Discussions forums—you can use the same ID for iWork.com. Otherwise, you must click Create New Account to sign up for a free Apple ID.

2   If necessary, enter your Apple ID and password, and click Sign In.

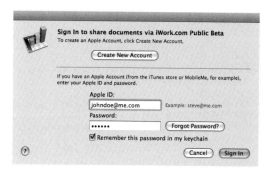

3   A new dialog opens and prompts you for information required to share the file.

   NOTE ▶ You must be connected to the Internet to share a file with the iWork.com Public Beta. You must also have an email account set up on your computer to send invitations to view the document.

4   In the To and Message fields, enter the email addresses to which you want to deliver your document, along with any message for the recipients of the presentation.

5   Modify the Subject field as necessary.

6 From the From pop-up menu, choose the email account that you want to use as the sender.

7 To enable viewer comments and downloads, leave the "Leave comments" and "Download the document" checkboxes marked.

TIP To set specific options for uploading and downloading files, click the Show Advanced button at the bottom of the dialog. Here you can choose which file formats to make available for download. The upload options also allow you to specify a name for the file to be posted. If you are reposting a previously shared document, you can choose to overwrite the old file or to enter a new name in the "Copy to iWork.com as" field.

8 Click the Show Advanced button to specify which files you want to make available in the Download Options.

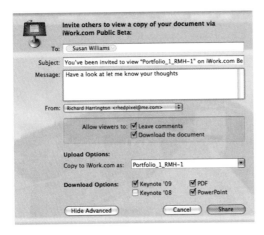

9 Click Share.

Keynote uploads any files you have chosen to share. When the documents are posted, Mail will send invitations. When the documents are online, Keynote will tell you and offer you a chance to view the webpage.

Sharing a Presentation with iChat Theater

At times, you may want to remotely share your presentation. By using iChat Theater, you can present your slides and talk to another person at a distance if both parties are running Mac OS X v10.5 or later. You'll also require a broadband Internet connection in order to share the file.

1   Open iChat and log in.

2   In iChat, choose File > Share a File With iChat Theater.

3   Select the Keynote presentation you want to share.

4   When you select a presentation, the first slide opens in the iChat video window. Keynote also opens the file so that you can control the slides.

5   When a message prompts you to start a video chat, select a name in your buddy list.

6   Choose Buddies > Invite to Video Chat to start the conference.

NOTE ▶ If your buddy doesn't have a video camera, choose Buddies > Invite to One-Way Video Chat. You can also click the Add (+) button at the bottom of the chat window to add additional buddies who are online.

7   Click the forward and backward arrows to control the slides.

8   When finished, close iChat and your Keynote document.

Making a DVD: Exporting to iDVD

In case your portable computer is lost or stolen, you may want to publish your presentation to a DVD as a safety measure.

You can also create DVDs to distribute your presentation to people who could not attend. Support for iDVD requires that you have both iWork '09 and iLife '09. In this exercise, you'll create a DVD of your photo presentation, including an interactive DVD menu.

1   If necessary, open **07Photo Portfolio.key**, and choose Share > Send To > iDVD.

2   For this presentation, from the Video Size pop-up menu, choose Widescreen (16:9).

This menu allows you to specify the size of the video you want to create, based on whether you will be showing it on standard or wide-screen video displays:

▶   Standard—Exports slides for viewing on a standard video display. Use this option if your original presentation has a 4:3 aspect ratio, such as 800 × 600 or 1024 × 768 pixels.

▶   Widescreen (16:9)—Exports the slides for viewing on a wide-screen video display. Use this option if your original presentation has a 16:9 aspect ratio, as used by HD video displays (such as 1280 × 720 or 1920 × 1080 pixels).

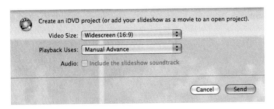

3   For this presentation, from the Playback Uses pop-up menu, choose Manual Advance.

This menu allows you to choose a presentation style:

▶   Manual Advance—Gives viewers total control over the slideshow as they click a mouse button or a skip button on a remote control to advance slides. This is a good option for self-paced reading or for creating a DVD version of your presentation.

▶   Recorded Timing—Uses timings that you previously recorded for your slideshow by choosing the command File > Record Slideshow.

▶   Fixed Timing—Runs the slideshow with no user interaction. You must set slide duration and build options. If slides contain automatic build timings, those will be used.

4   Click Send. Then give the file a unique name and choose your Movies folder as the Save destination.

5   Click Export.

A QuickTime movie file writes to disk. Depending upon the number of slides, the process can take a few minutes to create the DVD video file.

Before exporting finishes, iDVD will open automatically. Do not click any buttons on the welcome screen. Wait for Keynote to complete its export.

The theme you were using the last time you used iDVD will be active, and the theme's soundtrack may be playing. You can click the Start or Stop motion button in the DVD main menu to stop the animation and sound.

6   When Keynote finishes exporting the DVD file, click the Play button in iDVD to test the DVD project:

▶   Click Play Movie to watch the entire movie.

▶   Click Scene Selection to see an index of the presentation.

Creating a DVD Menu

Now let's choose a theme for the main menu of your DVD, a theme that will match the look of the slideshow.

1 Click the Themes button to view all available themes.

2 From the pop-up menu, choose 7.0 Themes.

3 Click the Modern theme to apply it to the main DVD menu.

A warning dialog explains that the DVD is going to perform a Change Project Aspect Ratio operation. That is, iDVD is going to switch the menus to a 16:9 ratio. This is OK, because that is the aspect ratio you used in the portfolio presentation.

4 Click Change to apply the theme.

5 Click OK to apply the theme family so that all submenus are also customized.

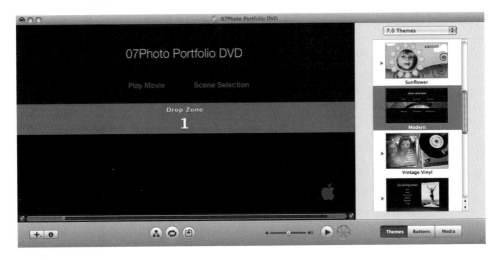

Now you can populate the DVD menu to complete its design.

6 Click the Edit Drop Zones button to access all of the drop zones for the project.

Drop zones are places in the menu layout where you can add your own content, giving you great flexibility when customizing a menu.

7 In the Lesson_07 folder on your hard drive, open the Portfolio Samples folder.

8 Drag the photo **Portfolio 1.jpg** into Drop Zone 1.

9 Drag the photos **Portfolio 2.jpg** and **Portfolio 3.jpg** into Drop Zones 2 and 3.

10 In the main DVD menu, click the Scene Selection button and press Delete.

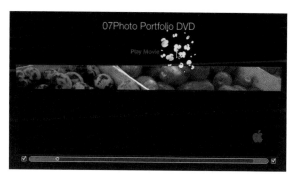

This removes the Scene Selection submenu. If the DVD were longer, this menu would be useful for jumping direct to a scene (where each scene would correspond to one of your Keynote slides). However, in this case, you want the viewer to watch the entire portfolio, so you can remove this element.

11 Click the Play Movie button to select it.

12 Click the Play Movie button again to edit it. Rename the button *View Portfolio.*

13 Click the menu title; then click again to rename it *Photo Portfolio DVD*.

14 Click the Preview button to preview the DVD.

Watch the project all the way through to ensure smooth playback. Because you chose Manual Advance, click the Play button on the remote control to advance to each slide. When finished with the preview, click the Exit button on the remote to stop previewing the DVD.

15 You can now click the Burn button to create the DVD.

The Burn button will open to reveal a yellow and black icon, and you will be prompted to insert a blank DVD. If you'd like to try burning a DVD, insert a blank disc. This step is optional.

16 When you are done with the DVD project, close iDVD and save your project.

Bonus Exercise: Exporting a Presentation for Editing in Final Cut Pro

If you're assembling a video from a meeting or event, you may want to combine live footage with Keynote slides to convey visual information. You can export the Keynote slides for use in iMovie, Final Cut Pro, or another video editing tool.

For this exercise, let's export some slides for editing in Final Cut Pro.

1   From the Lesson_07 folder, open **07Financials.key**. This presentation contains a single animated chart.

2   Open the Document inspector and examine the slide size. The document is currently 1280 × 720, proportions that work well for many HD video formats. Select one of the following values depending upon your video editing format; for this file, we chose to leave it at 1280 × 720.

NTSC DV—choose 720 × 534 (choose Custom slide size in the Document inspector)

NTSC D1—choose 720 × 540 (choose Custom slide size in the Document inspector)

PAL—choose 768 × 576 (choose Custom slide size in the Document inspector)

1080 HD—choose 1920 × 1080

720 HD—choose 1280 × 720

3   Click OK. The slide is resized to a video-ready proportion.

Next, let's make sure that no elements are too close to the edge of the slide, so we avoid cutting off part of the slide when it's converted to video (called *video overscan*).

> **TIP** ▶ When designing graphics for video, leave the outermost 20 percent of your image as video padding. The area inside these borders is called the *title safe area.*

4   If necessary, choose View > Show Rulers.

5   Drag alignment guides from each ruler to the 40 percent mark for the left, right, bottom, and top edges of the image.

Keynote measures from the center, so you are marking off a 10 percent margin in each direction, leaving the innermost 80 percent as your title safe area.

> **NOTE** ▶ Rulers in Keynote are set by default to display as a percentage of the screen area. If your rulers do not match those here, choose Keynote > Preferences > Rulers and select "Display ruler units as percentage."

6   Adjust the sizes and positions of the graphic elements so that they are contained inside the yellow lines.

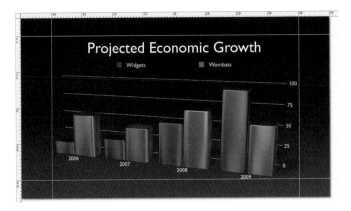

TIP ▶ Thin lines in a graph can shimmer on a television screen due to video interlacing. You can increase the thickness of the lines by clicking a line and then modifying its thickness in the Graphic inspector.

7 Choose Share > Export and click QuickTime.

8 For Playback Uses, choose Fixed Timing; then enter a build duration that meets your needs.

9 From the Formats pop-up menu, choose Custom.

Choose a size that matches your video editing system (in nonsquare pixels for SD formats or square pixels for HD formats). Here, we chose 720 HD.

NTSC DV—choose 720 × 480

NTSC D1—choose 720 × 486

PAL—choose 720 × 576

1080 HD—choose 1920 × 1080

720 HD—choose 1280 × 720

10 In the Video area, click the Settings button to customize the output file.

The Standard Video Compression Settings dialog opens.

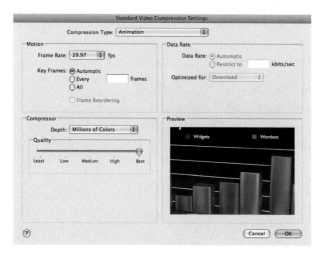

Select the Compression Type and Frame Rate to match the video you're editing; here, we've selected Animation as the compression type, 29.97 frames per second, and Automatic key frames.

Although Final Cut Pro can handle many different codecs, it's a good idea to match the sequence settings of your footage to minimize rendering time.

11 Click OK to apply the settings, and then click Next.

12 Specify a name and destination for the file and click Export. The file is written to your computer's hard drive and is ready for import into Final Cut Pro.

TIP Keynote can export an animation with transparency. Just open the Slide inspector and choose the Appearance tab. Choose None from the Background pop-up menu, then export using the above steps. If you pick the Animation codec, you can choose "include transparency" in the QuickTime export. This adds a standard alpha channel that Final Cut Pro can see.

Lesson Review

1. How can you print presenter notes?
2. How can you export your presentation as a movie file to your hard drive?
3. Which three Internet-ready formats can Keynote export?
4. What is a good method for exporting a presentation for viewing on a television or a computer?
5. How can you share a presentation with others over the Internet and allow for real-time conversation?

Answers

1. Choose File > Print; then choose Keynote from the Print options pop-up menu, and choose Slides With Notes.
2. Choose Share > Export; then click QuickTime.
3. Keynote can create QuickTime, PDF, and HTML files.
4. Keynote can export your project to iDVD, so you can create a DVD.
5. Using iChat Theater is a great way to share your presentation and talk to your buddies at the same time.

Pages: Publishing
Made Easy

8

Lesson Files

Time

This lesson takes approximately 60 minutes to complete.

Goals

Add and format text in a word processing document

Use styles to format a document

Add graphics

Proofread a document

Use research and reference tools

Create an envelope and merge addresses

Lesson 8
Word Processing

At its core, Pages is an easy-to-use word processing application. It features a wealth of tools—including functions to check spelling, find and replace text, and format text with styles as well as refined word processing templates to make great-looking letters, envelopes, forms, résumés, and reports.

Pages shares interface elements with its iWork companions, Keynote and Numbers. If you've explored the Keynote or Numbers lessons, you have a head start on learning Pages because the toolbar, format bar, and inspector are very similar. Activities such as formatting text, inserting photos, and creating charts are nearly identical in each part of the iWork application suite.

In this lesson, you will create a customized letter and a series of addressed envelopes. While doing so, you'll gain an understanding of the word processing tools in Pages.

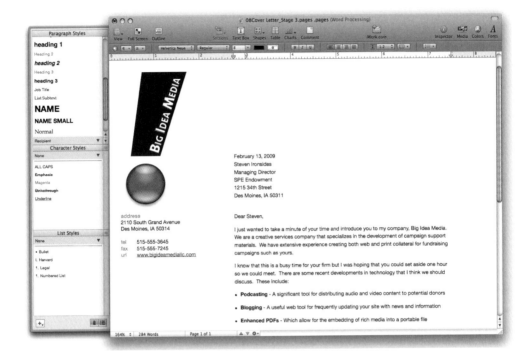

Opening Pages

You can open the Pages application of iWork in three ways:

▶   In your Applications folder, open the iWork '09 folder and then double-click Pages.

▶ In the Dock, click the Pages icon.

▶ Double-click any Pages document.

For this exercise, you'll open Pages from your Applications folder.

1   From the Finder, choose Go > Applications.

2   Locate the iWork '09 folder and open it.

3   Double-click the Pages application icon to open the application.

> **NOTE ▶** If you have not yet copied the lesson files from the DVD to your hard drive, do so before continuing this lesson. For information on copying the files, see "Getting Started," the introduction to this book.

Choosing a Template

When you first launch Pages, the Template Chooser appears, providing access to Apple-designed templates (and any templates you may have saved). Templates contain formatting and layout settings to help present your information and offer a quick way to start a project.

The Template Chooser contains templates that are useful for home, work, and school purposes. You can display all of the word processing templates at once or select a specific category, such as Letters, and view only those templates.

You can edit templates to include new content, as well as modify color and font styles. Examining templates also gives you a good idea of what is possible using Pages. Let's begin by choosing a template for your letter.

1   If the Template Chooser is not already displayed, choose File > New from Template Chooser.

The Template Chooser opens and displays several categories.

The chooser includes 17 letter templates. Some are designed for informal personal correspondence, while others have a very corporate, professional look. Each letter template has a corresponding envelope template. Together, the letter and envelope templates offer great design options for creating attractive stationery.

2   For this lesson, click the Letters category and then select the San Francisco Letter.

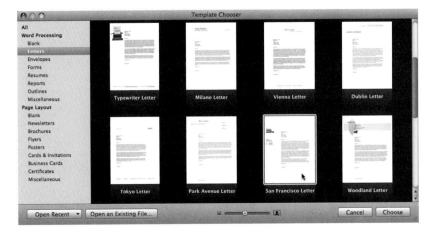

This template works well for corporate correspondence, as it has a wide column on the left suitable for a company logo.

NOTE ▶ San Francisco Letter is near the bottom of the Template Chooser window. You can scroll to the bottom using the scroll bar.

3 Click Choose to open a new document based on the template.

The new template opens. Placeholder text is present in the body of the letter, and information from your Address Book is automatically inserted into the document.

NOTE ▶ You can modify the information placed automatically into the sender fields by updating your personal card in Address Book.

4 Choose File > Save and name the file *08Cover Letter.pages*. Store the file on your local hard drive.

NOTE ▶ In addition to opening a Pages template, you can open and modify a Microsoft Word document file. Choose File > Open; then navigate to the .doc file you want to use. Pages imports the file and opens it as a word processing document. You can edit the imported document and save it as a Pages template.

Writing in Full-Screen Mode

Viewing your Pages document in full-screen mode can help you to stay focused on the writing task at hand. Pages displays controls when you need them, while hiding floating windows and email.

Let's enter full-screen mode:

1 Choose View > Enter Full Screen, or in the toolbar, click Full Screen.

The document appears in full-screen mode. Pages displays only the document, as well as document information (such as word and page count) at the bottom of the screen.

NOTE ▸ Although hidden, the menu and format bar are still accessible by moving your pointer to the top of the screen.

You can modify the appearance of full-screen mode using the View and Background controls, which appear on the far right of the format bar.

Let's make room for the company logo (which you'll add later in this lesson).

2   Click the text box containing the text *from the desk of,* and press Delete to remove it. The text box is removed. You will add a new logo shortly.

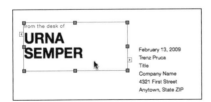
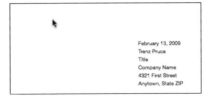

Now let's open the Inspector window so we can precisely modify the document.

3   Choose View > Show Inspector.

The Inspector window offers precise control over the elements in your document. Let's explore your navigation options.

4   Move the pointer to the top of the screen, and when the toolbar appears, set the view to 200%.

Pages zooms in on your document, making the text easier to read. The entire page no longer fits on the screen, so let's scroll down.

5   Move your pointer to the right of the document.

A scroll bar appears, allowing you navigate the document. You can also scroll your document using the scroll button on an Apple Mighty Mouse or a two-finger drag on a Multi-Touch trackpad.

TIP ▶   To quickly switch pages in a multipage document, move the pointer to the left edge of the screen to view Pages thumbnails of each page. You can click a thumbnail to switch to a specific page.

You're now ready to edit your letter. For the rest of the lesson, let's edit your document using the format bar controls and the menu items at the top of the screen. If you want to exit full-screen mode, choose View > Exit Full Screen or press Esc at any time.

Replacing Placeholder Text

One of the first things you'll want to do with your document is replace the Lorem Ipsum placeholder text with your own text.

Dear Trenz,

> Lorem ipsum dolor sit amet, consectetur adipiscing elit, set eiusmod tempor incidunt et labore
> et dolore magna aliquam. Ut enim ad minim veniam, quis nostrud exerc. Irure dolor in
> reprehend incididunt ut labore et dolore magna aliqua. Ut enim ad minim veniam, quis nostrud
> exercitation ullamco laboris nisi ut aliquip ex ea commodo consequat. Duis aute irure dolor in
> reprehenderit in voluptate velit esse molestaie cillum. Tia non ob ea soluad incom dereud facilis
> est er expedit distinct. Nam liber te conscient to factor tum poen legum odioque civiuda et tam.
> Neque pecun modut est neque nonor et imper ned libidig met, consectetur adipiscing elit, sed
> ut labore et dolore magna aliquam is nostrud exercitation ullam mmodo consequet. Duis aute in
> voluptate velit esse cillum dolore eu fugiat nulla pariatur. ¶

1   To replace the placeholder text, simply begin typing in the body of the letter.

    The entire placeholder text was selected, by default, when you first opened the new document.

2   Type the following text: *I just wanted to take a minute of your time and introduce you to my company, Big Idea Media.*

    Dear Trenz,

    I just wanted to take a minute of your time and introduce you to my company, Big Idea Media|

    The remaining text can be entered manually, but you can save time by inserting a file that contains the rest of the letter.

3   With the insertion point placed at the end of the last sentence, choose Insert > Choose.

    NOTE ▶ Inserting or pasting text to add text to a document preserves any formatting in the source text. If you want the additional text to assume the properties of the placeholder or current text, choose Edit > Paste and Match Style.

4   From the Lesson_08 folder, choose the file **08Letter Copy.rtf**, and click Insert.

    The text is added, but it requires some additional formatting because the inserted text does not match the text you've typed into the document.

Dear Trenz,

I just wanted to take a minute of your time and introduce you to my company, Big Idea Media. We are a creative services company that specializes in the development of campaign support materials. We have extensive experience creating both web and print collateral for fundraising campaigns such as yours.

I know that this is a busy time for your firm but I was hoping that you could set aside one hour so we could meet. There are some recent developments in technology that I think we should discuss. These include: Podcasting - A significant tool for distributing audio and video content to potential donors, Blogging - A useful web tool for frequently updating your site with news and information, Enhanced PDFs - Which allow for the embedding of rich media into a portable file.
I will contact your office shortly so we can arrange a meeting. I will work around your schedule and am willing to meet before or after your normal workday. Thanks agin for your considerration.

5   Drag to highlight the three paragraphs of text that you added to the document.

6   In the format bar, click the Styles pop-up menu and choose the Body paragraph style.

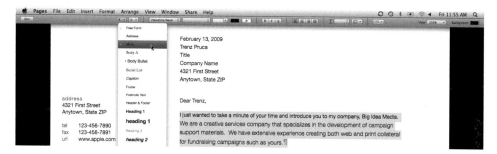

The text is reformatted to match the original template styles. If you look closely, however, the text formatting isn't quite consistent. Some of the text is in 8-point size, while other text is in 9 point. Additionally, the text mixes Light and Regular versions of the Helvetica Neue font. This variation occurs because the inserted text already had its own formatting. When you apply a paragraph style, the style respects any existing formatting.

You can override the existing formatting and force the text to update to the paragraph style. To do this, you'll access the Styles drawer.

7   Press Esc to exit full-screen mode, and in the format bar, click the blue Styles icon. The Styles drawer opens.

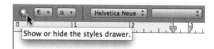

8   Click the disclosure triangle next to the Body paragraph style and choose Revert to Defined Style to update the text.

TIP ▶ You can also double-click a style to revert selected text to the defined style.

Let's finish the letter by addressing the recipient. You can use an Address Book card file to do so.

9   From the Lesson_08 folder, drag the **Steven Ironsides.vcf** card onto the addressee fields. You can also drag individual contacts into Pages directly from Address Book or drag multiple cards at once to create a mail merge.

Steven Ironsides

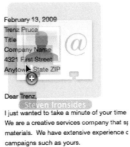

10   Return to full-screen mode and replace the text in the document as follows:

   ▶   Add your name after the *Sincerely Yours* text.

   ▶   Enter a personal address into the return address fields.

11   Save your work.

You can compare your document with the file **08Cover Letter_Stage 1.pages** in the Lesson_08 folder.

Formatting Text and Lists Using Styles

You can quickly format text using styles, so that you can concentrate on your writing and not on its appearance. Styles maintain visual consistency within a document and between related documents. Each template includes default styles that you can use, modify, or add to with your own styles. In this lesson, you'll use existing styles to format your letter.

1 In the second paragraph of the letter, click to place the insertion point after *These include:*.

> I know that this is a busy time for your firm but I was hoping that you could set aside one hour so we could meet. There are some recent developments in technology that I think we should discuss. These include: Podcasting - A significant tool for distributing audio and video content to potential donors, Blogging - A useful web tool for frequently updating your site with news and information, Enhanced PDFs - Which allow for the embedding of rich media into a portable file.

2 Press Return once to insert a line break and wrap the sentence to the next line.

3 Repeat step 2 to insert more line breaks so that each service appears on its own line:

> Podcasting - A significant tool for distributing audio and video content to potential donors,
>
> Blogging - A useful web tool for frequently updating your site with news and information,
>
> Enhanced PDFs - Which allow for the embedding of rich media into a portable file.

Now let's add emphasis to each service name so that they are easier for a reader to spot.

4 Select the word *Podcasting*.

5 In the format bar, click the Character Styles pop-up menu and choose Emphasis.

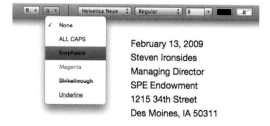

NOTE ▶ Styles can be accessed in the format bar and in the Styles drawer.

6   Repeat step 5 to apply the Emphasis character style formatting to the words *Blogging* and *Enhanced PDFs.*

> **Podcasting** - A significant tool for distributing audio and video content to potential donors,
>
> **Blogging** - A useful web tool for frequently updating your site with news and information,
>
> **Enhanced PDFs** - Which allow for the embedding of rich media into a portable file.

Now that the text is formatted, let's turn it into a bulleted list to add visual order.

7   Select the three services texts.

> **Podcasting** - A significant tool for distributing audio and video content to potential donors, ¶
>
> **Blogging** - A useful web tool for frequently updating your site with news and information, ¶
>
> **Enhanced PDFs** - Which allow for the embedding of rich media into a portable file.

8   In the format bar, click the List Styles button and choose Bullet.

The texts are now formatted as a bulleted list.

9   Now that the text is formatted as bullets, you can remove the unnecessary punctuation at the end of each bullet. Remove two commas and a period so that the text matches the following figure.

> • **Podcasting** - A significant tool for distributing audio and video content to potential donors
>
> • **Blogging** - A useful web tool for frequently updating your site with news and information
>
> • **Enhanced PDFs** - Which allow for the embedding of rich media into a portable file

10   Save your work.

You can compare your document with the file **08Cover Letter_Stage 2.pages** in the Lesson_08 folder.

Adding Graphics

What helps set Pages apart from other word processing applications is its robust support for graphics, from importing images to supporting many graphics formats.

Your corporate letterhead will look more official if you add your company's logo on the page to reinforce your branding. Pages helps you to add that graphic flair.

1   To more easily work on positioning the logo, press Esc to exit full-screen mode.

2   Switch to the Finder and open the Lesson_08 folder.

3   Locate the **BIM.ai** file.

4   Drag the logo into your document.

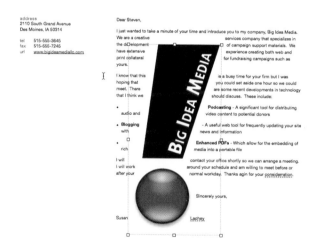

Pages imports the logo and adds it to the page. The logo causes the text in the document to wrap. You'll want to reposition the logo.

NOTE ▶ **BIM.ai** is an Adobe Illustrator file. Pages imports it as a vector-based PDF file.

5   Drag the lower right corner of the logo to resize it to a width of 1.5 inches.

6   Drag the logo to reposition it above the sender's address box at the left side of the page. Pop-up alignment guides will help you to position the logo.

   NOTE ▶ If you don't see the alignment guides, choose Pages > Preferences. Click Rulers and select the checkboxes for "Show guides at object center" and "Show guides at object edges."

   Let's help the logo stand out a bit on the page.

7   In the format bar, choose the Shadow option.

   NOTE ▶ If you'd like to customize the drop shadow, open the Inspector window (choose View > Show Inspector) and use the Graphic inspector to modify shadow properties such as color, blur, and opacity.

   Let's match the red text to the red logo.

8   Highlight the word *address*.

9   In the format bar, click the color well, and in the color matrix that appears, click Show Colors to open the Colors window.

10 Click the magnifying glass to select it, and then click the center of the red logo.

   The text color updates to match. Let's store the color for future use.

11 Drag the red color from the large strip to the color palette at the bottom of the Colors window to store it.

TIP   If you want more room in the color palette to store your favorite colors, drag the handle at the bottom of the Colors window to expand the palette.

Now that the color is stored, let's recolor the phone number text that currently uses the magenta style.

12 Click the word *tel* to select it; then click the new red swatch to apply that color.

Because the text was formatted with a character style, you can redefine it to update other instances in the document.

13 Move your pointer over the character style Magenta, and then click the disclosure triangle and choose Redefine Style from Selection.

All instances of the Magenta character style update to red.

14 Save your work.

You have successfully written and formatted your document. You are almost done, but you should proofread your letter for errors.

Proofreading a Document

Before your letter is completed, you will want to thoroughly proofread it. Pages includes a robust set of proofreading and spell-checking tools, as well as a handy thesaurus.

1 Choose Edit > Spelling > Spelling.

The Spelling window opens.

Pages highlights the first suspected word, *agaen.*

2 Pages displays a list of suggested replacement words. Choose *again* and click Change.

TIP ► If you know a word is correct and want to add it to your user dictionary, click Learn. If you want to skip all instances of a flagged word for this document—but you do not want to add it to your dictionary—click the Ignore button.

3 The next misspelled word, *considerration*, has one *r* too many. Choose the correct spelling, *consideration*, and click Change.

NOTE ► Some items on the page, such as web URLs, may be underlined in red to indicate a spelling error. If you want the spell checker to look at all text on the page, from the Check Spelling In pop-up menu, choose Entire Document.

4   Close the Spelling window.

TIP You can also right-click an underlined word. Pages will suggest correct spellings to replace the word.

5   Choose Edit > Proofreading > Proofreader.

The Proofreading window opens, and you're ready to check for errors. Pages highlights *services* in the first paragraph and suggests that if *services* is intended as a verb, *serves* is a better choice.

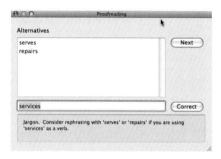

6   Because you are using *services* correctly, as a noun, click Next.

The Proofreader highlights no more words in your letter, so your proofreading is completed.

7   Close the Proofreading window.

TIP If you'd like to proofread while you create your document, Pages can be configured to underline potential problems in green. Choose Edit > Proofreading > Proofread as You Type.

8   Save your work.

You can compare your document with the file **08Cover Letter_Stage 3.pages** in the Lesson_08 folder.

In Pages, you can access other research and reference tools when finding and verifying information for a document:

▶ Dictionary and thesaurus—Pages includes both a dictionary and a thesaurus. To check a word using the Mac OS X dictionary, select the word and choose Edit > Writing Tools > Look Up in Dictionary and Thesaurus. The Thesaurus can check for words with a similar or opposite meaning.

> **TIP** ▶ If you want to do a quick lookup without leaving Pages, move your pointer over a word and press Command-Control-D to open a mini-dictionary. Here you can see the definition for the current word. Near the bottom of the window, click Dictionary to switch to a thesaurus. If you want to stay in this mode, release the D key, while still holding down Command-Control, and skim your pointer over new words to look them up.

▶ Google—You can open a Google search in Safari from within your document. Select a word and choose Edit > Writing Tools > Search in Google. If you're writing a letter, this is a handy way to check an address or search a map.

▶ Wikipedia—If you decide to dig a bit deeper and do research, Pages can connect you to Wikipedia, the online encyclopedia. Select a phrase and choose Edit > Writing Tools > Search in Wikipedia to find Wikipedia results in Safari. You can quickly browse and read more on almost any subject.

Creating Addressed Envelopes

Pages can address envelopes for mailing your documents and also merge contact info from Address Book into your Pages documents. This saves you time by allowing you to reuse a letter, contract, envelope, or other document for multiple recipients. Several of the Pages templates contain Address Book fields.

Let's address an envelope using an Envelope template.

1   Choose File > New from Template Chooser.

    The Template Chooser opens and prompts you to make a choice.

2   From the Word Processing category, select Envelopes. Scroll to the bottom of the list and select the San Francisco Envelope. Click Choose.

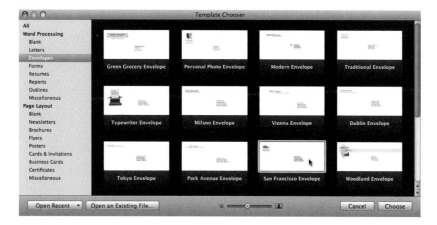

The envelope template is automatically filled in with information from your personal card in Address Book. This information is placed in the sender fields, but it can be modified.

3   Using the methods you learned earlier in this lesson, change the text and colors as in the following figure:

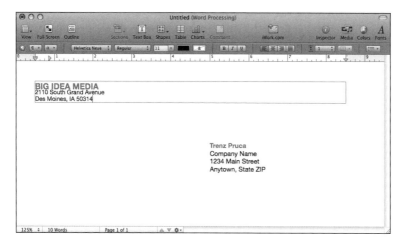

You may now fill in the recipient fields.

4   In the Finder, open the Lesson_08 folder.

5   Double-click the **Steven Ironsides.vcf** file to add it to your Address Book.

This is a vCard, which contains Address Book information for your client. You used it earlier to address the letter. Your Address Book application opens, and Steven Ironsides is added to your list of addresses.

NOTE ▶ You can select the card and delete it from your Address Book after you've completed this exercise.

6   Drag Steven Ironsides's card from your Address Book to the recipient fields.

Pages adds and formats the information from the vCard to the envelope template. Unlike the letter, the envelope doesn't insert the contact's job title.

TIP ▶ To add a customizable field, choose Insert > Merge Field. You can also open the Link inspector and click the Merge button to customize fields. Be sure to examine the template before creating the merge. Some templates are set to use work addresses, and others use home addresses. Work-oriented templates access corporate info, while more casual templates access home info. You can change which data is entered into template fields by using the inspector.

If you want to send an envelope or letter to multiple recipients, you can perform a merge. By specifying which cards you want to use, you can personalize the document for each recipient. For best results, create a group of cards within the Address Book application.

1   Return to Address Book and click the Add + (plus sign) button in the Group column. Name the group *Clients to Market to*.

2   Click the All group and drag five of your Address Book cards into the new group.

For the purpose of this exercise, any card is acceptable, although cards with business contacts will work best.

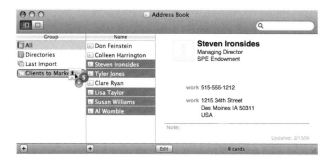

3   Return to Pages.

4   Choose Edit > Mail Merge.

You can specify a group of contacts for which you'd like to print envelopes.

5   In the Select a Mail Merge Source dialog, leave the Address Book radio button selected.

6   From the Address Book Group pop-up menu, choose the "Clients to Market to" group.

For quicker results without editing, you could choose Merge to: New Document for further editing or Merge to: Send to Printer.

> **TIP**   To smooth things along, Pages can intuitively substitute missing information with the closest match. The option is selected by default in the Merge dialog.

7   From the "Merge to" pop-up menu, choose Send to Printer. Click Merge.

The Printer dialog opens.

8   Click the Preview button to see how your envelopes will look.

9   Close the Preview application and return to Pages.

10   Close the Pages document, but don't save your work.

Lesson Review

1.   How can you access styles?

2.   How do you add a graphic from your hard drive to a Pages document?

3.   How can you check an address in your document using the Internet?

4.   Which view is best suited to help you focus on your writing?

5.   How can you create multiple envelopes or letters addressed to individual recipients?

Answers

1. You can access styles using the format bar or the Styles drawer.

2. You can locate the file and drag it into your document, or choose Insert > Choose and navigate to the file on your hard drive.

3. Highlight the address and choose Edit > Writing Tools > Search in Google to open a Google search in Safari. A Google Maps entry will be one of the first results on the page.

4. You can use the full-screen view to primarily display your document.

5. Choose Edit > Mail Merge to use a specified group from your Address Book.

9

Lesson Files	Lessons > Lesson_09 > 09Phoenix Mission_START.pages
	Lessons > Lesson_09 > 09Phoenix Mission_FINAL.pages
	Lessons > Lesson_09 > Leg_Deployment.jpg
	Lessons > Lesson_09 > Touchdown.jpg
Time	This lesson takes approximately 60 minutes to complete.
Goals	Use styles to format text and lists
	Add graphics to a document
	Create headers and footers
	Use tracked changes and comments
	Add a table of contents to a document
	Share a document on iWork.com

Lesson 9
Building a Report

In the last lesson, you explored word processing features in Pages and created a professional-looking letter and matching envelope. In this lesson, you'll explore the more advanced word-processing features of Pages that are particularly useful when creating long form documents such as reports.

You'll manage large documents by using section breaks; discover how to format margins, headers, and footers; and use printing commands for special purposes (such as binding). You'll also enhance a report by adding pictures and charts that help the reader to more clearly understand the information.

Opening an Existing File

In this lesson, you are going to work with an existing document. A colleague has started a report but wants you to review the document, make some additions, and then return the document with comments. Pages offers several tools that make these tasks a snap. Let's open a previously created document to make some additions and edits.

1   If necessary, open Pages by clicking its icon in the Dock.

2   In the Template Chooser, click the Open an Existing File button.

3   Navigate to the Lesson_09 folder and select the file **09Phoenix Mission_START.pages**.

4   Click Open to ready the document for editing.

Pages opens the document and displays the first page. The document contains a comment from your colleague, as well as some potential changes that you can make to improve the report.

It is a standard editorial practice for each editor of a shared document to save that document with a different name to identify the version that each participant modified and to retain a complete record of the document's changes. This process is often called *version control*, and it clarifies which variation of a document is being viewed.

To maintain version control, let's save the document under a new name.

5   Choose File > Save As.

The File Navigation Services dialog opens.

6   Navigate to the Lesson_09 folder.

7   Name the file *Phoenix Mission Revision 1.pages* and click Save.

You have successfully opened a peer's document and resaved it with a new version number. You are now ready to start to enhance and format the document for printing.

Tracking Changes

Pages incorporates powerful collaboration features that make it easy for you to share documents with other users and develop a document as a group. One of those features, *tracked changes*, accurately tracks changes as each collaborator works on a document.

By using tracked changes, the collaborators on a document can review the changes you have made and decide whether to accept or reject those changes. Because tracking changes requires multiple users, you will simulate it in this exercise.

1   Choose Edit > Track Changes to start tracking changes.

The document window changes slightly, displaying comments as you work and showing the tracking bar below the format bar.

NOTE ▶ When tracked changes is turned on, all document changes are recorded. Choosing Edit > Turn Off Tracking will prompt you to review all of the changes and decide whether or not to apply them. If you want to pause tracking, click the Pause button in the tracking bar.

2   On page 1, select the title, *The Phoenix Lander.*

3   In the format bar, click the Bold button.

4   Move the insertion point after the word *Lander,* then type *Project.*

As each change is made, Pages records the change, along with its author, time, and date.

TIP You can change the color of change bubbles for clarity. Click the Action menu in the upper right corner just below the format bar. Here you can choose Author Color and choose one of seven colors. Each author can use one of the colors. This makes it easier to spot changes and who made them.

Pages assigns unique colors to each author's change bubbles, making it easier to see who suggested which changes.

NOTE ▶ The author name is initially set using information in the default card in the Address Book application. You can change the author name, as well as which markup style is used, by choosing Preferences from the Action menu.

5   Examine the change bubbles to see what already has been changed in this document.

TIP The tracking bar allows you to quickly step through changes one at a time. This bar is visible when tracking is turned on. You can click the up and down arrows in the bar to review changes. Changes can be accepted or rejected individually or all at once using the Action menu.

Normally a colleague or supervisor would examine your document and suggest changes. With tracked changes enabled, you can quickly review her suggestions.

TIP Several advanced controls are available when you're tracking changes. Here are a few tips for getting more from this powerful tool.

▶ To show or hide all tracking bubbles, click View in the toolbar. You can then select Show Comments and Changes Pane or Hide Comments and Changes Pane.

▶ If you only want to see tracking bubbles for a specific section of text, select the text, and from the Tracking Bubbles pop-up menu, choose Show Only for Selection.

▶ If you don't want to see tracking bubbles for minor formatting edits (such as for-matting text with italics), click the Tracking Bubbles pop-up menu and make sure no checkmark is present next to Show Formatting Bubbles.

▶ If you want to simplify the way tracked changes are displayed, from the View Markup menu, choose View Markup Without Deletions. You'll see how the final text will read, but edits are displayed in a different color by author.

Using Comments

Placing comments into a document is a great way to make a point without actually edit-ing the text. If you or another reader wants to suggest a document change, you can insert a *comment*. Comments can include questions to other authors, or any suggestion or obser-vation about a document's content.

1 Examine page 1 to locate a yellow comment bubble.

A colleague asked you to make a change to the document.

Samuel Jones Today, 1:54 PM ⊗

Can you add a Figure Here?

2 Click in the empty space next to the comment where you would insert the figure.

3   Choose Insert > Choose.

A file navigation dialog opens that allows you to choose a photo.

4   Navigate to the Lesson_09 folder and choose **Touchdown.jpg**.

5   Click Insert to add the photo to the page.

A Brief Introduction to Mars

The photo is added to your document and fills the entire width of the text box. Let's resize the photo so that it is a little smaller.

6   Drag the resize handle in a corner of the photo until the picture is approximately 5 inches wide.

A Brief Introduction to Mars
Mars, our planetary neighbor, has long been the subject of human fascination. Just like Earth, it has deserts, mountains, valleys, and volcanoes. It is a terrestrial planet that is fourth

The picture is better sized for the page. Let's stylize the image with a custom border so that it stands out more clearly.

7 In the format bar, click the "Choose line style" button and choose the second picture
frame, as in the following figure.

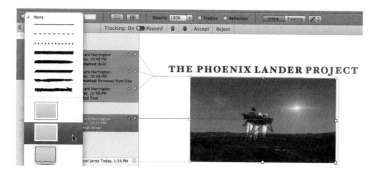

Now the photo is easier to see and matches the other photos throughout the report.
However, with the border added, the photo is bigger and has pushed a few lines of
text to the next page. (You can see this in the thumbnail view.) You can reduce the
size of the photo and avoid the title page's being broken up.

8 Drag a resize handle to scale the photo to approximately 4.5 inches wide.

Now that the text fits on one page, let's add a comment for the original author.

9 In the toolbar, click the Comment button.

An empty comment is added to the document, ready for text input.

> **TIP** ▶ Before entering a comment, press the Down Arrow key; otherwise, the com-
> ment's author and time stamp will be erased.

10 Add the comment in the following figure to the document:

> Richard Harrington Today,
> 10:55 PM
> I think this is a strong image to
> start the section with.

> **NOTE** ▶ Reviewing comments is similar to working with change bubbles. Click the X
> in the comment to delete a comment.

11 Choose File > Save to save your work.

> **TIP ▶** When you choose to print your document, what you see is what you get. If comments are visible, they will print on the page. This is a useful way to print a document for review purposes. If you don't want to print your comments, you'll want to hide them. To remove comments temporarily, choose View > Hide Comments.

Inserting a Cover Page

A cover page is commonly added to a report before it is distributed. This helps to identify the contents of the report and its authors. When using the report templates provided by Pages, you'll find that most include a cover page.

Let's add a cover page to your mission report and credit its authors.

1 In the toolbar, click the Sections button.

> **NOTE ▶** Each template in Pages offers one or more sections that contain formatting and placeholder text and media. When you want to add a page to a word processing document, click the Sections button. If you're working in the Page Layout mode, this button will be called Pages.

2 Choose the Cover section.

A new page 2 is added to your document after the current page. You can move this page to the top of the thumbnail view to reorder it in your document.

3   In the thumbnail view, drag the thumbnail for page 2 above the page 1 thumbnail.

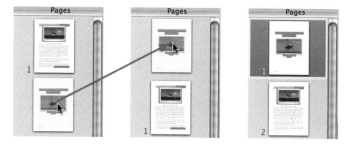

Now that the pages are in the right order, you can replace the placeholder text and media on the new page.

4   Click the placeholder title labeled *Astronomy 101 Report*, and type *The Phoenix Lander Project*.

5   Replace the other text on the cover page to match the following figure. Be sure to replace only one line of text at a time to preserve formatting.

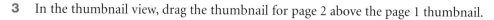

THE PHOENIX LANDER PROJECT

A Journey to Mars in Our Time

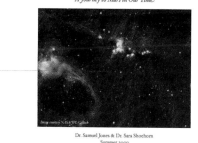

Dr. Samuel Jones & Dr. Sara Shoehorn
Summer 2009

After the text is replaced, you can customize the photo area. Pages can use images in a wide range of file formats, including TIFF, PSD, and JPEG. Let's add a photo to the first page.

6   Select the space photo.

7   Choose Insert > Choose and navigate to the Lesson_09 folder.

8   Choose **Leg_Deployment.jpg**.

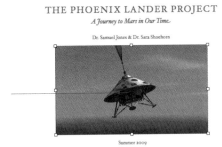

The photo is added to the page, but the text shifts position due to the different size of the new photo. You may adjust the image to place the names and dates below the picture.

9   Option-drag the image's lower right resize handle.

The image enlarges in all directions at the same time. Resize the image to a width of approximately 5.5 inches.

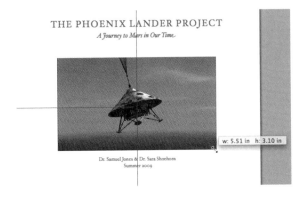

If you give the photo a custom border, it will stand out more on the printed page.

10 Click the Line Style button and choose the second picture frame.

Dr. Samuel Jones & Dr. Sara Shoehorn
Summer 2009

The photo looks good, but a little more space between the edge of the photo and the bottom text would improve readability.

11 Choose View > Show Inspector and click the Wrap inspector.

12 Increase the Extra Space value to 24 pt.

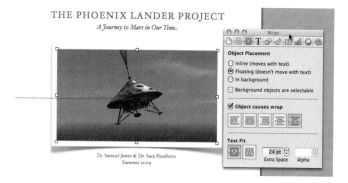

The text is now farther from the photo and easier to read.

13 Choose File > Save to save your progress.

Managing Section Breaks

When working with a Pages document, it's a good idea to use sections. Sections help keep a large document organized by keeping together all of the pages for each part of a report. When sections are present in your document, you will find it much easier to reorganize or add to it.

Many template documents have sections already inserted for elements like cover sheets or tables of contents. You can also manually add a section break where you'd like to split a report by choosing Insert > Section Break. Your Phoenix mission document has seven sections. Let's split some sections apart to help reorganize the document.

1 In the thumbnail view, select the page 12 thumbnail.

   NOTE ▶ You might have to scroll down to see all the page thumbnails in your document.

   The conclusion of the document and a two-page listing of Mars Missions are currently placed in the same section. These pages can be moved only as a group. However, you've decided that you want the Mars Missions section relocated after the conclusion. To do so, you'll want to split the section.

2 Click to place the insertion point before the title *Annex - Mars Missions.*

3 Choose Insert > Section Break.

   A new section break (and a blank page) is added. Don't worry, you'll clear the extra space later.

   You can place the Bibliography page earlier in the document.

4 Click and hold the thumbnail for page 15 (the Bibliography).

5 Drag the current page 15 thumbnail higher in the Pages thumbnails list so that it goes after the current page 12.

   The Bibliography now appears before the Mars Missions section.

MORE INFO ▶ The bibliography in this report was built using EndNote X2. Many research and academic professionals use EndNote X2 to manage their citations and bibliographies. Pages '09 works with EndNote X2 software, so that you can search and manage references as well as create bibliographies. To use these features, you must install EndNote X2 and assign Endnote X2 a default library. See the Help article "Adding Citations and Bibliographies Using EndNote" for more information.

6   Choose File > Save to capture your progress so far.

TIP ▶ Pages includes a Bibliography section template if you want to create a bibliography manually.

Congratulations—you have successfully reordered the sections of your document. Using sections is the best way to keep a long document organized.

Adjusting Margins

When you prepare a document for printing, you'll often want to adjust its margins. Every Pages document uses margins that define how much empty space exists on the left, right, top, and bottom borders of the page. It is traditional to leave empty space in this area to improve the document readability. The default margins for Pages templates are set to 1 inch around all four sides of a document; however, you can easily modify these margin sizes.

NOTE ▶ Be sure you understand the capabilities of your output device. Many printers can't print to the farthest edge of a page, and most documents require at least some margin.

Let's adjust the margins of the current document so that it is ready for printing and binding. You'll want to leave extra space on the inside edge of each page so that the printed document can be placed into a binder or sealed with a bound edge. This area of the page is unusable for text or graphics, so you'll adjust the margins.

1   Open the Document inspector.

2 Select the Facing Pages checkbox to print the document as a double-sided report.

Because you are preparing a document that is going to be printed on both sides of the page and bound, you will want to make room for that binding. In the Document inspector, you can increase the inside margin by the necessary amount. Pages will automatically put the larger margin on the side closest to the binding.

> **TIP** ▶ You can display the page margins by choosing View > Show Layout.

3 Change the Inside margin field to 1.5 in to allow more room for the binding.

Changing the margin size has modified your page breaks because you have reduced the overall area available for the text. You can adjust the Outside margin by .5 inches to restore the text area to its previous capacity.

4 Change the Outside margin to .5 in.

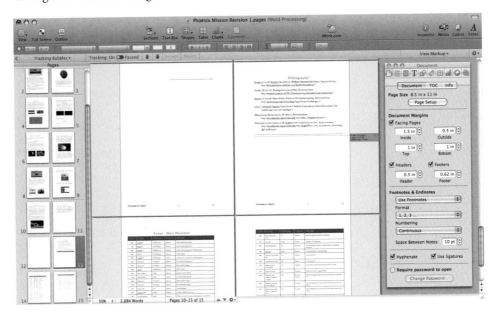

The document now has the same pagination as it had previously. What's important is that you still have the larger inside margin. The extra space is used by the binding for the printed report.

Starting Chapters on Right-Facing Pages

It is standard to start each section on a right-facing page. You will notice that the chapters of some books include blank pages at the end so that the next chapter can start cleanly on a right-hand page. This is an easy task for you to perform in Pages.

1   Switch to the Layout inspector.

You should select all the pages so that your changes will affect every page in the report.

2   Click in the thumbnails view and press Command-A to select all the page thumbnails.

3   In the Layout inspector, click the Section button to modify only the Section properties.

4   Select the "Use previous headers & footers" checkbox to retain the current headers and footers. (You'll change them in the next exercise.)

5   From the "Section starts on" pop-up menu, choose Right Page.

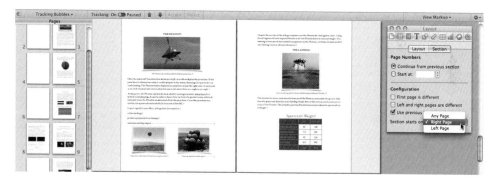

Each section now begins on a right-facing page (like chapters in a book). To accomplish this, Pages has added some blank pages to the document. This is a publishing standard and makes it easier to find the start of each section.

Adding a Footer to Your Document

When writing a report, you'll often want to repeat some of the same information on multiple pages. Among the most common information repeated on multiple pages is page numbers. When combined with a table of contents, page numbers help the reader to find information more effectively.

You can choose to add recurring information at the top of a page (which is called a *header*) or at the bottom (a *footer*). You can choose to add your own text manually or to employ formatted text fields that update automatically.

Let's add page numbers to your Phoenix report.

1   Choose View > Show Layout to make the headers and footers easier to see by displaying the layout of your document.

Boxes on the page help identify the header, footer, and body areas.

2   Select page 3, and then click to place the insertion point in the footer area.

Adding the filename to the footer will help identify which document is being read, which is particularly helpful when people are reviewing physical printouts for comments.

3   Choose Edit > Select All and press Delete.

This clears the current content of the footer.

4   Choose Insert > Filename.

Pages adds the document's full filename to the footer. You can simplify this filename by removing the *.pages* extension, which isn't necessary for this kind of label.

NOTE ▶ If you want to place unique headers for each section, you can open the Layout inspector and deselect the "Use previous headers & footers" checkbox.

5   Double-click the filename text; then deselect the "Always show filename extension" checkbox.

lenges·in·interplanetary·travel:·landing·on·Mars
☐ Show directory path
☐ Always show filename extension
PHOENIX.MI

6   Click after the filename text to move the insertion point.

7   In the format bar, click the Left Justify button, then press Tab twice to align the next text field with the right edge of the footer.

8   Choose Insert > Page Number.

PHOENIX.MISSION.REVISION.1 → → ₃

9   Highlight the page number, and in the format bar, click the Bold button to reformat just the page numbers.

NOTE ▸ The method for adding a header to your document is nearly identical to adding the footer.

Formatting Text and Lists Using Styles

You can quickly format your document text by using styles. Highlight the desired text and click a style in the Styles pane. Using styles allows you to concentrate on your writing and lets Pages attend to its appearance. Styles maintain consistency within and among your documents. Each template includes default styles that you can use, modify, or enhance with your own styles. Styles are also used when creating a table of contents or using outline mode, as they let Pages identify titles and headings.

Pages offers three types of styles for text and list formatting:

▸   Paragraph styles—In a Pages document, a paragraph is defined as any block of text that is followed by a Return character. A paragraph style can include specifications for font, size, text color, and so on. If you don't find a suitable paragraph style, you can modify an existing style or create a new one.

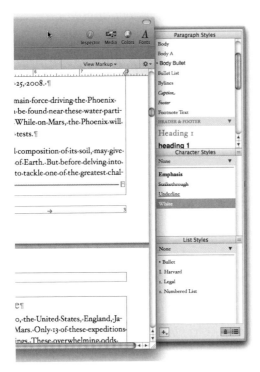

▶ Character styles—These styles apply attributes to a section of text without changing the style of the rest of the paragraph. For example, you might change a single phrase to a bold style and change its font color. If you can't find a suitable character style, you can modify one of the existing character styles or create a new one.

▶ List styles—Pages includes preformatted bullet and numbering styles for creating ordered lists. These are useful for visually organizing information for the reader. Just as you can customize character and paragraph styles, you can modify a list style to match your requirements.

Updating a Paragraph Style

Every Pages document contains several styles that define the text appearance. These styles are set by default, but you can easily update them for your current document.

1   In the thumbnails view, select page 5.

2   Triple-click the section title, *The Mars Curse*, to select it.

Let's adjust the text formatting for this style.

NOTE ▶ Styles are available in the format bar and in the Styles drawer. If the Styles drawer is not visible, you can open it by clicking the Styles Drawer button in the format bar.

3   In the format bar, click the Bold button so that the text stands out.

4   Change the section title's point size to 20 pt.

> ### The·Mars·Curse¶
> Sixty·percent·of·all·missions·to·Mars·have·failed.·Since·1960,·the·United·States,·England,·Ja-

The text is now bolder and larger, which makes it easier to read. The section title stands out more clearly.

5   Closely examine the Paragraph Styles list.

Heading 1 (the current style) has a red triangle icon next to it that indicates the style has been overridden. Let's make your style change global and apply it to this entire document.

6   Click the red triangle icon and choose Redefine Style from Selection.

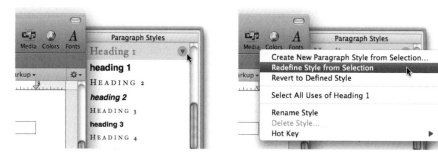

The red triangle turns black as the modified style is applied and saved. Throughout the current document, all instances of text using the Heading 1 style are updated.

7   Choose File > Save to save your progress.

Using Character Styles

The key advantage to using character styles is that they can be used to make part of a paragraph more visible. For example, you could italicize all cited references in a report to make them easier to spot.

1   Switch to page 15, a page titled, "Learning from the Past."

2   Select the reference at the bottom of the page, *(Ulivi, 2007, p. Page 147; Wikipedia, 11 November 2008)*.

> tists·speculate·that·the·Mars·2·entered·the·atmosphere·at·too·steep·an·angle·and·the·para-
> chute·failed·to·deploy.(Ulivi,·2007,·p.·Page·147;·Wikipedia,·11·November·2008).¶

Let's italicize the text with a character style.

3   In the format bar, click the Italic button.

The text is italicized.

4   Closely examine the Character Styles list.

The red triangle next to the word *None* indicates that the style has been modified. Let's create a new style that can be reused in future documents.

5   Click the red triangle and choose Create New Character Style from Selection.

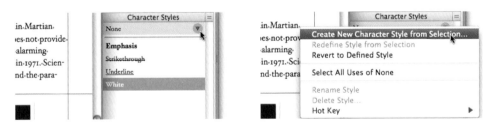

A dialog opens asking you to name the style.

6   Name the style *Italicize*.

You can take precise control over how this style is applied.

7   Click the disclosure triangle next to "Include these character attributes."

8   Click Select Overrides to keep only those properties that have been changed.

In this case, only Italic: On remains selected.

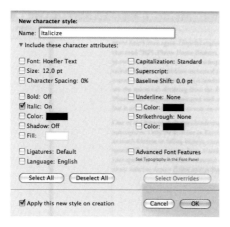

9   Click OK to create the new character style.

Let's reuse the style on another citation.

10   In the Pages thumbnails list, select page 8.

11   Select the citation, *Wikipedia, 19 November 2008.*

12   Click Italicize Character Style to apply your new character style.

You've used character styles to change the appearance of your document.

> **MORE INFO** ▶ On this page of your document, you'll notice that complex visual formulas are displayed. Pages can work with MathType to display mathematical expressions and equations. You must install MathType 6 or later on your system to create and manipulate an equation. After an equation is inserted into a Pages document, it is treated as a graphic. If you open the document on a system that does not have MathType installed, the equations still display correctly. If the current system includes MathType, you can double-click the equation to edit it. See the Help menu entry "Adding Mathematical Expressions and Equations Using MathType" for more information.

Formatting a List Using List Styles

Let's use list styles to format a list. By adding bullets or numbers, a list is easier to spot and comprehend.

1   Select page 12, titled "The Descent."

2   As in the following figure, highlight the last three lines of text above the photos: *soften landings*, *protect equipment from damage*, and *minimize landing impact.*

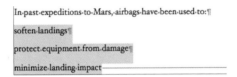

These three items are a list and should be formatted as such. Because they are not a list of numbered steps, the use of a bulleted list style is most appropriate.

3   In the List Styles area, choose the Bullet style.

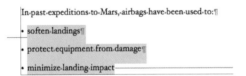

The text is reformatted as a bulleted list. You can improve its readability by tweaking the default formatting.

4   Open the Text inspector and click the List button.

5   Set both the Bullet Indent and Text Indent fields to 0.25 in to move the text inward.

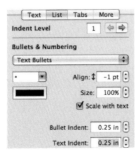

The text is easier to read, so you'll want to store the formatting for continued use.

In·past·expeditions·to·Mars,·airbags·have·been·used·to:¶
•   soften·landings¶
•   protect·equipment·from·damage¶
•   minimize·landing·impact

6   Click the red triangle icon next to the Bullet list style and choose Redefine Style from Selection.

This saves the changes you made to the style.

7   Choose File > Save to save your progress.

You have successfully formatted the text in your document using styles. In our next exercise, you'll create a table of contents for your document. Pages uses the styles to help identify the levels of headings in the document, so the work you have done with styles is important.

MORE INFO ▶ To learn more about adding and modifying styles, see "Modifying Paragraph Styles," "Modifying Character Styles," and "Modifying List Styles" in the Help menu.

Adding a Table of Contents

Creating a table of contents is easy in Pages '09. Pages can automatically generate a table of contents based on the use of paragraph styles for document headings. A good TOC helps the reader to quickly find sections in a document and provides an overview of the contents.

1   In the thumbnails view, select page 1.

2   In the toolbar, click the Sections button and choose Table of Contents.

NOTE ▶ A table of contents can be added to any word processing document. If the template you are using doesn't offer a Table of Contents section, simply choose Insert > Table of Contents.

A new page is added as a left-facing page. Because other sections of your document start on a right-facing page, you'll want your TOC to start that way, too.

3 Open the Layout inspector and click Section.

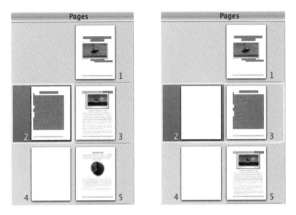

4 From the "Sections start on" pop-up menu, choose Right Page. The document layout is fixed and the TOC starts on page 3. Now let's modify that table of contents.

5 Open the Document inspector.

In the Document inspector, you can modify the formatting of your TOC.

6 Click the TOC button.

7 In the Document inspector, for the Title style, deselect the checkbox in the #'s column.

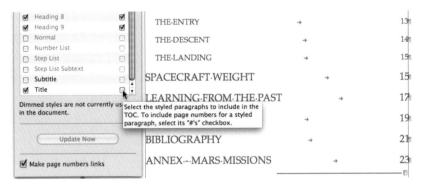

Pages removes the page numbers for the Title headings in the TOC. This simplifies the TOC and avoids unnecessarily repeating a page number for page 5.

8   Choose File > Save to save your progress. You can compare your work with the file **09Phoenix Mission_FINAL.pages**.

You've added a table of contents to your document. It's now ready to post online for your other team members to review.

NOTE ▶ When you change your document, in the Document inspector you can click the Update Now button (or the table of contents itself) to force an update to your table of contents. Note that the table of contents updates automatically whenever you close and save the document.

Sharing a Document on iWork.com

To facilitate collaboration with others, you can post word processing documents on iWork.com, a document-sharing site. This site is in beta, which means it is currently being developed and enhanced but open to public trial. The service is free, and allows others to view, comment on, or download your word processing document.

1   Choose Share > Share via iWork.com.

If this is your first time using the iWork.com service on your current computer, you'll have to sign in.

NOTE ▶ If you already have an Apple ID from the iTunes store, MobileMe, or the Apple Discussions forums, you can use that ID to log in to iWork.com. Otherwise, you must click Create New Account to sign up for a free Apple ID.

2   If necessary, enter your Apple ID and password, and click Sign In.

3   A new dialog opens and prompts you for important information required for sharing the file.

NOTE ▶ You must be connected to the Internet to share a document on the iWork.com Public Beta. You must also have an Apple Mail account set up on your computer to send invitations to view the document.

4   In the To and Message fields, enter the email addresses and a message for the intended recipients of the word processing document.

5   Modify the Subject field as necessary.

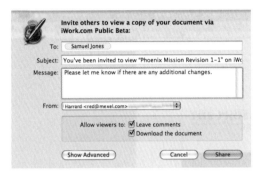

6   In the From pop-up menu, choose an email address as the sender.

7   To enable viewer comments and downloads, select the "Leave comments" and "Download the document" checkboxes.

> **TIP** ▶ To set specific options for uploading and downloading files, click the Show Advanced button at the bottom of the dialog. Here you can choose which file formats to make available for download. The Upload options also allow you to specify the name of the file to be posted. If you are reposting a previously shared document, you can choose to overwrite the old file or to enter a new name in the "Copy to iWork.com as" field.

8   Click Show Advanced to specify download options.

Deselect the Word checkbox so that you post only a PDF and a Pages '09 file.

9   Click Share.

Pages uploads the document and sends an invitation to anyone you listed in the To field. When the job is done uploading, you can click View Document Now to see it posted online.

You've opened and modified a multipage word processing document. By turning on change tracking, you've enabled others to identify and comment on any changes you've made. The skills you've learned in this lesson will be important because you'll frequently use styles, sections, and document sharing in your day-to-day work.

Lesson Review

1. Identify two ways to access styles.

2. How can you add a graphic on your hard drive to a Pages document?

3. How can you adjust the margins in a document?

4. What is the easiest way to add a table of contents to a Pages document?

5. Which document formats can you use to share a Pages document on iWork.com?

Answers

1. You can access styles through the format bar or the Styles drawer.

2. There are three ways to do this: You can use the Media Browser (see Lesson 3, "Adding Media to Your Presentation"), you can drag the file from your hard drive, or you can choose Insert > Choose and navigate to the file on your hard drive.

3. Open the Document inspector and modify the Top, Bottom, Left, and Right fields as necessary.

4. Click the Sections button in the toolbar and choose Table of Contents, or choose Insert > Table of Contents.

5. You can post a Pages '09 or Pages '08 file as well as a PDF or a Microsoft Word document.

10

Lesson Files

Time
This lesson takes approximately 60 minutes to complete.

Goals
Use a Pages template

Replace placeholder text

Edit placeholder images

Resize an object

Use a mask to crop an image

Flow text and wrap text around objects

Format text using styles

Export to PDF

Creating a Newsletter

In Pages, a powerful layout mode allows you to create beautifully designed brochures, flyers, and newsletters. Its contextual format bar, rich graphics support, and robust selection of Apple-designed templates give you many options to use in creating your page layouts.

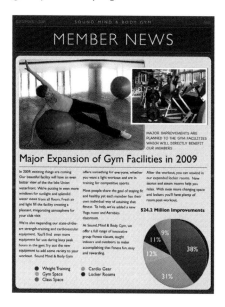

In this lesson, you will open a Pages newsletter template and populate it with content as a newsletter for members of a gym. Then you will export the document as a PDF file that is ready for Internet distribution.

Choosing a Newsletter Template

Pages offers 14 newsletter templates in a variety of styles that you can browse in the Template Chooser. A cover-page thumbnail allows you to preview each layout style, but you can also skim the pointer over each template to see more of each template's pages. A template contains several layout options for interior pages that can be further modified to match your specific needs.

Let's start by choosing a template.

1   Choose File > New from the Template Chooser.

Because you are about to build a newsletter, let's explore the newsletter templates in Pages.

2   For this exercise, choose the Page Layout group, then the Newsletters category. Skim your pointer over each template to see the page designs it offers.

3   Choose the Informal Newsletter template and click Choose to open a new document based on the template.

4   Choose File > Save and name the file *Gym Newsletter.pages*. Store the file in the Lesson_10 folder on your local hard drive.

Working with a Template

Most templates include several page designs that help you quickly format your document. These layouts often contain placeholders for text, images, tables, charts, and other formatting options you may want to use. The newsletter you are designing in this lesson requires a total of four pages. By choosing the template, you've already chosen a suitable layout for the first page; now let's choose the layouts for the other three pages.

1   On the toolbar, click the Pages button, and choose a page design from the pop-up menu. For this newsletter, choose the 2 Column with Sidebar layout.

This design works well for a single story with some extra information next to it.

2   Add two more pages to the layout: Sidebar & 3 Notecards and Mailer.

The Sidebar design is well-suited for short stories, and the Mailer design is meant for the back cover of a newsletter.

NOTE ▶ When a preformatted page is added to your document, a section break is automatically inserted between the pages. So, when you edit an individual page, it will not affect those that precede or follow it.

3   Choose File > Save to save your document.

Formatting the Title

Similar to the word processing templates, page layout templates in Pages use Lorem Ipsum placeholder text. You'll add your own text to a page by replacing this text.

It's been a busy year for the Thompsons

Sociis mauris in integer, a dolor netus non dui aliquet, sagittis felis sodales, dolor sociis mauris, vel eu libero cras. Interdum at. Eget habitasse elementum est, ipsum purus pede porttitor class, ut adipiscing, aliquet sed auctor, imperdiet arcu per diam dapibus libero duis. Enim

eros in vel, volutpat nec pellentesque leo, temporibus scelerisque nec. Ac dolor ac adipiscing amet bibendum nullam, massa lacus molestie ut libero nec, diam et, pharetra sodales eget, feugiat ullamcorper id tempor eget id vitae. Mauris pretium eget aliquet, lectus

tincidunt. Porttitor mollis imperdiet libero senectus pulvinar. Etiam molestie mauris ligula eget laoreet, vehicula eleifend. Repellat orci eget erat et, sem cum, ultricies sollicitudin amet eleifend dolor nullam erat, malesuada est leo ac. Varius natoque turpis elementum est.

1   In the thumbnail view, choose the Page 1 thumbnail.

If you can't see thumbnails, click the View button in the toolbar and choose Page Thumbnails. Let's customize the title page of the newsletter.

2   Double-click the title text (which currently reads *THE THOMPSONS*).

3   Type *member news*.

4   Select the smaller text at the top of the page (which currently reads *ANNUAL UPDATE*).

5   Type *sound mind & body gym*.

6 In the upper left corner of the page, double-click the date to select it.

7 Choose Insert > Date & Time to change the date on the document.

The current date is inserted automatically. However, because you're preparing the gym newsletter for September delivery, you'll want to change that date.

8 Double-click the newly added date to select it.

9 Click the Calendar icon; then choose September 1, 2009.

10 From the Choose Date Format pop-up menu, choose September 1, 2009.

This changes your date's appearance to the desired format.

11 Click an empty area of the canvas to close the calendar.

The date is now properly formatted; however, the graphic additions to the masthead aren't really appropriate for a gym newsletter. Let's remove them.

12 Click the outside edge of the rightmost fleur-de-lis; then Command-click the fleur-de-lis on the left.

Both objects are now selected and highlighted with bounding boxes.

13 Press Delete to remove the two objects.

14 Choose File > Save to capture your work so far.

Building the First Page

You are now ready to add content to the first page of your newsletter. Several objects can be added to a Pages document, including text boxes, photos, shapes, tables, and charts. As you add more objects to a page, you can adjust the layout to maintain an orderly look that improves the readability.

Adding Text

Let's start by adding the first story to your newsletter, replacing the placeholder text. You can choose to type text directly into any text box, or you can insert text from a document file. First, let's simplify the front-page layout by removing some unnecessary graphic placeholders.

1 Click outside the page (in the white area); then drag to select the three photos and captions at the bottom of the page.

2 Press Delete to remove the placeholder images.

You now have more room for your first story. Remember, you can easily modify any Pages template to serve your own needs.

3   Click the bottom edge of the tan rounded rectangle to select it.

4   Click the center resize handle and drag the edge of the rounded rectangle to extend the box to the bottom of the page.

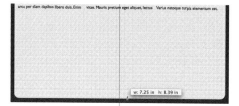

5   Click the main text box to select it.

6   Drag the resize handle at the bottom of the text box so that it fills more of the page, as shown in the following figure.

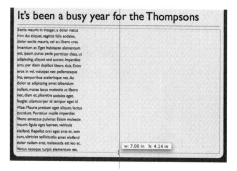

Before   After

You can replace the default headline with one of your own.

7   Double-click the headline placeholder text. It currently reads, *It's been a busy year for the Thompsons.*

8   Type the following text: *Major Expansion of Gym Facilities in 2009.*

9   Click an empty area of the page to deselect the text box.

> **TIP** You can press Command-Return to stop editing a text box object. Pages exits the text editing mode and selects the box as an object.

While you could type your articles directly into Pages, to speed up the rest of the text entry for this exercise, you'll cut and paste the articles from a Pages document.

> **NOTE** ► The same technique would work well if you were emailed text to use in a Pages document.

1   In the Lesson_10 folder, open **10Source Text.pages**.

You'll start by copying the photo caption text from the source document onto your Clipboard.

2   In the Pages source document, select the photo caption text and choose Edit > Copy.

3   Return to your Pages newsletter and select the text in the photo caption area on page 1.

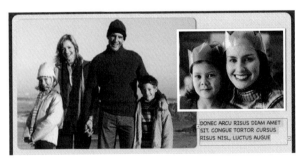

4 Choose Edit > Paste and Match Style.

This copies the text from your Clipboard yet maintains the formatting on the template page. The end of the text is cut off, however, because the text is too long to fit in the text box.

5 Click in an empty area of the page to deselect the text box.

Pages puts a + (plus sign) at the bottom of the text box to indicate the presence of overflow text. The text box contains too many characters to display completely at its current size. The text box must be made larger or the text must be made smaller—or both—so that the entire text can be seen.

6 Click the + symbol and drag down to resize the text box. Stop dragging when all the text is visible in the box.

 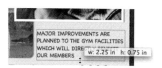

7 Return to the source text document. Select the main story text and copy it.

Story Page One

Major Expansion of Gym Facility

Story Body

In 2009, exciting things are coming. Our beautiful facility will have an even better view of the the lake Union waterfront. We're putting in even more windows for sunlight and splendid water views from all floors. Fresh air and light fill the facility creating a pleasant, invigorating atmosphere for your club visit.

We're also expanding our state-of-the-art strength-training and cardiovascular equipment. You'll find even more equipment for use during busy peak hours in the gym. Try out the new equipment to add some variety to your workout. Sound Mind & Body Gym offers something for everyone, whether you want a light workout and are in training for competitive sports.

Most people share the goal of staying fit and healthy, yet each member has their own individual way of attaining that fitness. To help, we've added a new Yoga room and Aerobics classroom. At Sound, Mind & Body Gym, we offer a full range of innovative group fitness classes, taught indoors and outdoors to make accomplishing that fitness fun, easy and rewarding.

After the workout, you can unwind in our expanded locker rooms. New saunas and steam rooms help you relax. With even more changing space and lockers you'll have plenty of room post-workout.

8 Return to your newsletter. Double-click the story text to select it.

9   Choose Edit > Paste and Match Style to paste the text into your story text box.

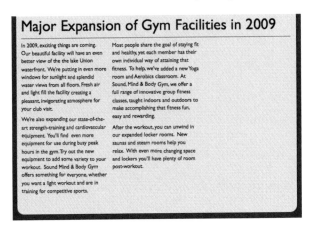

The text fills only the first two columns. You'll fill the third-column space with a chart graphic that illustrates the improvements being made to the gym. You can copy a chart from a Numbers document and add it to your Pages newsletter.

MORE INFO ▶ When a story spans multiple text boxes or pages, you can link text boxes, which causes overflow text to automatically flow to the next text box. You will explore this feature in Lesson 11, but it can also be useful when laying out a multi-page document such as a newsletter.

Adding a Chart

You often may want to add a chart or graph to a Pages document to help illustrate numerical information. Numbers is a spreadsheet application included with iWork '09 that can display data in easy-to-understand visual formats such as pie charts. You'll explore the application in depth starting in Lesson 13, "Spreadsheet Essentials." For this exercise, let's just copy a chart from a Numbers document. Because Numbers is part of the iWork suite, it is easy to copy data between Numbers and Pages.

TIP ▶ If a chart doesn't already exist, you can create it in Pages. In the toolbar, click the Charts button and choose a chart type. Enter your data into the Chart Data Editor window and format using the Chart inspector.

1   In the Finder, navigate to the Lesson_10 folder.

2   Double-click the file **10Chart.numbers** to open the spreadsheet in Numbers.

3   Click the chart and then Shift-click the legend to select them both.

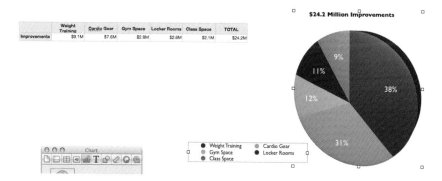

4   Choose Edit > Copy; then return to Pages.

5   Choose Edit > Paste to paste the chart and legend into your newsletter.

When the chart is added to the page, the text partially wraps around the chart and is partially hidden. Let's resize and reposition the chart.

NOTE ▶ You can control the way text wraps in the Wrap inspector.

6   Drag the chart and legend toward the bottom of the page.

7   Press Command-Shift-A to deselect all elements on the page.

8   Click the chart to select it by itself. The resize handles reappear for the chart.

9   On the chart, drag the upper left corner handle down and to the right to make it smaller. Resize so the chart's width is approximately 2.76 in. Then drag the chart to the bottom right of the page, as shown in the following figure.

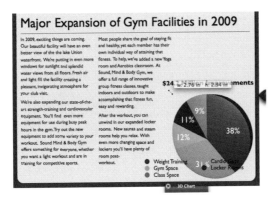

The text and other elements automatically reflow.

NOTE ▸ The circular refresh button next to the chart allows you to update its data. Pages maintains a link to the original Numbers document. If you change the original chart in Numbers, you can click the update button in Pages to force the chart to update and display the new data.

The chart is now an appropriate size for the layout, but it overlaps the legend and makes it difficult to read. You can fix this by repositioning the legend.

10   Drag the chart legend to the left and place it below the article text.

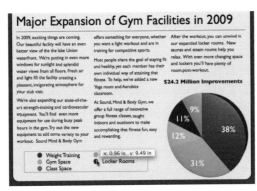

The text automatically reflows to make room for the object because object wrapping is turned on for the pasted chart. You can control how text flows around a graphic or turn wrapping off by using the Wrap inspector.

11 Choose File > Save to save your work.

Editing Image Placeholders

You've added the story and headlines to the first page of the newsletter and inserted a chart; let's add more visual interest by inserting photos. You can add images to your Pages document in several ways, including using the Media Browser, which functions just as it does in Keynote. (For more details, see Lesson 3, "Adding Video and Animation.") For this exercise, we'll assume that you have not added photos to your iPhoto library, so you'll navigate to them manually.

1 Select the large photo on page 1 (the image of the family).

2 Choose Insert > Choose.

A file browser dialog opens.

3 Navigate to your Lesson_10 folder. Open the Artwork folder and choose **01 Yoga Class.tif**. Click Insert.

The photo is scaled and added into your page layout.

The photo appears cropped to match the shape defined in the template. However, the image hasn't been edited. Part of the image is simply hidden behind a mask. iWork uses masks to conceal portions of an image without permanently altering them. Masks allow you additional flexibility when altering image size, shape, and placement.

Let's work with this image to focus on the subject.

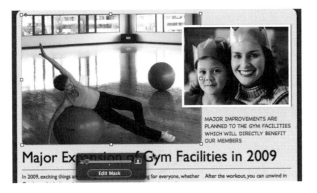

4   Click the Edit Mask button to resize the image within the mask and adjust the position of the mask.

5   Drag the scale slider to enlarge the image within the mask.

The image changes size and remains contained within the mask.

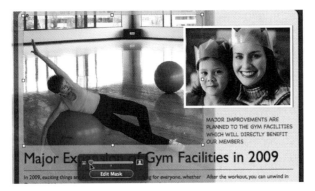

The image still shows too much of the windows at the top and doesn't center on the subject. You should move the focus to the important parts of the image.

6   Drag the image up to reposition it within the mask and hide the windows.

The subject now receives much more attention in the shot.

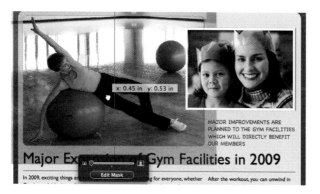

Ghosted parts of the photo indicate areas of the image that exist outside the mask. These ghosted areas won't display in your final newsletter.

7   Click the Edit Mask button to reapply the mask to the image.

The ghosted areas disappear, leaving just the part of the photo within the mask visible.

Now that you've replaced one photo, you can place a second photo on the page.

8   Click the second placeholder image to select it.

9   Choose Insert > Choose, and choose Lesson_10 > Artwork > **02 Weight Equipment.jpg**.

The second photo is added to the page. It appears a little washed out compared with the first. Thanks to the image-adjustment tools in Pages, this is an easy fix.

10 Choose View > Show Adjust Image.

The Adjust Image window appears. The tools contained here allow you to fine-tune an image's appearance. The tools are similar to the adjustment commands available in iPhoto.

11 Drag the Saturation slider to the right to increase the color intensity.

A value of 70 boosts the color in the image to more closely match the color in the first photo. The colors in the image now have greater richness and depth.

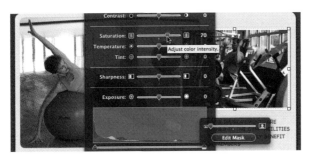

12 Click the Enhance button to adjust the contrast within the image.

The computer attempts to properly balance the relative amounts of light and dark.

13 Close the Adjust Image window.

14 Save your document.

Laying Out More Pages

Now that you've had some practice, you'll find that completing the newsletter is a much easier task. The newsletter has three additional pages. Although each page has a unique layout, all of them can be completed using techniques similar to those you used to customize page 1.

1   Select the thumbnail image of page 2 to switch to that page.

2   Click the large camping photo and choose Insert > Choose. The Lesson_10 > Artwork folder should still be visible in the dialog. Select **03 Trainer.tif** and click Insert.

The new picture replaces the placeholder image.

3   Using the techniques you've already learned, replace the four images on the right by inserting the following images from top to bottom:

▶   **04 Boot Camp.jpg**

▶   **05 Cardio Machines.jpg**

▶   **06 Basketball.tif**

▶   **07 Circuit Training.jpg**

Before image replacement   After image replacement

Now you've added all the photos on the second page, you can complete the page by adding new text. All of the text you need can be found in the **10Source Text.pages** document. Be sure to use the Paste & Match Style command.

4   Select the text for the photo caption on the main image and replace it by typing *personal training has become a cornerstone of the health and fitness industry.*

5   Select the headline and replace it by typing *Finding and Working with a Qualified Personal Trainer — The Key to Reaching Your Long-term Fitness Goals.*

6   Replace the text for the main story (it begins with *Personal training, once thought…*).

     The article is added to the page, but it wants a little additional formatting.

7   Select the phrase, *Tips on Choosing Trainers.*

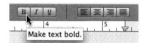

8   In the format bar, click the Bold button to add visual emphasis to the text.

Let's cleanly split the text across the two columns. This will help balance the text on the page.

TIP ▶ To set the number of columns on a page and their widths, use the Layout inspector.

9   In the last line of the fourth paragraph, click between the terms *courses for* and *continuing education credit.*

10   Choose Insert > Column Break to split the columns at the insertion point.

The text is now properly divided between the two columns.

11   Replace the text for the four photos on the right of the page with the following:

Fall Fitness

Boot Camp

Cardio Gear

Basketball

Weight Training

You can copy and paste the new text (choosing Edit > Paste and Match Style to keep the template styles) or simply type it directly into the layout.

NOTE ▶ Pages underlines *Cardio* in red to indicate that it may be misspelled. Some slang or jargon words might not be in your computer's dictionary. You can choose to ignore a spelling warning if you know a word is spelled correctly. Alternatively, you can add the correct spelling to your dictionary. To do so, select the word; then right-click and choose Learn Spelling from the shortcut menu.

12 For reference, compare your document with this completed page.

Don't worry if items are not an exact match; just do your best to have a neat and organized presentation of the information on the page.

13 Save your document.

Good work—you've successfully customized a Pages template that started out as a family newsletter and turned it into a professional-looking commercial document to distribute among gym members.

Inserting a Page into a Layout

Sometimes, you'll want to combine an existing Pages document with another Pages document. Using Pages to copy a page from one document to another can save you time, compared with cutting and pasting individual elements or redesigning an entirely new page. For your gym newsletter, let's replace page 3 with a previously laid-out page from another Pages document.

1   Open Lesson_10 > **10Spotlight & Classes.pages**.

2   Click the page's thumbnail and choose Edit > Copy.

3   Return to the active newsletter document.

4   Click the page 3 thumbnail and press Delete. An alert dialog appears to confirm that you want to delete the page.

5   Click Delete.

6   Choose Edit > Paste to add the page to the newsletter document.

Completing the Layout

You have successfully completed three of the four pages of your gym newsletter. The fourth page is a mailer page, which is designed for addressing the newsletter.

Replacing Photos

To complete the layout of the fourth page, let's replace the placeholder photos. By now, you should be quite comfortable with the process of adding your own images to a template.

1   Click the thumbnail for page 4.

2   Click the larger picture of the family walking to select it.

3   Choose Insert > Choose and choose Lesson_10 > Artwork > **08 Weights.jpg**. Click Insert.

The new photo replaces the placeholder image. However, the shot is a bit loose and doesn't focus on the action.

4   Double-click the photo to edit it.

5 Drag the resize handle and reposition the image so that it is better masked. When you're done, click the Edit Mask button. You can use the following figure as a visual guide.

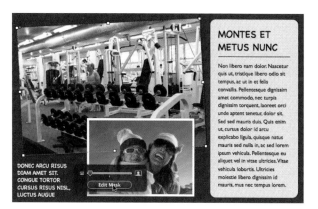

6 Select the second image on the page and replace it with Lesson_10 > Artwork > **09 Bike.jpg**.

The default placement masks the figure poorly and hides the rider's head.

7 Click the Edit Mask button and drag the image so that it is better framed. When you're finished, click the Edit Mask button to exit.

Before   After

8 In the lower left corner of the main photo, select the caption.

9   Press Delete to remove it.

10 Save your work.

Adjusting Text Size

You are almost done with the layout of this Pages document. Let's quickly add your last story so that you can proof the document and output a PDF file for the web.

1   Click the story headline and type *WEEKLY EVENTS*.

The text is a little too large and wraps to a second line, which leaves a bad break in the line and a lot of empty space. You can reduce the text a little so that it fits on one line.

2   Drag through the headline to select it.

3   Press Command- – (minus sign) to reduce the text by one point size. The text now fits on a single line and looks cleaner.

Before

After

TIP ▶ Pressing Command- – (minus sign) reduces the selected text one point size at a time. To enlarge text by one point size, press Command-+ (plus sign).

4   Return to the source text document and copy the page 4 story text to your Clipboard.

This time you are going to retain the formatting of the copied text.

5   Return to your Pages newsletter and click the placeholder text to select it. Choose Edit > Paste to insert the new text.

The new text is added to the Pages document with its existing formatting, including bold text. Additionally, the web URL is automatically formatted when Pages detects a properly formatted web address. However, in this case, you want to remove the formatting so that the URL appears as plain (unlinked) text.

6   Click within the text box (but not on the web link, or else you'll go to the website).

7   Press the arrow keys to move the insertion point until the web link is selected.

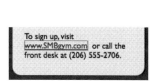

8   Open the Link inspector and deselect the "Enable as a hyperlink" checkbox.

Formatting the Address Field

The last area on the page that requires reformatting is the address field. You will want to replace the text with the correct business address. Additionally, you can enhance the address field by adding a business logo.

1   Replace the return address in the template with the following:

▶   Sound Mind & Body Gym

▶   437 North 34th Street

▶   Seattle, WA 98103

2   Click the right edge of the text box, and drag the resize handle to make it bigger. This will allow more room for the logo.

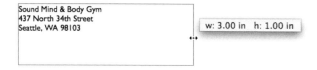

This newsletter will be distributed primarily online. Therefore, the mailing address area is going to be used only occasionally for sending a few copies.

3 Select the addressee name text box and press Delete.

You can still add a logo to the page. However, the logo you'll use has some extraneous text beneath it. By masking the image, you can hide the unnecessary text.

ORIGINAL – "S" enlarged

Throughout this lesson, you've only added images to placeholders. Pages offers a free-form graphics canvas, however, so you can add more images to your layout and create additional masks to define image borders. The logo has a circular shape, so let's create a circular mask to hold it.

4 Click an empty area on page 4 to make sure that nothing is currently selected.

5 In the toolbar, click the Shapes button and choose an oval.

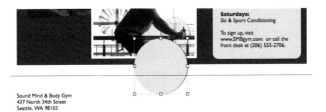

A shape is added to the center of the page. The circle can be sized to either an oval or a circle.

6 Shift-drag a corner handle to make the circle smaller. Size the circle to a diameter of about 1.00 inches.

Holding down the Shift key while dragging retains the original proportions of the image and, in this case, retains the circular shape.

7   In the Wrap inspector, select "Object causes wrap."

You will reposition the circle to jut into the address field. Let's make it easier to accurately position the logo.

8   Choose Pages > Preferences, and choose Rulers.

9   Select the "Show guides at object edges" checkbox.

This will display pop-up guides to help you position the logo.

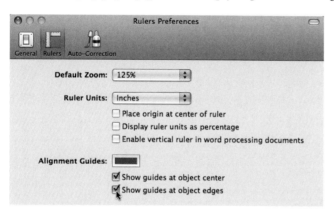

10 Close the Preferences window.

11 Reposition the circle on the page to closely match the following figure:

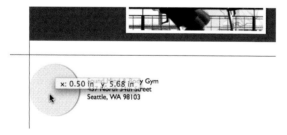

The alignment guide will show you when the edge of the circle is aligned with the edge of the newsletter content. Now that the circle is on the page, you can use it to mask your logo to a clean shape.

12 Switch to the Finder. Open the Lesson_10 > Artwork folder and drag **10 Logo.jpg** on top of the circle in the Pages document.

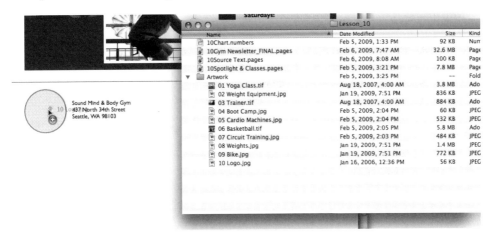

The logo is added to the page and is masked by the circle. Still, you'll want to adjust it within the mask.

13 Click the Edit Mask button. Drag the scale slider and resize the logo so that it fits within the circular mask. Then drag the logo to reposition it within the mask.

14 Click the Edit Mask button to apply the mask.

The logo has an unnecessary drop shadow and stroke. You can easily remove these.

15 Verify that the logo is selected, and in the format bar, deselect the Shadow checkbox.

16 In the format bar, set the stroke to None.

17 Save your document.

You can compare your work with **10Gym Newsletter_FINAL.pages**, a completed version of the newsletter in the Lesson_10 folder.

Exporting to PDF

Congratulations! Your gym newsletter is complete. It is now time to save it in an Internet-ready format. By sending a newsletter over the Internet, you can save a lot of postage costs. Using the PDF format ensures that your document maintains its appearance, no matter what hardware displays it; and it can be printed or viewed by Mac, Windows, and even Linux users.

1   With your newsletter open in Pages, choose Share > Export.

2   Click the PDF button to choose that format.

3   From the Image Quality pop-up menu, choose Better; then click Next.

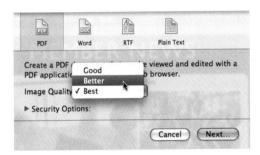

The menu offers three quality choices: Good, Better, and Best. When choosing one of these, you will want to consider a balance between file-size constraints and image quality. Choosing Better balances a compact Internet-friendly file size with image quality that is suitable for printing.

4   Name the document *SMB_GYM_FALL09_WEB.pdf* and save the file to the Lesson_10 folder.

When choosing a filename, avoid spaces and long names if your file is meant to be downloaded. The name you entered here identifies the company and the year, and indicates that the file is optimized for the web.

5   Click Export to write the PDF file to the save location.

You can now send your newsletter to others as a PDF file as an email attachment or by posting it to a website.

6   Close and save your Pages document.

Lesson Review

1. Describe two methods for replacing a placeholder image.
2. How can you adjust an image's appearance after the image has been added to Pages?
3. What's the first step you perform when you want to edit the mask of a selected image?
4. How do you wrap text around an object?
5. How do you scale a shape proportionally?

Answers

1. Drag a new image onto a placeholder image; or select a placeholder image and choose Insert > Choose and select a new image in the Finder.
2. Choose View > Show Adjustment Image to open the Adjust Image window.
3. Click the Edit Mask button to edit an image mask.
4. Select the object. In the Wrap inspector, select the "Object causes wrap" checkbox.
5. Shift-drag a scale handle.

11

Time This lesson takes approximately 60 minutes to complete.

Goals Add assets to the Media Browser

Modify masked images

Group and edit objects

Format hyperlinks

Link text boxes

Wrap text around an object

Add connection lines between two objects

Add sound files to a Pages document

Save a flyer as a template

Lesson 11
Creating Promotional Materials

One of the major benefits of Pages is its design flexibility. Supporting a wide range of graphic formats and Apple-designed templates, Pages makes it easy to create and customize media-rich content, such as marketing brochures and flyers.

Brochures are a convenient medium for conveying a lot of information in a well-organized layout. They are also relatively inexpensive to manufacture because they often use common paper sizes. Flyers, on the other hand, tend to display less information, but do so in a highly visual manner. Flyers are meant to quickly catch the eye and entice the viewer to action.

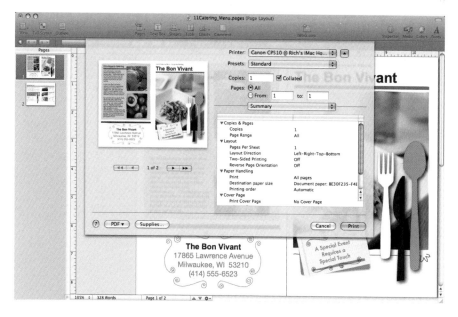

In this lesson, you'll complete the designs for a marketing brochure and flyer using several advanced controls in Pages. You will learn how to build your own library of assets and will design professional-looking printed marketing items.

Customizing the Media Browser

One way to speed up the Pages design process is to gather the images you'll use and place them close at hand. By default, the Media Browser provides access to all the media files in your iPhoto library, your iTunes library, your Aperture library, and your Movies folder.

Although the default media libraries on your Mac are readily available, you can customize the Media Browser to temporarily add a folder of project media from your hard drive without importing the images. By adding a folder to the Media Browser, you can use drag and drop within Pages.

1   Choose View > Show Media Browser to open the Media Browser.

As you are customizing the Media Browser, you'll want to precisely arrange the windows to suit your workflow.

2   Switch to the Finder and select the Lesson_11 folder.

3   Position the folder so that it is not obscured by the Pages application.

4   Return to Pages.

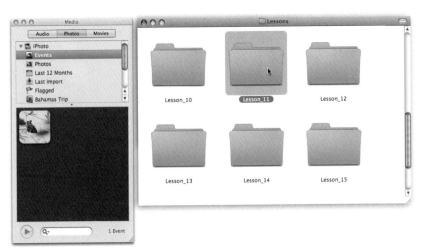

5   In the Media Browser, click the Photos button and then drag the Lesson_11 folder from the Finder into the Media Browser.

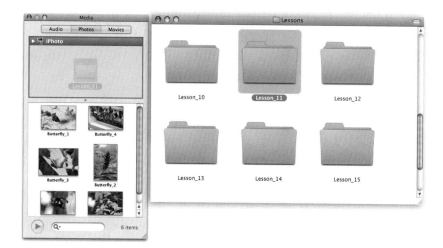

Two folders of images are added to the Media Browser. Let's add some audio files that you'll use later in the lesson.

6   In the Media Browser, click the Audio button and drag the Lesson_11 folder from the Finder into the Media Browser.

TIP▸   You can drag any media folder to the Media Browser to secure quick access to its media. To remove the main folder from the Media Browser, Control-click (or right-click) the folder you want to remove and choose Remove folder.

Creating a Brochure

Brochures can be printed inexpensively and then left on counters or packed with purchases. The brochure is a popular and affordable tool for explaining services or products to your customers. Pages includes several brochure templates. In the next exercise, you'll start your brochure with a partially built document.

1   Choose File > Open.

2   Navigate to the Lesson_11 folder.

3   Select the file **11Catering_Menu Start.pages**.

4   Click Open.

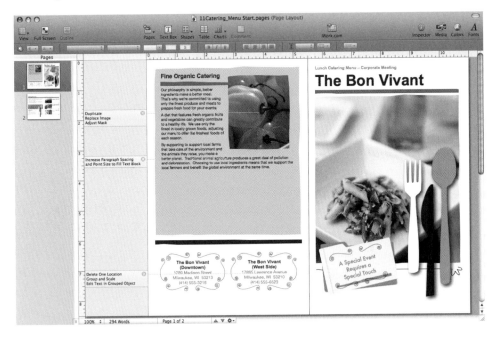

Pages opens the partially completed document. You'll see that some comments have been left in the document to help you finish the project.

> **TIP** Before settling on a final design for material you intend to print, output a sample file on your printer or at your printing shop. Be sure your file matches the capabilities and requirements of your output method.

Modifying Masked Images

In this brochure, you'll find several images with custom masks. The original designer drew a custom shape and then used that shape to mask the photo. A great feature of Pages is that the custom masks remain editable, so you can further modify their appearance. Let's add an image to the layout and give it a unique border.

1   Click the thumbnail for page 1 to select it.

2   Click the pepper image on the left-hand page to select it.

Let's create a duplicate of the image to fill out the page.

3   Option-drag a duplicate of the pepper image directly below the first. Use the alignment guides to help you align the duplicate with the original image.

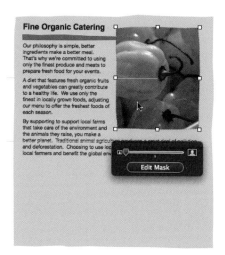 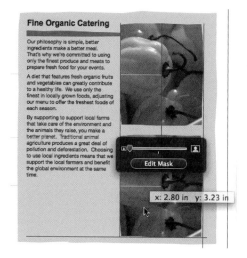

A duplicate that can be customized is placed on the page.

4   In the Media Browser, click Photos and select the Food Shots folder. Select the image **Back Cover 2.jpg** (a picture of avocados) and drag it onto the second peppers image.

Now that the avocados image is placed, you can modify its mask so that it looks different from the image above.

5   Click the Edit Mask button. Pages displays the mask as a series of red dots that indicate the points drawn with the custom shape tool.

These points can be dragged to new positions if you'd like, but they can also be quickly modified using the Metrics inspector.

6   Open the Metrics inspector.

7 Click the Flip Horizontal button to create a mirror image of the mask.

Now let's rotate the mask 180 degrees so that it looks even more different. The current mask already is rotated 90 degrees, so the new value is 180 degrees plus 90 degrees, for a total of 270 degrees.

8 Enter *270* into the Angle field.

The custom mask now looks substantially different.

9 Click the Edit Mask button to stop editing the mask.

10 Close the two comments with the instructions about modifying the images.

11 Choose File > Save As.

12 Name the file *11Catering_Menu.pages* and save it to the Lesson_11 folder.

Adjusting Text to Fit a Layout

One objective of professional design is to have a clean layout of text without any extraneous space. The current page looks good, but filling out the text box would make the page more balanced. Instead of adding more words, let's format the text to improve its readability.

First, adjust the size of the text.

1 Double-click in the large text box on the first page.

2 Press Command-A to select all of the text.

A blue highlight indicates all of the selected text. Let's make the text bigger.

3 Press Command-+ (plus sign) two times to increase the size of the text by 2 points.

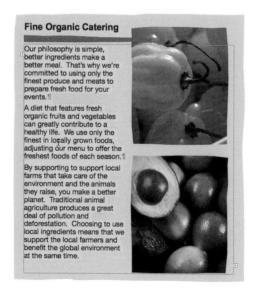

The text almost fills the box. You can now adjust the space between each paragraph to further refine the layout of the text box.

4   Open the Text inspector.

5   Increase the space between paragraphs by entering *12* in the After Paragraph field and press Return.

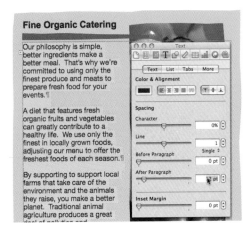

The text now fills the text box properly.

6   Close the comment about the text box.

7   Choose File > Save to save your work.

Group and Edit an Object

If you have a complex layout comprising several objects, grouping can make them easier to handle. In this document, you'll see two sets of addresses at the bottom of the first page as well as several graphic flourishes. The restaurant has stopped offering catering at the Madison Street location, so let's modify the brochure to remove that address.

1   Click at the top of the left address and drag on the canvas to select all of its elements.

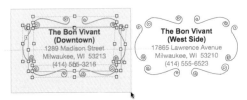

2   Press Delete to remove the address and its graphics.

Now that the one address is gone, the other should be scaled and modified to balance the page design. By grouping the floating objects together, you'll find it easier to move and resize the address as a single object.

3   Click at the top of the address and drag on the canvas to select all of its elements.

4   Choose Arrange > Group to combine the objects into a single, editable object.

> **TIP** ▶ To ungroup an object, choose Arrange > Ungroup. If the group is locked, you will have to unlock it first by choosing Arrange > Unlock.

5   Drag the selection handles to scale the image to a height of 2.00 inches. Position the object so that it is centered horizontally on the page. You can use the alignment guides for assistance.

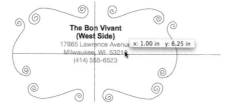

The size looks better, but the text is now too small to properly match the graphic flourishes. The text also should be edited. Fortunately, you can edit text inside a group without ungrouping it.

6   Click within the grouped object to edit the text.

> **NOTE** ▶ If a single click doesn't select the object, keep clicking until the object you want is selected.

7   Delete the text *(West Side)* from the text box. Be sure to remove the empty line break.

8   Press Command-A to select all the text in the block.

9   Press Command-+ (plus sign) to increase the point size 1 point for each press. Press the key combination nine times to achieve the desired effect and complete the first page.

10   Choose File > Save to save your work.

You have completed the first page of your brochure layout. By combining the controls of the inspector with advanced commands, you precisely edited the content on the page. Let's switch to the second page to finish your brochure.

Connecting Text Boxes

When designing page layout documents, it is common for text to flow from one area of the page to another (or even onto a second page) to accommodate a long story or a design objective. If you have more text than will fit in a single floating text box, you can create a linked text box and configure text to flow from one text box to the next. The advantage of using this technique is that you can easily edit the text in all of the boxes at one time.

Your brochure design has three featured items on the right of page two. Every time the menu is updated, different items are added. The photos have already been placed, so let's quickly add the text to all the boxes at one time.

1   Click the thumbnail for page 2 to select it, then click in the first text box (containing Menu Item #1) to select it.

Let's link to the next text box.

2   Click the blue square on the right side of the text box.

The pointer changes to a plus symbol and prompts you to click another text box on the page.

TIP ▶ To create a new linked text box, choose Format > Text Box > Add Linked Text Box.

3   Click the next text box on the page for Menu Item #2.

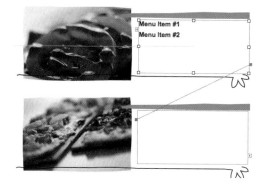

Pages shows a blue connection line to indicate that the boxes have been linked.

NOTE ▶ If the blue connection lines aren't visible, choose Format > Text Box > Show Connection Lines.

Let's connect the third text box.

4   Click the blue square on the right side of the second text box; then click the third text box (labeled Menu Item #3).

Now that the text boxes are linked, let's insert the menu descriptions.

5   Double-click the first linked text box and press Command-A to select all the text.

6 Press Delete to remove the placeholder text.

> **NOTE ▶** To break a connection between linked text boxes, choose Format > Text Box > Break Connection into Text Box, or Format > Text Box > Break Connection out of Text Box. You can also drag the connection line from the blue square to break the link.

Let's add more text.

7 From the Lesson_11 folder, open **New Menu Items.pages**.

8 Select all of the text in the document and choose Edit > Copy.

9 Return to the catering menu.

10 Click in the first text box and choose Edit > Paste.

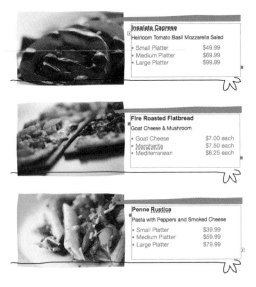

The added text automatically flows from the first text box through the other linked text boxes.

NOTE ▶ To split text between linked text boxes, choose Insert > Column Break.

11 Delete the comment about linking text boxes.

12 Choose File > Save to capture your work.

NOTE ▶ You can link text boxes at any time. If a plus symbol appears at the bottom of a text box, it means you have overflow text. You can choose to expand the current text box or to link it to another text box. Linking is a great way to solve layout problems as it lets you continue to overflow text to another part of the page or to another page altogether.

Your brochure is almost finished,—all that is left is to format an email address to make it interactive in its PDF version.

Format a Hyperlink

One way to make a brochure drive customers to your business is to add interactive links. When you save a brochure as a PDF, you can include web links or email addresses that allow clickable action. To do this, you'll use the Link inspector.

1 In the leftmost page, locate the email address *chef@thebonvivantcatering.com*.

2 Select the full email address.

> This menu is meant as a sample for planning a lunchtime meeting with clients. Send us an email at chef@thebonvivantcatering.com for a complete menu to choose from.

3 Open the Link inspector.

4 Select the "Enable as hyperlink" checkbox.

The inspector automatically sets the Link To pop-up menu to Email Message and addresses the To field because you highlighted a properly formatted email address.

5   In the Subject field, enter *I'd like to place an order.*

Now, when a customer clicks the link, her email program will open and create a new message addressed to the catering department with a complete email address and subject line.

NOTE ▸   For best results, be sure to choose Share > Export when creating your PDF.

6   Delete the final comment.

7   Press Command-S to capture your work.

You can compare your work to the file **11Catering_Menu End.pages**.

8   Close the brochure document.

Creating a Flyer

A flyer is a common promotional tool that provides a cost-effective way to promote an event, cause, or product. Flyers are best used when promoting a single item because they are most often only quickly glanced at.

TIP Pages includes pull-tab flyer templates, which feature removable tabs along the bottom. After printing, you should cut a short distance vertically (use the thin line for guidance). This makes the pull tabs easier to rip off. A pull tab is a great way to let a passerby get a phone number or web address for future follow-up.

You will use Pages to create a flyer to promote a band called the Nadas. The flyer is partially designed but could use some additional work. When the flyer is complete, you can save it as a template so that it can be quickly updated in the future.

1   Choose File > Open.

2   Navigate to the Lesson_11 folder.

3   Select the file **11Band_Flyer Start.pages**.

4   Click Open.

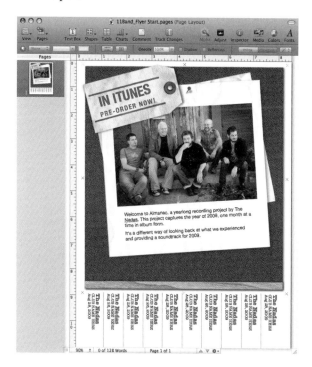

Pages opens the mostly completed flyer.

Wrap Text Around an Object

When you add an image to a page, you can choose to flow text around the object. Let's add the CD cover for the band's latest release to the page.

1   In the Media Browser, select the Lesson_11 folder.

2   Select the image **Almanac_Cover.jpg.**

3   Drag the CD cover to the page near the bottom right corner of the bulletin board.

NOTE ▸ Be careful not to drag the album cover on top of the band photo or you'll replace that photo.

The photo is added to the page. Let's adjust it so that the text wraps around the cover image.

4   In the format bar, click the Wrap button and choose the first wrap option.

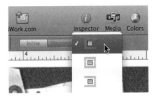

The text wraps around the top, bottom, and left edges of the object.

TIP If you want precise control over how much extra space is placed around the wrapped image, adjust it in the Wrap inspector.

5   In the Metrics inspector, enter a width of 2.5 in (inches) to precisely size the cover image.

6 Position the image on the page so that it fits in the right corner, without affecting any of the pull tabs.

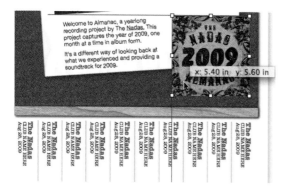

Let's add and format a picture frame so that the CD cover looks like another item on the bulletin board.

7 In the format bar, click the Line Style button and choose the pushpin-style frame.

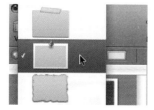

It looks right stylistically, but the border is a bit thick and the pushpin is too large compared with the other pin on the board.

8 Open the Graphic inspector.

9 Drag the scale slider to 50% to shrink the border and the pushpin. Your CD cover is almost complete. Let's help it stand out a bit so that the white border and white paper are separated.

10 In the Graphic inspector, select the Shadow checkbox.

11 In the Metrics inspector, rotate the image to 354° so that the picture looks angled like others on the bulletin board.

12 Reposition the album cover if necessary.

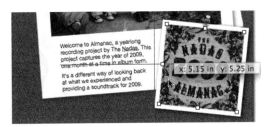

13 Choose File > Save As.

14 Name the file *11Band_Flyer.pages* and save it to the Lesson_11 folder.

Your final design is under way. Let's connect the album cover with the callout for the iTunes store.

Using a Connection Line

If you want to place a line between floating objects, iWorks offers an easy way to do so called a *connection line*. The new line stretches between the objects even if you reposition them. Additionally, the line can be stylized to make it appear as a hand-drawn element on the page.

Let's connect the album cover to your "call to action" graphic.

1 Verify that the album cover is still selected.

2 Command-click the tag graphic at the top of the page.

   NOTE ▶ Be sure to click at the edge of the tag graphic so that you select the image and not the text box.

3 When both objects are selected, choose Insert > Connection Line to add the connection line.

Pages adds a thin black line between the objects. Let's modify it to match other elements in the flyer. First, curve the line so that it arcs around the photo of the band.

NOTE ▶ When two objects are connected, you can move either object and the line will move with it.

4   Drag the white editing point near the center of the line to the right, using the preceding figure as a guide. Now that the line is curved around the photo, let's stylize it to match the flyer design.

5   In the format bar, click the line style button and choose the first rough stroke.

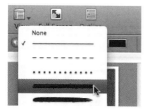

6   In the format bar, change the line width to 10 pt.

7   Change the line color to red.

TIP ▶ You can use the magnifying glass in the Colors window to choose a shade of red already present on the flyer.

Let's add an arrowhead to guide the reader's eyes.

8   In the format bar, click the first Endpoints pop-up menu and choose the first arrowhead. If you want, you can drag the blue dot at the end of the line to offset the arrowhead.

Let's make the arrow stand out a bit more dimensionally.

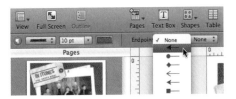

9   Select the Shadow checkbox to add a drop shadow to the line.

10   Choose File > Save to save your work.

The flyer is almost complete. Let's make just two small enhancements.

Updating Placeholder Text

When designing marketing materials, you will often want to perform small updates to text (such as a time, location, or date). Pages makes it easy to insert placeholder text that can be easily replaced or updated.

1   Double-click the center pull tab to edit its text. The text box rotates 90 degrees for editing.

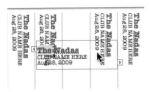

2   Highlight the second line of text.

NOTE ► Be sure to highlight only the words CLUB NAME HERE and not the line break. If you highlight the line break symbol (¶), you have selected too much.

3   Choose Format > Advanced > Define as Placeholder Text.

The text can now be easily replaced just like the placeholder text you worked with in a Pages template. Let's format the date to automatically update when the document is opened.

4   Double-click the date located on line three of the pull tab.

5   In the date format window, select the "Automatically update on open" checkbox. The date will now change to the current day when the document opens. Let's copy the text in this pull tab and use it to replace the others.

6   Click inside the current text box and press Command-A to select all the text.

7   Choose Edit > Copy.

8   Double-click in the first text box and press Command-A to select all the text.

9   Press Command-V to paste the text from your Clipboard.

10 Repeat steps 8 and 9 for each text box in the pull-tab section.

11 When finished, choose File > Save to capture your work.

You have updated the text in your flyer. Let's add a few media files to complete the project.

Adding Sound to a Pages Document

A little-known feature of Pages is its support for movie and sound files. These files are playable only inside of Pages, but they are still worth exploring. For instance, you might choose to include a media file as inspiration or reference in a design document.

In the case of your band flyer, you can include music tracks that could serve as an incentive for fans to download the Pages document to print and display in their neighborhood. Let's explore how you add audio media to a Pages document.

1 Open the Media Browser, click the Audio tab, and navigate to Lesson_11 > The Nadas.

2 Click **02 Blue Lights.mp3**.

3 Shift-click **09 Feels Like Home.mp3** to select all three media files.

4 Drag the three media files to the canvas.

Pages adds three partially transparent speaker icons to the canvas. Each icon represents a sound file. These icons are visible only inside Pages and will not print or show up in an exported document.

5 Adjust the speaker icons so that they are in a single row. Use the alignment guides to help with alignment and distribution.

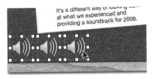

6 Double-click a speaker icon to play the song. Click the icon again to pause playback.

   NOTE ▶ The audio files can be played only within the Pages document. If you don't hear the sound, make sure your computer's volume is turned up.

7 Choose File > Save to save your work.

Saving a Flyer as a Template

Your flyer is finished. In this exercise, you'll create a web-ready version that you can print or electronically distribute. You'll also save your file as a template so that you can reuse it to create other flyers. Any document that you'll want to update frequently with new information (such as venues and performance dates) should be saved as a template.

1   Choose File > Save as Template.

2   Name the template *Nadas Flyer.template* and select the "Include preview in document" checkbox. The preview makes it easier to look at the document using Mac OS X v10.5 and its QuickView feature.

3   Choose Save.

> **NOTE ►** Be sure to save to the default location that Pages chooses so that your template will appear in the Template Chooser.

Now that your flyer is saved as a template, let's make sure it is stored correctly.

4   Choose File > New to create a new document and access the Template Chooser.

The new template appears in the My Templates section.

> **TIP ►** You can manually remove any unwanted templates by deleting them from your home folder in Library/Application Support/iWork/Pages/Templates/My Templates.

5   Because you're not going to create a new document at this time, click Cancel.

Now publish the Pages file to an iWeb page to share with others.

6   Choose Share > Send to iWeb > Pages.

iWeb opens and prompts you to choose a page type. You will not need to create an actual website in this lesson, but you can explore iWeb on your own.

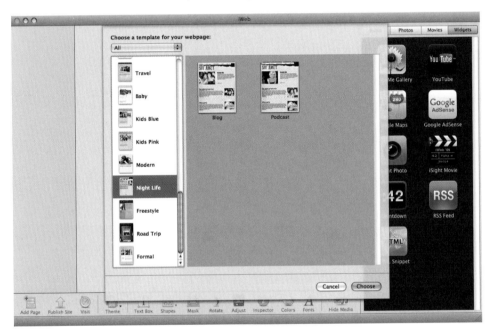

TIP ▶ You can use iWeb to create a website for sharing your Pages documents. When you offer the poster file for download, multiple users (such as a street team) can customize it as necessary.

MORE INFO ▶ For more about iWeb, see Apple Training Series: iLife '09 (Peachpit Press, 2009)

Close iWeb and return to Pages.

7   Save and close your flyer document.

Lesson Review

1.   How can you add a folder of photos to the Media Browser?

2.   How can you combine two or more objects so that they are treated as a single object?

3.   How do you set properties for an email address?

4.   How do you rotate text or objects?

5.   How can you save a frequently used document layout for quick customization in the future?

Answers

1.   Drag a folder of images into the Media Browser.

2.   Select the objects and choose Arrange > Group.

3.   Use the Link inspector to generate email messages from a valid email address.

4.   Use the Metrics inspector and enter a specific rotation amount in degrees or Command-drag a corner selection handle.

5.   Choose File > Save as Template.

12

Lesson Files

Lessons > Lesson_12 > 12Academic Certificate FINAL.pages

Lessons > Lesson_12 > 12Butterfly Garden Poster_FINAL.pages

Lessons > Lesson_12 > 12Club_Roster.numbers

Lessons > Lesson_12 > Monarch.jpg

Lessons > Lesson_12 > Butterfly Photos

Time

This lesson takes approximately 90 minutes to complete.

Goals

Work with Poster and Certificate templates in Pages

Add and subtract elements in a template layout

Format and replace placeholder text

Add project photos to your iPhoto library

Adjust images for optimum appearance using iPhoto

Send a Pages document via email

Address multiple certificates using the Mail Merge command and a Numbers spreadsheet

Creating Materials for the Classroom

The classroom is a great place to integrate visually rich documents to help communicate with students. By harnessing Pages, an educator can quickly make posters, certificates, lab notes, and quizzes. Students can also use Pages for many word processing tasks, from simple essays to complex reports.

In this lesson, you will use two template projects for two typical classroom tasks: making a poster and generating a certificate for a school's science club. You'll also use iPhoto to refine and repair photos for use on the page. Even if you don't need to make classroom materials, you will still explore useful page layout features in this lesson that allow you to create a variety of highly visual posters and documents.

Designing a Poster

Pages includes 11 Apple-designed poster templates, many of which are specifically intended for use in school-oriented activities. You'll find starter templates for events like musicals, sporting events, science fairs, and community projects. These templates can be modified using your own photos and text. Let's explore making a poster for a community project.

Choosing a Poster Template

The Template Chooser is a great tool you can use to start your project by choosing a poster template that closely matches your needs. With a proper template in hand, you can choose the correct page size for your project and customize other print and design options. Let's choose a starting template for your poster project.

1   If the Template Chooser is not already open, choose File > New from Template Chooser.

2   In the Template Chooser, from the Page Layout group, choose the Posters category.

    Pages includes 11 starting projects in two sizes: small and large. If you're working in inches, a small poster is 8.5 by 11 inches, the standard print size. Larger posters use tabloid-sized paper, measuring 11 by 17 inches. You can always modify the page size by opening the Document inspector and clicking the Page Setup button.

3   Click the Garden Project Poster Large thumbnail, and click Choose.

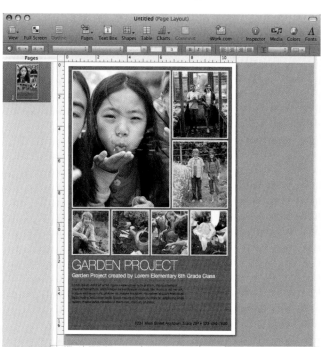

The poster opens, and some of its information, such as the address field, is already entered, based upon the default card in your Address Book.

Let's see the entire document onscreen at once.

4   Click the View pop-up menu and choose Fit Page.

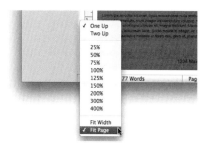

The entire page shrinks so it can fit in the Canvas window.

Customizing Text

Now that you've opened the starting template, you can populate it with your own content. You'll notice that the placeholder uses a standard text called "Lorem ipsum," which uses several Latin words that are only there for layout purposes. This placeholder text is meant to give you a good idea of how the finished text will appear. You'll want to fill in the document with your own information to customize it for your event.

1   Double-click the poster title (*Garden Project*) and replace the text with *Butterfly Garden*.

2   Replace the poster's subtitle by clicking to highlight it, then typing *Garden Project created by Lincoln High Science Club.*

Now that the title and subtitle are suitable for your project, let's fill in a few details about the event.

3   Double-click the large text box to select the entire placeholder text.

4   Type the following information into the poster template:

Come see some of the most beautiful creatures on Earth in our relaxing butterfly garden. Our students have researched and designed a garden with the right plants and flowers to attract all of the beautiful butterflies in our area.

The garden itself is also a great way to explore the local plants in our region. Stroll peacefully and relax with nature. The garden is free to visit and is open daily from 1 p.m. until 4:30 p.m. for the months of April, May, and June.

This text easily fits in the template but can be more attractively formatted. Let's increase the spacing between the two paragraphs to fill up the text box and improve the separation between the two thoughts.

5   Press Command-A to select the text you just entered, then open the Text inspector and set the After Paragraph field to 12 pt.

This automatically inserts 12 points of space between the two paragraphs. Let's keep improving the text formatting. Look closely at how the time information is split across the last two lines. This makes the poster harder to comprehend at a quick glance.

6   In the second-to-last line, place the insertion point before the number *1*.

7   Press Return to break the text to the next line.

Keeping the *1* and *p.m.* on the same line makes the text easier to read, but the extra space between the lines doesn't look right.

8   Choose Edit > Undo to undo the previous step.

9 With the insertion point still located before the number *1*, press Shift-Return to insert a line break.

The text is wrapped to the next line, and the correct spacing between lines is preserved.

10 Triple-click in the lower text box on the page to select all of the placeholder text.

NOTE ▶ Pages automatically inserted information based on the Address Book card that's designated My Card. If you find that you use one address frequently, be sure to open Address Book and fill in your address card.

11 Enter the following information into the last field to indicate the address for the butterfly garden: *Opening in April • 14228 Wentworth Avenue • Calumet City, IL 60409.*

Opening in April • 14228 Wentworth Avenue • Calumet City, IL 60409

TIP ▶ To place a bullet symbol in your text, press Option-8.

The text is looking good, but different formatting could help it to stand out.

12 Select all of the text in the address box.

13 In the format bar, click the Bold button to make the font bold.

14 In the format bar, click the Font Size field and enter 22 pt to enlarge the text.

15 Next to the Font Size field, click the Text Color well to change the text color. In the color matrix, choose a bright blue to make the text stand out more clearly.

Opening in April • 14228 Wentworth Avenue • Calumet City, IL 60409

16 Choose File > Save and name the poster *Butterfly Garden Poster.pages*.

You have finished adjusting the text in your poster. You'll find that modifying text in future posters will be just as easy.

Customizing a Layout

The current poster has several photos already placed in the layout. While you could use these pictures in your final poster, you'll usually want to replace most media placeholders with your own photos.

This poster contains seven placeholder images. For this poster, you have only six photos you'll want to use, so let's adjust the layout.

1 Select the photo of the two children with the pitchfork.

2   Press Delete to remove the image.

The seventh photo is removed from the layout, but the deletion leaves a large gap in the layout that should be corrected.

3   Select the photo of the two children inside the greenhouse.

You can easily adjust the mask of the media placeholder to accommodate a different layout. Let's make this photo tall and skinny to fill in the right edge of the poster.

4   Click the Edit Mask button.

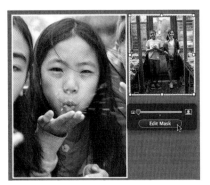

5   Click in the middle of the mask's bottom edge and drag the selection handle down.

6   Size the mask so that it is 8.5 inches tall and matches the height of the largest image on the page.

7 Drag the resize slider for the photo to make it larger, and then drag the image inside the masked area until it fills the frame.

8 Click the Edit Mask button to apply the mask.

9 Choose File > Save to save your progress.

You have successfully adjusted the page layout and are ready to insert your own photos.

Adding Photos to Your iPhoto Library

One way to store images for use in Pages is to add them to your iPhoto library. iPhoto provides easy, flexible image-management tools. Let's add your butterfly photos to iPhoto.

1 In the Finder, open the Lesson_12 folder.

2 Drag the Butterfly Photos folder onto the iPhoto icon in your Dock.

If it's not open already, iPhoto opens. The photos are automatically loaded to an Event called Butterfly Photos.

NOTE ▶ iPhoto uses Events to organize images that were photographed within one day of each other. For more information about organizing images with iPhoto, see *Apple Training Series: iLife '09* (Peachpit Press, 2009).

3   Carefully examine all six photos for improvements that can be made.

You should notice that the first photo looks a little bright, the fourth looks too dark, and all of them are a little washed-out. You can use iPhoto to touch up all of your images.

▶ Taking Pictures with the iSight Camera

In a classroom, you'll often use a lot of photos. Conveniently, your Mac is a flexible tool that allows you to import photos from digital cameras or to digitally capture printed images with a scanner. Additionally, you can also locate websites that offer royalty-free photos for classroom use. What many users forget, however, is that computers like the iMac include a built-in iSight camera that can be used to capture photos.

If you are using an iMac or a Mac laptop, it probably has a built-in iSight camera. While the most common use for this camera is iChat video conferencing, it can also be used to take pictures. Using the Photo Booth application, you can easily capture still photos with the iSight or any digital video camera connected to your Mac.

▶ **Taking Pictures with the iSight Camera** *(continued)*

1 In your Applications folder, open Photo Booth.

2 Choose the type of snapshot you want to take by selecting one of three buttons at the bottom of the Preview window:

  ▶ Still Picture

  ▶ Four Quick Snapshots

  ▶ Movie Clip (which can be used in Keynote)

3 When you are ready to take a photo (or record a movie), click the red shutter button below the preview image.

4 Photo Booth performs a three-second countdown. If you're taking a picture of a person, it's time for him or her to smile. Otherwise, hold the object you want to shoot in front of the camera.

5 The screen flashes when Photo Booth takes the picture. If you're recording a movie, be sure to click the Stop button to end the recording.

  A thumbnail of the image is added to the bottom of the window.

  You photos are automatically stored in a folder named Photo Booth, located in your Pictures folder in your home folder. You can open the folder by selecting a thumbnail and choosing File > Reveal in Finder. To delete a photo, select a thumbnail and press the Delete key.

6 When you're finished, close Photo Booth.

  Your pictures will automatically appear in the Media Browser. This method makes it easy to add an image to any Pages (or Numbers or Keynote) document. The pictures are not high-resolution images, so you should keep them small if you intend to print your document.

Fixing Overexposed Images

If a photo is shot in very bright conditions or with the lens pointed into a bright sky, the image may become overexposed. iPhoto can fix these problems with just a few clicks.

1   In iPhoto, select the first butterfly photo.

2   Click the Edit button.

The image opens to fill the window and is ready to be edited.

3   Click the Adjust button to open the Adjust window.

4 Drag the Exposure slider to the left to decrease the overexposed areas.

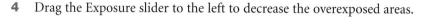

A value of approximately –0.25 works well for this image.

5 Drag the Saturation slider to the right to boost the color vibrancy in the image. Use a value of 80.

The image now has increased color intensity but lacks detail.

6 Select the "Avoid saturating the skin tones" checkbox to protect the reds from becoming oversaturated.

NOTE ▶ This option is really designed to avoid saturation in skin tones. In this photo, the option works well because of the reddish-orange in the butterfly's wings.

The image color looks good, but the image itself could be a little sharper. To fix this, iPhoto provides two types of commands.

7   First, drag the Definition slider to the right to a value of 70.

The Definition command can improve clarity and reduce haze in your photos without adding too much contrast. Now let's sharpen the image. Sharpening works best when you are viewing the image more closely.

8   Press the 1 key to view your photo at 100 percent.

A Navigation window opens to make it easier to view your image.

9   Drag the small rectangle so that you can see the butterfly centered in the window.

10   In the Adjust window, drag the Sharpness slider to the right until the image looks crisp. For this image, try using a value near 25.

NOTE ► You may have to move the Navigation window to see the adjustment controls.

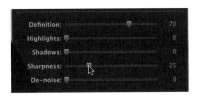

TIP ► If you want to compare the before and after states while sharpening, hold down the Shift key to see the original image. When you release the Shift key, you can see the adjusted image.

Congratulations! You have successfully enhanced the first photo, so let's tackle another problem.

Fixing Underexposed Images

If a photo is shot in low light, you may find that it is underexposed. The best way to prevent this is to use a flash when taking photos. However, if you choose to fix underexposure after the fact, iPhoto can help.

1   Click the thumbnail of the butterfly and red flower.

This picture is too dark. Let's correct its exposure.

2   In the toolbar, click the Enhance button to have iPhoto attempt to automatically fix the image.

In the Adjust window, you'll see that the Levels, Saturation, and Temperature values have been adjusted for the image.

NOTE ▶ You'll also find a useful Enhance button near the bottom of the Adjust Image window inside iWork.

3   Drag the middle slider of the Levels controls to the left to increase the brightness of the image's middle tones.

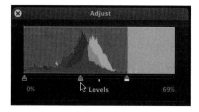

Adjusting the mid-tones makes an image appear brighter without washing out the dark areas or over-brightening the light areas.

4   Adjust the Definition and Sharpness controls using the techniques you learned in the previous exercise.

This photo's exposure balance now looks much better, so let's enhance the remaining images.

Quickly Improving Multiple Images

You can view more than one photo at a time in edit view, which makes it easier to compare images when making an adjustment.

1   Select the second photo thumbnail.

You'll want to compare this with the three remaining photos.

2   Command-click the thumbnails for images 3, 5, and 6 to add them to edit view.

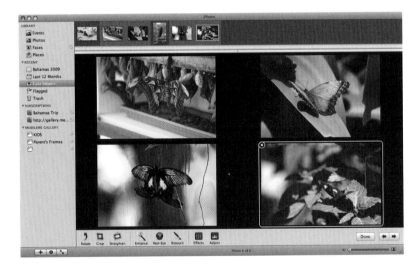

All four images now appear in edit view. The white outline indicates the photo currently being edited.

3   Click the first image in the upper left corner.

4   Click the Enhance button to automatically fix the photo.

5   Make any additional adjustments you desire using the tools in the Adjust window.

6   Click each of the remaining images and repeat steps 4 and 5 until you are happy with the photos' appearance.

7   When finished, click the Done button to close edit view.

8   Choose iPhoto > Quit to close iPhoto and return to Pages.

Adding Photos to Your Layout

Now that you have imported, organized, and enhanced your photos, you can add them to your layout. In iWork, you can access all of your iLife content using the Media Browser, including photos from iPhoto, movies from iMovie, and audio from GarageBand.

> **NOTE ▶** If you choose not to fix your photos in iPhoto, you can make several essential adjustments within Pages in the Adjust Image window.

Let's add your butterfly photos to your layout.

1   Click the Media button (or choose View > Show Media Browser) to open the Media Browser.

2   Click the Photos button to find photos.

3   In the Source list, click the disclosure triangle next to iPhoto to view all albums and Events.

4   Click Events to display only iPhoto Events.

TIP If you want to jump to the last photos you loaded, click Last Import.

5 Double-click the Butterfly Event to open it and see only the butterfly images.

6 Drag the six images into the media placeholder areas one at a time.

Use butterfly photos 1 and 2 for the top two images; then use photos 3–6 for the bottom row. You can use the following figure as a guide.

After the photos are added, you can adjust the images' masking and positioning to improve the layout.

7 Double-click the large butterfly photo.

8 Drag the slider above the Edit Mask button to enlarge the photo within the mask.

9 Click the image inside the mask and drag to reposition the photo within the mask's edges. Use the following figure as a guide.

10 Adjust the five other images using the following figure as a guide.

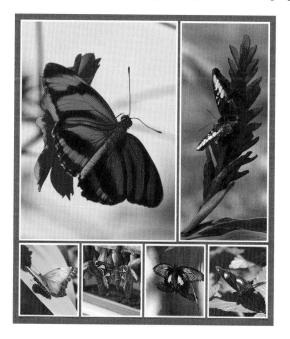

11 Press Command-S to save your progress.

Congratulations—the poster is complete! In the next exercise, you'll send the document to a local printing facility to create multiple copies.

> **NOTE** ▸ You can compare your final poster layout to the file **12Butterfly Garden Poster_FINAL.pages**.

Distributing a Poster via Email

Now that the poster is complete, you can distribute it via email. You might want to email it to multiple recipients so that they can print their own copies as needed. However, you might find that it is less expensive to use a dedicated printing facility or copy shop if lots of color copies are required. Fortunately, Pages helps you email the document as a high-quality, print-ready PDF.

1　Choose Share > Send via Mail > PDF.

　　A dialog may ask you to confirm the attachment of a large file.

2　Click Proceed to continue.

3　A PDF file is created in the background while Mail opens.

　　The new PDF file is attached to a blank message and is ready to send.

4　Address your message, and add a short note describing the document and providing any other appropriate information for the printer.

5　When you're ready to deliver your message, click the Send button.

Designing a Certificate

Awarding certificates to students is an excellent way to mark their progress toward an educational goal or to recognize a significant contribution of time or effort. Pages offers two templates that can be easily customized. In this lesson, you'll design a certificate to honor the students who made outstanding contributions to the butterfly garden activity.

Customizing a Design

You can customize your certificate to tie it to the butterfly garden activity. By removing some template elements and adding others, you'll create a themed certificate that commemorates a student's participation in the program.

1   In Pages, choose File > New to open the Template Chooser.

2   In the Page Layout group, select the Certificates category.

3   Click the thumbnail for the Student Certificate template, and click the Choose button.

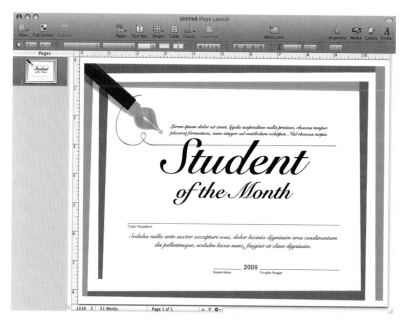

A new document based on the Student Certificate template opens. Let's remove some unnecessary template elements.

4   Click the pen graphic; then Shift-click the left edge of the line graphic, being careful not to select the text box.

The graphic items are selected, but they display *X*'s instead of the expected selection handles. This is because the elements have been locked to prevent accidental movement or deletion. To modify these elements, you must unlock them.

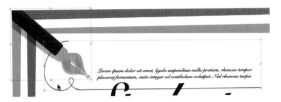

5   Choose Arrange > Unlock to release the selected elements for editing.

6   Press Delete to remove the elements from the certificate.

7   Above the word *student*, select the text box and press Delete to remove it.

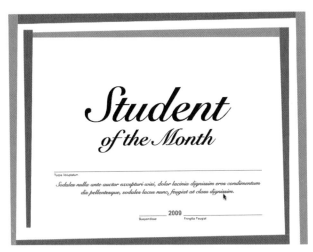

Now that you've removed the unnecessary template elements, you will customize the page with new artwork.

8   Choose Insert > Choose.

9   Navigate to the Lesson_12 folder. Select the file **Monarch.jpg** and click Insert.

A butterfly image is added to the center of the page but covers part of the certificate. You can remove the white background so that the certificate can be seen using Pages' Instant Alpha tool.

10   Select the monarch image, and choose Format > Instant Alpha.

11   Click the white background that you want to make transparent, and then drag slowly over it.

As you drag, the selection grows to include adjacent colors. You can control how much of the area is selected by dragging less or more.

> **TIP** If you hold down Option while you drag when using the Instant Alpha command, all instances of the selected color will be removed from the image. If necessary, you can restore the colors that you removed from the image by choosing Format > Remove Instant Alpha.

12 Repeat the drag process as many times as necessary to remove all of the white background from the monarch image.

13 Press Return to apply the Instant Alpha effect.

14 Drag the selection handle to make the butterfly smaller, and position it in the lower left corner of the page. Use the following figure as a guide.

15 Choose File > Save to capture your progress so far. Name the document *Academic Certificate.pages* and save it to the Lesson_12 folder.

Adjusting and Replacing Placeholder Text

Now that your certificate has the correct look for your event, you can further customize it by replacing the placeholder text with your own text, working your way from top to bottom.

1 Select the *Student of the Month* text box and drag it up toward the top of the page. Use the following figure as a guide for positioning. The goal is to balance the design across the certificate's height.

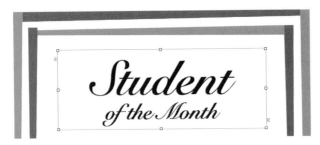

Now widen the text box so that it can accommodate more text.

2 Option-drag the selection handle at the side of the text box until the box is as wide as the image frame.

Holding down the Option key while dragging scales the box in both directions at the same time. This keeps the box centered as you resize it.

3 Replace the word *Student* with *Science Club*; then replace the words *of the Month* with *Outstanding Service*.

TIP Be sure to do one line at a time to preserve the template formatting.

4 Click in an empty area of the certificate; then drag to select the next three elements (two text boxes and a line).

If you click incorrectly on an element, you can Command-click a single element to add it to, or remove it from, your selection.

5 Press Shift–Up Arrow to implement a *supershift* that moves the selected items up 10 pixels at once.

6 Press Shift–Up Arrow three more times to nudge the items up.

7 Select the text and the line next to the date, and press Delete to remove them.

8 Click the date field to select it and display the selection handles.

9 Drag the selection handle to the left to increase the size of the date field.

10 Double-click the date text to select it. In the format bar, click the Right alignment button.

The text now stays aligned with the right edge of the text box. You can set the date field to insert the current date whenever the document is opened. The current date will be automatically added whenever the certificates are printed.

11 With the placeholder date selected, choose Insert > Date and Time.

The current date is added to the text box.

12 Double-click to select the date.

The Date Format window opens.

13 From the Choose Date Format pop-up menu, choose the Month, Day, Year format and select the "Automatically update on open" checkbox.

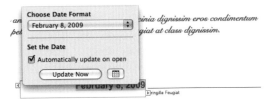

You're almost done—your last task is to adjust the remaining placeholder text.

14 Double-click the first placeholder text (*Turpis Voluptatum*) to select it, and type *Student Name*.

15 Double-click the large box of blue cursive text to select it, and type *For outstanding service and leadership, as shown in the development of Lincoln High School's Butterfly Garden project.*

The text looks good, but the school's name breaks across two lines, which doesn't look as professional as it might.

16 Place the insertion point before the word *Lincoln* and then press Shift-Return to add a line break.

For outstanding service and leadership, as shown in the development of Lincoln High School's Butterfly Garden project.

17 Double-click the first placeholder text (*Fringilla Feugiat*) to select it, and type *Faculty Advisor*.

18 Choose File > Save to save your progress.

Customizing Certificates Using Mail Merge

Now that the certificates are designed, let's add the students' names. Instead of addressing the certificates one at a time, you can perform a mail merge to customize the name line. In Lesson 9, "Building a Report," you performed a merge using the Address Book application. In this lesson, you'll merge information from a Numbers spreadsheet containing the roster of the Lincoln High School Science Club.

Your first step is to add a text box that will contain the name of each student.

1 In the toolbar, click the Text Box button to add a new placeholder text box to the page.

Format the text box so that it matches the rest of your certificate.

2   In the format bar, click the Bold button and change the point size to 36 pt. Then click the Center alignment button.

The text box must be resized.

3   Click outside the text box to deselect the placeholder text; then click the box to select it.

4   Drag the selection handles so that the text box matches the width of the student name line.

> **TIP** ▶ Hold down Option while dragging to scale in both directions at once.

5   Open the Text inspector and click the Bottom alignment button.

Let's add two merge fields to use when addressing the certificates.

6   Double-click the placeholder text and press Delete to remove it.

7   Choose Insert > Merge Field > Name > First Name.

Pages adds a special text field that can merge data from a Numbers spreadsheet or Address Book.

8   Press the Right Arrow key to deselect the merge field; then press the Spacebar twice to add spaces between the first and second text fields.

9   Choose Insert > Merge Field > Name > Last Name.

You are now ready to complete the merge. Let's first explore the Numbers document.

10 Go to the Finder and open the Lesson_12 folder.

11 Double-click the file **12Club_Roster.numbers** to open the Science Club's membership roster.

Numbers opens, along with the roster spreadsheet.

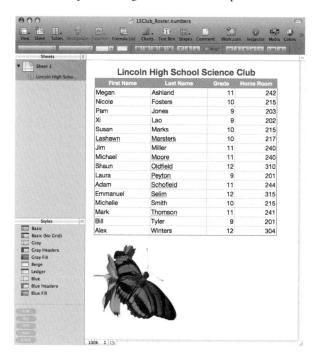

12 Closely examine the spreadsheet, especially the First Name and Last Name columns.

It is essential to keep the first names and last names in separate fields for easy sorting.

NOTE ▶ To use a Numbers spreadsheet in a merge, you have to follow a couple of guidelines:

▶ Keep all your data in a single table.

▶ Create at least one header row and one or more rows of data in your table. Each row of data will be used to generate a unique document in Pages.

13 Close the spreadsheet and return to Pages.

> **NOTE** ▶ You can compare your poster with the file **12Academic Certificate FINAL.pages** to check your progress.

14 Choose Edit > Mail Merge to perform the merge.

15 Choose Numbers Document.

The file-browser window opens.

16 Navigate to the Lesson_12 folder and select the file **12Club_Roster.numbers** and click Open.

17 Click the disclosure triangle next to Merge Fields, and verify the Merge Field and Target Name pairings.

Pages correctly matches the Merge Fields and Target Name pairings because the Numbers dialog uses an identical format.

> **NOTE** ▶ If your fields don't match exactly, you can click the Target Name pop-up menu in the Merge window and choose another target. You can also use the Link inspector's advanced controls to customize merge fields.

18 In the "Merge to" pop-up menu, choose Send to Printer to print a certificate for each student.

19 Click Merge to open the Print dialog.

20 Click the disclosure triangle near the Printer pop-up menu to display advanced printing controls.

Pages indicates that it will create 16 certificates.

21 Click the next arrow to preview each certificate that will be printed.

If you were ready to print, you'd click the Print button. Because this is a practice exercise, you probably don't want to print 16 copies of the certificate.

22 Click Cancel to cancel the printing process; then click Cancel again.

23 Close the document and save your progress.

▶ Other Classroom Options

Both Pages and Numbers offer additional timesaving templates. Be sure to explore
the following templates and categories in each application.

Pages

The following Pages templates are useful in the classroom:

Reports—Students can create reports that combine text and graphics.

Word Processing Miscellaneous—Teachers will find two templates in the Word
Processing Miscellaneous category: The Evaluation and Quiz templates can be used
to help assess student performance.

Page Layout Miscellaneous—The Miscellaneous category for Page Layout
offers Lab Notes and Scrapbook templates for collecting data and memorabilia,
respectively.

Flyers and Posters—Several more templates are available, including flyer and
poster templates suitable for promoting school events.

▶ **Other Classroom Options** *(continued)*

Numbers

The following Numbers templates are useful in the classroom:

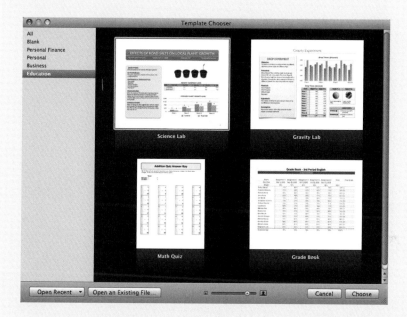

Personal—In the Personal category, you'll find several templates for comparing and organizing data. Try using the Team Organization template to track a school sports team. The Comparison template is a great way for students to compare two items in a personal finances exercise.

Education—Numbers offers four templates specifically intended for classroom use. Two templates are useful for tracking lab experiments. The Math Quiz template can quickly create quizzes for addition, subtraction, multiplication, or division, and assign higher or lower point values for each problem. The quiz also generates an answer key for quick grading. The Grade Book template is ideal for tracking student performance and progress.

TIP ▶ For more ideas on using iWork and iLife in the classroom, see *Apple Training Series: A Teacher's Guide to Digital Media in the Classroom* (Peachpit Press, 2008).

Lesson Review

1.   If you want to modify a locked element, what must you do first?

2.   How can you access your iPhoto library in iWork '09?

3.   What is the fastest way to send a Pages document via email?

4.   Which two sources can the Mail Merge command access?

5.   How do you scale an object equally in two directions?

Answers

1.   You select the object and then choose Arrange > Unlock if you want to reposition, remove, or resize an object.

2.   Open the Media Browser to display all of the Events and albums in your iPhoto library.

3.   Choose Share > Send via Mail to attach a Pages, PDF, or Microsoft Word version of your document to a new Mail message.

4.   When performing a merge, you can access data in Address Book or a Numbers spreadsheet.

5.   Option-drag a selection handle.

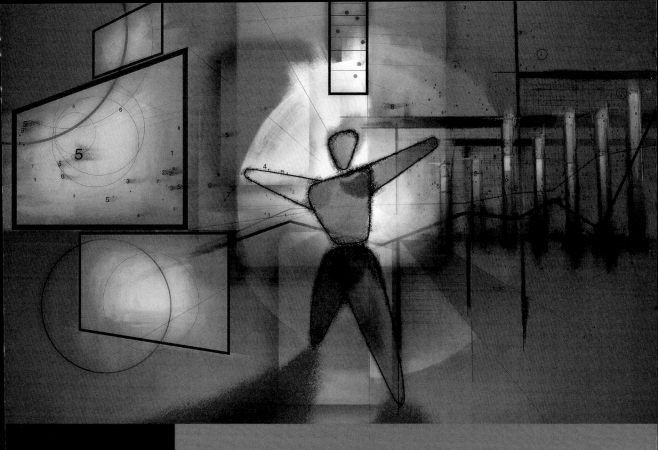

Numbers: Working
with Spreadsheets

13

Lesson Files Lessons > Lesson_13 > 13_Starter Budget.xls
Lessons > Lesson_13 > 13_Budget_End.numbers
Lessons > Lesson_13 > 13_Draft.png

Time This lesson takes approximately 60 minutes to complete.

Goals Create a basic to-do checklist and a travel budget
Work with templates in Numbers
Understand key spreadsheet terms
Convert a Microsoft Excel file into a Numbers spreadsheet
Add header rows, header columns, and footer rows
Format cell contents
Format a table using styles
Use formulas and functions to calculate cell values
Add and resize a graphic object
Size and print a spreadsheet
Save a spreadsheet as a PDF or an Excel file

Lesson 13
Spreadsheet Essentials

Numbers is an easy-to-use spreadsheet program with a flexible, free-form canvas that you can use to organize data, manage lists, create tables and charts, insert graphics, and place text anywhere on the page. The program supports over 250 math functions that perform complex calculations with just a few mouse clicks.

If you've used other spreadsheet programs, such as AppleWorks or Microsoft Excel, Numbers will seem familiar from the moment you open it. The good news is, Numbers offers some innovative features that let you create great-looking spreadsheets with less work—features like intelligent tables, customizable checkboxes and sliders, 2D and 3D charts, and ready-made templates for home, education, and business uses.

Robert Carman Travel Expense Sheet

	Per	Cost	Quantity	Subtotal
Plane	Trip	$375.00	1	$375.00
Rental Car	Day	$63.00	3	$189.00
Hotel	Night	$265.00	3	$795.00
Meals Stipend	Day	$64.00	3	$192.00
Supplies	Fee	$215.00	1	$215.00
Taxi Fare	Fee	$35.00	4	$140.00
Airport Parking	Day	$23.00	4	$92.00
Total				$1,998.00

DRAFT

In this lesson, you'll use Numbers to create a simple to-do checklist and a travel budget. Along the way, you'll learn spreadsheet essentials—the basics of working with data tables and calculations—as well as how to use templates and how to import, enhance, and export Microsoft Excel spreadsheets.

We'll start by opening a blank Numbers spreadsheet. After exploring the Numbers interface, we'll create a to-do checklist and use the inspectors and format bar to make adjustments to the rows, columns, and cells. Next, we'll create a basic business travel budget and use the tools in Numbers to calculate expenses. We'll also format the report to present the data in a clear and accurate way that helps make it more readable. Finally, we'll save the completed budget as both Numbers- and Excel-compatible spreadsheets that you can share on the Internet.

Opening Numbers

You can open Numbers in three ways:

▶ In your Applications folder, open the iWork '09 folder and double-click the Numbers icon.

▶ In the Dock, click the Numbers icon.

▶ Double-click any Numbers document.

For this exercise, you'll open Numbers using the first method.

1 In the Finder, choose Go > Applications.

2 Open the iWork '09 folder.

3 Double-click the Numbers icon to open the program.

> **NOTE** ▶ If you're starting this book with the Numbers section and haven't yet copied the Lessons folder from this book's DVD-ROM to your hard drive, please refer to "Copying the Book Files" in Getting Started.

Choosing a Template

When you first open Numbers, you'll see the Template Chooser, which lets you choose Apple-designed templates (along with any custom templates you've created and saved).

1   Choose File > New from Template Chooser to open the Template Chooser.

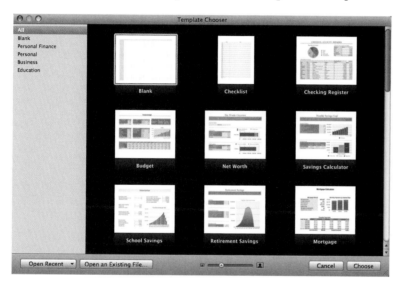

Templates are the quickest way to begin a project, because much of the formatting has already been done for you. They're great starting points, with ready-made data, formulas, charts, and formatting that can save you loads of time and make data calculation easier (and even fun). You can edit templates to suit your content, modifying everything from font style and color to chart types and formulas.

Take a moment to browse through the various templates for home, work, and school by clicking each of the five categories. This will also give you a visual overview of some of the capabilities of Numbers.

▶   Move the pointer over a thumbnail to preview each template.

▶   Drag the resize slider at the bottom of the Template Chooser to see larger thumbnails.

▶   Click the Open Recent button at the bottom of the Template Chooser to access recently opened documents with a single click.

Now let's open a blank template and get started on a basic spreadsheet with a to-do checklist.

2 In the Template Chooser, click to select the Blank category, and then select the Blank template.

3 Click Choose to open a new document based on the Blank template.

▶ ## Choosing the Right Template for the Job

The Template Chooser in Numbers is organized into five categories that make it easier to find the right template for your needs. Here's a quick guide to some particularly useful and well-designed templates in Numbers.

Blank

Only two templates are in this category, but both are useful. Blank is a standard spreadsheet with no formatting. Use it when you want to build your spreadsheet from scratch. Checklist is a good starting point for creating to-do lists, packing lists, order forms, or any other list-based data. These are the basic starting points for all custom spreadsheets.

Personal Finance

This category contains some great tools that can help you manage individual or household finances. Look here for financial management templates such as Budget, Checking Register, Mortgage, and Savings Calculator, as well as financial planning templates such as School Savings and Retirement Savings.

▶ **Choosing the Right Template for the Job** *(continued)*

Personal
This category contains some beautiful project-planning forms for uses ranging from special events and dinner parties to garden and home improvement. Thanks to their rich graphics, these templates are great for personal and home improvement and offer easy starting points for organizing your life in an attractive way that can be easily shared. In particular check out Dinner Party, Home Improvement, and Travel Planner.

Business
Designed primarily for small businesses, this category includes some great templates for standard business needs, like invoices and expense reports, along with some more complex financial analysis templates. Don't miss Invoice, which helps you bill clients in a professional manner, and Financials, for analyzing your company's performance.

Education
The Education category brings organization to the classroom. It includes two useful projects for elementary and high school science labs, which help students document their research with both data and graphics. Teachers will also find templates for generating grade books and math quizzes.

You can find even more templates created by the Apple community by visiting iWorkCommunity.com Template Exchange (www.iworkcommunity.com) and Numbers Templates (www.numberstemplates.com).

Working with Sheets

Now let's get to work on our starter spreadsheet and learn the basics of managing sheets, entering data, and formatting cells to best display the information. The first step is to understand how Numbers organizes information.

Each Numbers spreadsheet includes one or more *sheets*. Think of sheets as tabs or subdivisions within your document. Typically, sheets are used to organize the spreadsheet information into smaller, more manageable groups. For example, you might put all your raw data and assumptions on one sheet and, on a second sheet, present your final conclusions and charts.

Our blank spreadsheet opens with only one sheet. You can see a list of all the sheets in the document in the Sheets pane, located above the Styles pane in the upper left corner of the canvas. In this exercise, we'll experiment with naming, adding, deleting, and reordering sheets.

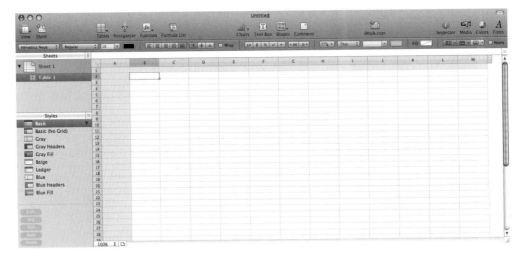

1   To rename the sheet, double-click its name (currently *Sheet 1*).

2   Enter a new name that better describes what the sheet is about. For this example, type *Expense Report*, and press Return.

Let's add a second sheet to the document.

3   To add a new sheet, click the Sheet button in the toolbar (or choose Insert > Sheet).

A second sheet, called Sheet 2, is added to the document. Notice that Numbers also added a second table on the new sheet. You'll look at tables in the next section.

4   Rename the new sheet *Raw Data.*

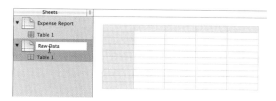

You can reorder your sheets to change how the data is presented for printing or viewing.

5   In the Sheets pane, click to select the Raw Data sheet; then drag it to the top of the Sheets pane to make it first in the list.

As you add sheets in a document, the Sheets pane can become crowded; it's sometimes useful to view just the sheets without their contents listed.

6   Hide the contents of both sheets by clicking the disclosure triangles to the left of each sheet's name.

TIP ▶   If you are using a laptop with Multi-Touch trackpad support, you can navigate between sheets with the three-finger swipe gesture (place three fingers on the trackpad and drag up or down).

That's all it takes to manage sheets in your document. Being able to rename and reorder sheets is important as your spreadsheets grow in complexity. Next, let's explore a table.

Working with Tables

Within a single sheet you can have one or more *tables*. Tables are simple grids, with horizontal columns and vertical rows, used to organize, analyze, and present data.

Typically, when you build a spreadsheet, you spend most of your time working with tables. A unique feature in Numbers is the ability to use multiple tables and, on a single sheet, mix them with other media such as charts or graphics. Numbers lets you build and format tables in numerous ways, and lets you handle different types of data intelligently within your tables. You can sort, sift, categorize, and conditionally format your data quickly and easily.

> **NOTE** ▸ Many of the templates include preformatted tables that make it faster to set up tables with your own data and images.

Let's take a moment to learn the "language" of tables. In this exercise, you'll practice with Numbers using a blank spreadsheet. Later in the lesson, you'll create a useful to-do checklist.

1   Click the middle of the Raw Data sheet on your canvas to select it.

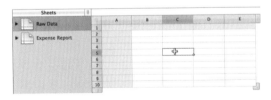

Notice that numbers and letters appear at the edges of the table. These *reference tabs* help you identify and navigate the contents of your spreadsheet.

By clicking in the sheet, you have selected a *cell*. A cell is an individual box within a table that can contain data.

2   Look across the top of the active sheet and click the letter C.

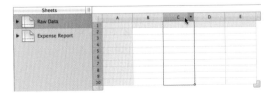

By clicking a letter, you have selected a *column*. Columns are a vertical array of cells that is one cell wide. Each column uses a letter in the reference tab for identification.

3   Look down the left edge of the active sheet and click the number 7.

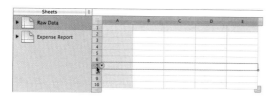

By clicking a number, you have selected a *row*. Rows are a horizontal array of cells that is one cell tall. Each row is labeled with a consecutive number in the reference tab on the left edge of the table.

Now that you know how to identify individual rows and columns, let's select a specific cell. A cell is identified by the intersection of its row and column.

4   Select cell B8.

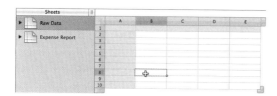

This cell is located at the intersection of column B and row 8.

All sorts of tables are available to choose from in Numbers, so now let's experiment with adding two specific kinds of tables to the spreadsheet: Basic and Checklist.

1   Click the disclosure triangle next to the Raw Data sheet to see all of its tables.

2   In the toolbar, click the Tables button and choose Basic from the pop-up menu.

Another table (called Table 2) is added to the sheet. This table is smaller than Table 1, but like all tables, it can be resized or repositioned to meet your needs.

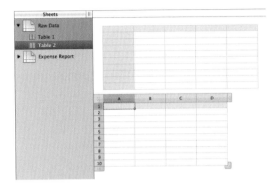

You can also add tables using a menu command. Let's create a to-do list by adding a Checklist table.

3   Choose Insert > Table > Checklist. Table 3 is added to the sheet.

Next, let's add some text.

4   Click in cell A1 and type *Status*. Press Tab to switch to the next cell.

5   In cell B1, type *Action Item*, and press Return.

The table is looking clearer. But a to-do list should have some dates to help organize the information. Let's add one more column to hold the date information.

6   In Table 3, the checklist table, click column B to select it.

7   Click the reference tab pop-up on the upper right corner of column B and choose
Add Column Before.

A third column is added to the sheet.

8   Label the newly created column B as *Due Date.*

9   To enter a date in the new column B, click in cell B2 and type *12/15/09.* Press Return.

Numbers interprets the data as a date and displays Dec 15, 2009. This is the default
format for displaying a date, but let's say you want a different format for the dates in
this checklist.

10 Click column B to select all the cells. By selecting the entire column, you can reformat
all the cells to match.

11 In the format bar at the top of your screen, click the Cell Format pop-up menu.
Choose Date & Time, and then choose from the list the display format that shows the
full month, date, and year.

The date will be reformatted in the selected column.

NOTE ▶ The date in the format menu will be based upon the current date and time. Your menu may look slightly different.

Next, let's resize the date column so that it takes up less room in the table.

12 Place the pointer between columns B and C in the table until it changes to a double arrow.

13 Drag to the left to make column B narrower.

A width of 2.00 in allows plenty of room for the date but avoids wasted space.

14 Choose File > Close to close this practice spreadsheet.

Save the starter spreadsheet only if you want to use it to practice more on your own.

Now that you know how to work with sheets, tables, rows, and columns, you can say good-bye to your starter spreadsheet and move on to the fun stuff: formulas, functions, and more sophisticated formatting of complex documents.

Importing Spreadsheet Data

In this exercise, we'll create and work with a business travel budget. To save you from having to type in the data, we'll start by importing a basic spreadsheet that already has the data entered. We'll then use Numbers to make the report more attractive, more readable, and more functional.

And to make it more interesting, the spreadsheet we'll import is a Microsoft Excel document. If you've worked with spreadsheets before, you've probably used an Excel workbook, a common format. Numbers has excellent support for opening, working with, changing, and saving Excel files, so it's easy to share documents with Microsoft Office users.

NOTE ▶ Numbers can import data from several other common formats, including files saved in comma-separated value (CSV) format, tab-delimited format, Open Financial Exchange (OFX) format, and AppleWorks 6. Numbers supports Microsoft Excel 2008 and earlier formats for both Mac and PC.

1 Choose File > Open and navigate to the Lesson_13 folder.

2 Choose **13_Starter Budget.xls** and click Open.

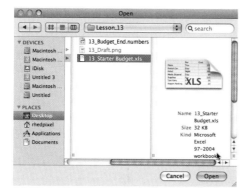

Numbers opens the Excel spreadsheet and imports it to a Numbers file. The new Numbers document has three sheets, each with a table. However, the second two sheets are blank, so let's go ahead and delete them now.

NOTE ▶ Empty sheets are commonly found in Excel documents because the standard Excel spreadsheet has three worksheets. Numbers converts each Excel worksheet into a new sheet.

3 Select Sheet 2 and click Delete. Numbers asks you to confirm that you want to delete the selected sheet. Click Delete.

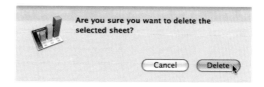

4 Select and delete Sheet 3.

5 Choose File > Save.

6 In the Save As field, name the file *13_Starter Budget.numbers*.

7 If your file folder isn't visible in the Where pop-up menu, click the disclosure triangle to the right of the Save As field.

8 Specify a location (such as the chapter folder) in which to store the file.

9 Click Save to save the file to your hard drive.

When you save a Numbers spreadsheet, all of the graphics and formatting are stored within the document so that it can be easily transferred to another computer.

NOTE ▸ Fonts cannot be embedded into a saved Numbers document. If you want to transfer a document to another computer, be sure the other computer has the same fonts installed.

Now that the data is imported to your spreadsheet, let's format the table to help us calculate and analyze the data.

Formatting a Table

To improve the readability of your tables, you can use formatting tools to stylize the cells and layout. Although you may think this is done only for aesthetic reasons, remember that in most instances, it's important to make your information easy to read. There are three primary ways to access formatting tools:

▸ Use the format bar (located across the top of the document) to quickly format a table with the most common controls.

▶ In the toolbar, click the Inspector button then choose the Table inspector or Cells inspector.

▶ You can also use menu commands to perform table formatting.

Using Header Rows and Columns

By using a header row and column, you can add a label that describes the contents of a table's rows and columns. Header rows and columns are usually formatted so that they stand out. A footer row can also call out data that has been totaled.

▶ A *header row* uses the topmost cell of each column.

▶ A *header column* is the leftmost column in the table.

> NOTE ▶ A major benefit of using header rows and columns is that they appear on each page when you print a table. This information ensures that your data is clearly labeled and makes the table easier to read.

In this exercise, you'll add a header row, header column, and footer row to your table:

1 In the canvas, select the table by clicking it.

   You will know a table is selected when the column and row labels appear.

2 Click the reference tab for column A to select the leftmost column.

3 Position your pointer over the reference tab of column A to display its disclosure triangle. Click the triangle, and from the pop-up menu, choose Convert to Header Column.

4 Click the reference tab for row 1 to select the topmost row.

5 Pause your pointer over the reference tab of row 1 to display its disclosure triangle. Click the triangle, and from the pop-up menu, choose Convert to Header Row.

	A	B	C	D	E
1		Per	Cost	Quantity	
2	Convert to Header Row	rip	375	1	
3	Add Row Above	lay	63	3	
4	Add Row Below	light	265	3	
5	Delete Row	lay	64	3	
6	Hide Row	ee	215	1	
7	Insert Category	ee	35	4	
8	Show More Options...	lay	23	4	
9					
10					
11	Total				

The table is already much easier to read because the information has been visually organized. Now you'll add a footer row to draw attention to the bottom row of the table. By formatting the Total row, you'll make your totals stand out more clearly.

6 With the table selected, click the Footer button in the format bar to add one. A new footer is added to the bottom of the table.

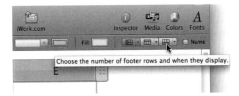

7 Click cell A11 to select it.

8 Choose Edit > Cut to move the selected text to the Clipboard.

9 Click cell A12 to select it.

10 Choose Edit > Paste and Match Style to write the text to the new cell but retain the formatting of the target cell.

11 Drag across rows 9, 10, and 11 to select them.

12 Pause your pointer over row 9. When the disclosure triangle appears, click it, and from the pop-up menu, choose Delete Selected Rows.

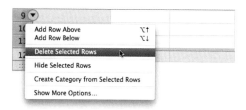

13 Press Command-S to save the changes to your document.

Formatting Cells

By formatting cells in a table, you display data in specific ways. For example, in this table, you can designate data in the Cost column as monetary values and display those values with a currency symbol (such as $, £, or ¥).

> NOTE ▶ When formatting cells, you are only setting the display characteristics of the cells (not changing their data). When a cell is used in a formula, its actual value is used.

There are two easy ways to define cell formats:

▶ Use the format bar to access the most common controls.

▶ Use the Cell Format pop-up menu in the Cells inspector.

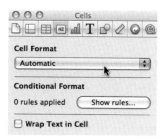

> NOTE ▶ Even empty cells can be formatted. When you add text to a formatted cell, it displays according to the cell's formatting. Deleting text from a formatted cell removes that value from the cell but retains the cell formatting.

1 Click the reference tab for column C to select the column.

2 In the toolbar, click the Currency Format button.

The cells with number values now have $ symbols and display two decimal places, which is standard with this type of currency.

TIP If the default currency style is not correct for your needs, the Cells inspector offers 25 currency formats. Additionally, you can choose Format > Create Custom Cell Format to make your own financial formatting styles.

3 Click the reference tab for column E to select it.

This column will be used as a subtotal column.

4 In the toolbar, click the Currency Format button.

5 Click cell E1 and type *Subtotal* to label the cell.

The data is formatted correctly but it's not as easy to read as it might be. To improve the readability, you'll now center some of the data in the cells.

1 Click the reference tab for row 1 to select all of the column labels in the header row.

2 In the format bar, click the Center Alignment button to center the labels on these columns.

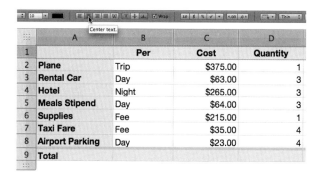

3   Choose Edit > Select All to select the entire table. Then, in the format bar, click the "Align text to the bottom of a table cell, text box, or shape" button to align the text labels to the bottom of the rows.

4   Click the reference tab for column B to select the column.

5   Command-click column D to add it to the selection. Pressing the Command key while clicking lets you select multiple items that are not adjacent.

6   In the format bar, click the Center Alignment button to center the text in these columns.

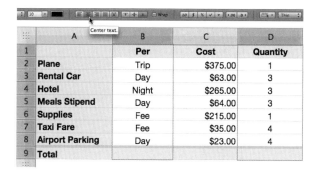

7   Press Command-S to save your travel budget.

Using Table Styles

Numbers offers powerful and flexible table styles to quickly change a table to a predefined visual format. By applying styles, you can ensure that tables are formatted consistently across your document. Numbers includes several default styles, but you can also create and save your own custom styles.

A table style can define the following attributes:

▶ The table's background (including color or image) and its opacity

▶ The stroke, color, and opacity of a body cell's outside border

▶ The outside borders of the header row, header column, and footer row

▶ The background (color or image and opacity) of table cells

▶ The text attributes of table cells

In this exercise, you'll apply and modify a table style to suit your travel budget.

1 On the canvas, select the current table.

2 In the Styles pane, click Beige; then try the various styles to see how the table changes as they are applied.

NOTE ▶ Because you previously formatted cells in the table, those cells retain their formatting. Changes made to an individual part of a table are called *overrides*. Applying a table style respects these overrides. To clear overrides, place your pointer near the style's name; then click the arrow to the right of the style you want to apply and choose Clear and Apply Style. For this exercise, you'll leave the overrides in place.

3 Choose the Blue Headers style to apply it to the table.

4   Click the reference tab for row 1 to select it.

5   In the format bar, click the Fill button and choose a dark blue fill color.

Some of the text is being clipped because the cells aren't big enough. Numbers can fix this problem quickly.

6   Click a cell in row 9 where the text is clipped. Open the Table inspector and click the Fit Row Height button to automatically adjust the height of the table's cells to fit the new style.

Now that you've created a new table style, you can save it for later use.

7   Choose Edit > Select All.

8   With the table selected, move the pointer over any existing style in the Styles pane. Click the arrow to the right of any style and choose Create New Style.

9   Name the style *Blue Two Tone* and click OK.

The style is added to the Styles pane of the document. You can easily reuse it on any future tables that you add to this document.

NOTE ▶ Custom table styles are stored only with the document in which they were created. To store a style for use in other documents, you must create a template from your document. To do so, choose File > Save As Template. Do not save this report as a template because you are not yet finished formatting it with formulas and functions.

10 Press Command-S to save the changes to your document.

Now that the table is formatted, you can finish it by using formulas to apply mathematical functions to the cell data.

Using Formulas and Functions

When you use formulas to calculate values based on your table data, you unleash the true power of Numbers. When you enter a formula into an empty table cell, it will display a new (and constantly updated) value in the cell that's the solution to that formula. In your example spreadsheet, formulas can be used to calculate a budget estimate.

Numbers has several tools for working with formulas and functions:

▶   The Formula Editor lets you create and modify formulas in the spreadsheet. To open the Formula Editor, select a table cell and press the = (equal sign) key.

   NOTE ▶ You can also open the Formula Editor by choosing Formula Editor from the Function pop-up menu in the toolbar.

▶   The formula bar is always visible beneath the format bar and can be used to create and modify formulas.

▶   You can also apply a *function*, which is a predefined operation that has a name (such as SUM, AVERAGE, or MEDIAN). Functions can be accessed using the Function Browser, or you can find the most common functions already calculated for you beneath the Styles pane.

Now you'll create some formulas to fill the Subtotal column in your travel budget:

1   In the canvas, select the table by clicking it.

2   Click cell E2 to make it active.

3   Press the = (equal sign) key to open the Formula Editor.

You will create a formula to multiply the cost of each item by its quantity and calculate a subtotal cost for each item.

4   Click cell D2.

You'll notice that the formula reads *Quantity Plane*. The Formula Editor uses the labels from your headers to make formula editing much easier.

NOTE ▶ Numbers also uses colors to make formulas easier to read. You'll notice that the color of the text matches the shading of the cells that are used in the formula.

5   Press the * (asterisk) key to indicate that these values will be multiplied.

MORE INFO ▶ Numbers uses standard mathematical operators:

+   Plus

-   Minus

*   Multiply

/   Divide

6   Click cell C2.

Numbers inserts the text *Cost Plane* into the formula. The formula now reads = *Quantity Plane * Cost Plane.*

 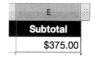

7   Press Return to apply the formula.

Numbers calculates the correct value of $375.

You can also write formulas in Numbers using only the keyboard, without a mouse or trackpad. Let's give it a try.

8   Click cell E3. Press the = (equals) key to open the Formula Editor.

9   Hold down the Option key while in the Formula Editor to reference cells with arrow keys. Press the Left Arrow to select the adjacent cell.

NOTE ▸ The formula now reads *Quantity of Rental Car.*

10   Press the * (asterisk) key to add a multiply calculation.

11   Hold down the Option key and press the Left Arrow key twice to select the next adjacent cell.

The formula now reads *Quantity of Rental Car * Cost of Rental Car.*

12   Press Return to apply the formula.

You can reuse this formula on similar cells in the spreadsheet.

Cost	Quantity	Subtotal
$375.00	1	$375.00
$63.00	3	=(Quantity Rental Car)*(Cost Rental Ca)
$265.00	2	

13   Click cell E3.

14   Place your pointer over the fill handle in the lower right corner of cell E3.

The pointer changes to a crosshair.

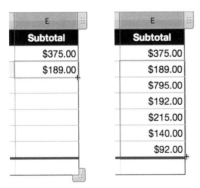

15 Drag the fill handle downward to apply the formula to other cells in the column. Drag through cell E8 to apply the formula to calculate all subtotal values in column E.

Now that accurate subtotals exist, we can add all of the subtotals together to create a total budget number. Let's use a function.

16 Drag through cells E2 to E8 to select them. These are the numbers you'll want to add.

17 From the area below the Styles pane, drag the SUM function to cell E9.

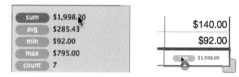

Numbers calculates a correct value of $1,998.00 for the budget estimate. Now you can review your calculations for accuracy.

18 In the toolbar, click the Formula List button to view a complete list of every formula in your spreadsheet.

19 Look at each formula to ensure accuracy.

You should see that the Quantity and Cost values are matched (that is to say, Quantity of Hotel * Cost of Hotel).

NOTE ▶ To quickly navigate to any formula, click it in the formula list.

20 In the toolbar, click the Formula List button hide the list of formulas.

21 Press Command-S to save the changes to your document.

Adding Media

Although Numbers is a spreadsheet application, it offers the same robust graphics capabilities as Keynote and Pages. The Numbers document is a free-form graphics canvas that provides great flexibility in arranging your information and graphics on the page:

► You'll find useful layout and graphics tools, including alignment guides; rulers; and Instant Alpha, masking, and drawing tools. These features are explored in the Keynote and Pages lessons of this book, as well as in the online help.

► You can add floating text boxes by clicking the Text Box button in the toolbar. These boxes can contain any text and be positioned anywhere on the canvas.

► You can add preset shapes or draw your own custom shapes in the spreadsheet.

► The iLife Media Browser lets you access photos, movies, and sounds stored on your hard drive, and drag them directly into your Numbers canvas.

Thanks to Numbers' free-form canvas, you have great visual control over your spreadsheet. To make use of it, let's add a graphic element and position it on the page:

1 In the Sheets pane, choose the sheet by clicking its name.

2 Choose Insert > Choose to choose a file to insert into the sheet.

3 Navigate to the Lesson_13 folder that you copied to your computer. Choose the file **13_Draft.png** and click Insert.

The graphic is added to the page, but it's a little large, so let's scale it down.

4 Click the image to select it. Then drag its selection handle until the image is about 3.5 inches wide. (You can see the width and height displayed next to the image as you drag.)

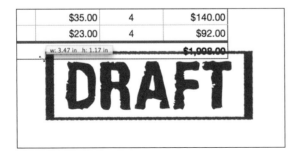

5   Position the image on the page using the figure for guidance.

	Per	Cost	Quantity	Subtotal
Plane	Trip	$375.00	1	$375.00
Rental Car	Day	$63.00	3	$189.00
Hotel	Night	$265.00	3	$795.00
Meals Stipend	Day	$64.00	3	$192.00
Supplies	Fee	$215.00	1	$215.00
Taxi Fare	Fee	$35.00	4	$140.00
Airport Parking	Day	$23.00	4	$92.00
Total				$1,998.00

DRAFT   x: 2.21 in y: 2.53 in

The blue alignment guides are useful for positioning the graphic on the page. You'll make minor adjustments to the image size and position in the next section.

6   Press Command-S to save the changes to your spreadsheet.

Printing Your Spreadsheet

A unique feature of Numbers is its interactive Print View, which makes it easy to prepare your spreadsheet for printing or sharing. Whenever you want to print a sheet or make a PDF for online review, you can use Print View to check the layout.

1   In the Sheets pane, choose the sheet you'd like to print.

2   In the toolbar, click the View button and choose Show Print View.

Notice that the page icon at the bottom of the document window is selected. You can toggle Print View on and off by clicking this button.

Next to the Print View button you'll find two buttons for page orientation. Currently, this document is set to portrait (vertical) orientation. Because this table is wider than it is tall, you should switch to Landscape orientation.

3 Click the Landscape (horizontal) button to change the page layout.

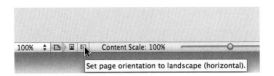

Now that the page is properly oriented, you'll notice that it doesn't fill the page as well as it could. Let's resize the content to get as large a printout as possible.

4 Drag the Content Scale slider to the right until its value is 175%.

This sizes the table as large as possible while still fitting it all onto one page. You'll notice, however, that the spreadsheet will print to as many as four pages because the red *DRAFT* graphic still is wrapping to other pages.

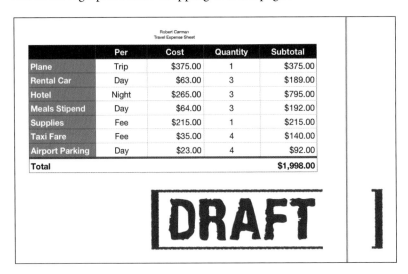

NOTE ▶ You can separately configure page attributes (such as page orientation and margins) for each sheet by using the Sheet inspector.

5 Click the DRAFT graphic and size it by dragging its selection handles.

A new width of about 2.5 inches will work well.

6 Reposition the graphic by dragging it so that it doesn't wrap to any additional pages.

Because you are in Print View, elements such as the page header are visible. The current text appears a bit small and could be better formatted for readability.

7 Click in the header to edit the text.

8 Delete the hard return between the two lines of text so that the page title appears on one line. Click at the start of the text *Travel Expense Sheet* and press Delete to remove the gap.

Let's add a single space between the words *Carman* and *Travel.*

9 Drag though the text to select it.

10 In the format bar, change the header text to Helvetica Neue Bold at 24-point size, as in the following figure.

11 Press Command-S to save the changes to your document.

Now that you've completed the spreadsheet and set the optimum print size, you can print the document.

12 When you are ready to print, choose File > Print.

13 From the Printer pop-up menu, choose the printer you'd like to use.

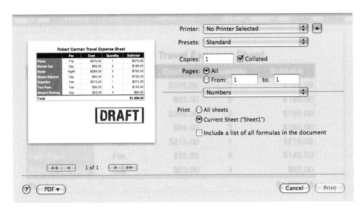

If the full print window is not visible, click the disclosure triangle next to the Printer field.

14 In the Copies field, type the number of copies you want to print.

NOTE ▸ In the print window, you can choose to print all sheets or just the current sheet. This makes it easy to print only the pages you want. Additionally, you can select the "Include a list of all formulas in the document" checkbox to print additional pages that will show all of the calculations performed.

15 Click Print.

Exporting Your Spreadsheet

Because spreadsheets are generally used collaboratively, it's useful to be able to export your Numbers spreadsheet to a variety of formats. Numbers files can also be easily emailed or posted to iWork.com for sharing over the Internet.

Sharing a PDF File

The Portable Document Format (PDF) is an industry-standard format that can be viewed using applications such as Preview on a Mac or Adobe Reader on a Mac or PC.

PDF files are compatible with most computer platforms and are an easy file format to use for document sharing. Many portable devices, such as handheld computers and iPhones, can display PDF files. You can also password-protect a PDF file against editing, which makes it a good choice when you want to retain a document, such as a budget, in its original form.

1 Choose Share > Export to open the Export controls.

2 Because you want to export a PDF file, click the PDF button.

3 Choose an option from the Image Quality pop-up menu.

Good quality is acceptable for email attachments. Choose Better or Best for printing.

4 In the Layout pop-up menu, specify how you want to print each sheet.

Choose Sheet View so that the PDF will look identical to its Print View.

5 Click the disclosure triangle next to Security Options to choose options that make the document secure for sharing.

6 Select the Open Document checkbox to require a password to open the PDF.

Enter the password *pumpernickel1972*.

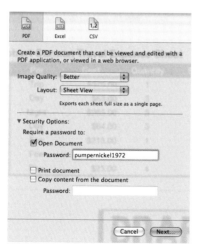

7 Click Next.

8   Specify a location in which to save your file.

You can target the chapter folder for temporary storage.

9   Click Export to save the PDF file.

Emailing an Excel File

If you want to share your spreadsheet with Microsoft Excel users, Numbers makes it easy to export your spreadsheet as an Excel document.

1   Choose Share > Send via Mail > Excel.

NOTE ▸ Microsoft Excel does not offer robust graphics support. Some of your formatting as well as embedded graphics may be lost in the export process. In this exercise, all information will successfully translate.

2   Apple Mail opens a new message with the Excel spreadsheet attached.

NOTE ▸ You can also choose File > Save As to save a copy of your Numbers document as an Excel file to your hard drive.

3   Address the message to the recipient and click Send.

NOTE ▸ Numbers converts each table into an Excel worksheet. If a document contains multiple tables, separate worksheets will be created. Note that some formula calculations may differ in Excel.

Sharing a Document with iWork.com

To make it easy to share iWork documents and collaborate with others, Apple created iWork.com. It's essentially a web-based document-sharing service, but what it means to the iWork user is that you now have an easy way to post documents for review with a few clicks. This service is currently in beta, which means it's still being developed, but is open to public trial. The service is currently free, and it allows others to view, comment on, or download your spreadsheet.

1 Choose Share > Share via iWork.com.

 If this is your first time using the service on this computer, you'll have to sign in.

 NOTE ▶ If you already have an Apple ID—from the iTunes Store, MobileMe, or the Apple Discussions forums—you can use that ID on iWork.com. If not, you must click Create New Account to sign up for a free Apple ID.

2 If necessary, enter your Apple ID and Password and click Sign In.

3 A new dialog opens and prompts you for important information required to share the file.

 NOTE ▶ You must be connected to the Internet to share a document with iWork.com Public Beta. You must also have a Mail account configured on your computer to send invitations to view the document.

4 In the To and Message fields, enter the email addresses and any message you want to deliver to the recipients of the spreadsheet.

5   Modify the Subject field as necessary.

6   In the From pop-up menu, choose an email address to use for sending the invitation.

7   To enable viewer comments and downloads, keep the "Leave Comments" and "Download the document" checkboxes selected.

> **TIP** ▶ To set specific options for uploading and downloading files, click the Show Advanced button at the bottom of the sheet. Here you can choose which file formats to make available for download. The Upload options also let you specify the filename to be posted. If you are reposting a previously shared document, you can choose either to overwrite the old file or to enter a new name in the "Copy to iWork.com as" field.

8   Click Share.

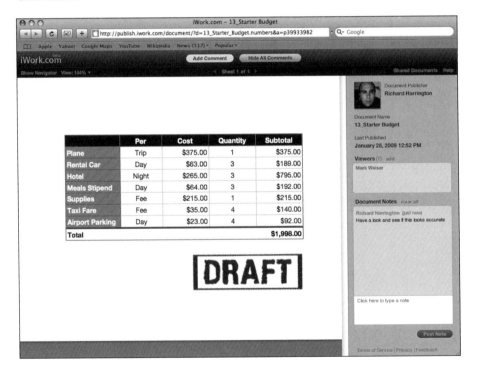

A copy of your spreadsheet is published to iWork.com. Unique invitations are sent to each individual you specified. The viewer can choose to leave comments and notes, or to download your spreadsheet.

You now know how to create and work with Numbers spreadsheets, as well as send them via email and share them via the Web.

Lesson Review

1. How can you import a Microsoft Excel file to a Numbers spreadsheet file?
2. How can you add a new table to a sheet?
3. How can you quickly format a table's appearance?
4. What is the first step to create a formula in the Formula Editor?
5. How do you interactively size a document for printing?

Answers

1. Just open the file; Numbers will import it when opening it.
2. In the toolbar, click the Tables button, or choose Insert > Table and pick a table layout.
3. Choose a table style in the Styles pane and apply it to change the format of your table.
4. Select the desired cell and press the = (equals) key.
5. Choose Print View and adjust the Content Scale slider to size your document's content to the desired layout.

14

Lesson Files   Lessons > Lesson_14 > Photos
Lessons > Lesson_14 > 14_Event_Planner_Final.numbers

Time   This lesson takes approximately 60 minutes to complete.

Goals   Use a Numbers template
Add media to a spreadsheet
Use Address Book cards
Edit and sort data
Use steppers, sliders, and checkboxes
Modify and save styles
Publish to the Internet with iWeb

Lesson 14
Creating an Event Planner

When it comes to getting organized, Numbers and its many useful templates should be your starting point. You'll find templates to help you organize home improvement projects, vacations, sports teams, and even your home inventory.

In this lesson, you'll organize an event and learn how Numbers can integrate your contact information to build a list of guests. Then, you'll calculate an event budget as Numbers helps you choose among several event options. You'll also learn how to add graphics to improve the appearance of your spreadsheet. With the help of Numbers, let's get organized.

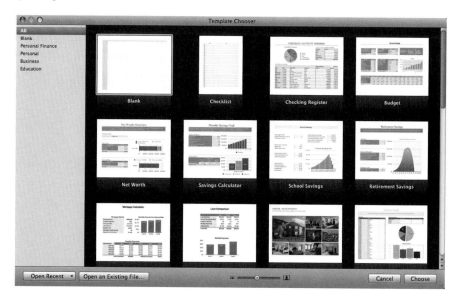

Choosing a Template

The Template Chooser in Numbers includes many templates worth exploring. For this exercise, you will open the Event Planner template and use it to organize a wedding. You will modify the template to include custom images and data, and adjust the formatting of cells. Finally, you'll publish your wedding spreadsheet to the Internet using iWeb.

To select a template:

1   Open Numbers, if necessary. If the Template Chooser is not open, choose File > New from Template Chooser.

2   Select a template. For this exercise, click the Personal category, and then, in the Template Chooser window, select Event Planner.

3   Click Choose to open a new document based on the template.

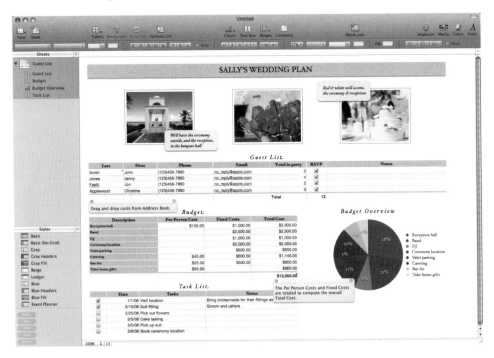

The template opens with placeholder text and images.

4   Double-click the placeholder text *Sally's Wedding Plan* and change it to *Martin & Lauren's Local Reception.*

> **NOTE** ▸ While this template is suited for weddings and receptions, you can use it to plan any social or business gathering.

5   Select the title text by dragging; then, in the format bar, click the Bold button.

6   Choose File > Save. Name the document *Event_Planner.numbers* and save it to your hard drive.

Adding Media to a Spreadsheet

While spreadsheets often focus on data, Numbers '09 also offers you a flexible graphics canvas. Using graphics, you can personalize a spreadsheet with a company logo, add custom shapes, or even insert relevant photos. As with the other iWork applications, you can use the Media Browser to add photos and movies to your spreadsheet.

> **NOTE** ▸ If you plan to share your spreadsheet as a Numbers file, you can insert rich multimedia such as audio and video that will be viewable by other Numbers users. For example, a movie or sound file could play if you double-click its icon. Adding media to your spreadsheet is a useful way to share clips for another person to review or to organize audio records.

Adding Images

Although the Media Browser is an easy tool for browsing photos, it's not the only available browser. If you haven't added photos to your iPhoto or Aperture library, you can also access them in the Finder and drag them directly into your spreadsheet.

1   Open a Finder window and navigate to the Lesson_14 folder. Open the Photos folder.

The folder contains three photos for use in your spreadsheet.

2 Drag the first photo, **Wedding 01.jpg**, onto the first placeholder image at the top of your spreadsheet.

3 You can also change the placeholder images by using a menu command. Click the second image placeholder to select it.

4 Choose Insert > Choose and navigate to the second photo, **Wedding 02.jpg**, in the Lesson_14 folder.

5 Use either method to add a third photo, **Wedding 03.jpg**.

The spreadsheet now has three custom photos. The photo captions, however, should be updated.

6 Click inside the first rounded rectangle to replace the text. Type the text *We invite you to celebrate our marriage.*

7 Click inside the second rounded rectangle and type *For those who couldn't be in Washington, DC…celebrate with us locally.*

8 Choose File > Save to save your work.

Adjusting an Image

You can adjust the exposure, saturation, and other properties of an image without ever leaving Numbers. This flexibility allows you to make instant graphics changes when you see your images combined on the page. In this exercise, you'll explore the Adjust Image window.

1   Click the second picture to select it.

2   Choose View > Show Adjust Image.

The Adjust Image window opens.

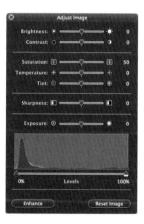

3   Drag the Adjust Image window to reposition it so that you can clearly see the entire image you want to modify.

4   Click the Enhance button to automatically adjust the image.

The Enhance function spreads the red, green, and blue tones evenly across the histogram and subtly fixes the image's color balance.

5   Drag the Brightness slider to the right to increase the image's white level.

A value of approximately 20 brightens up the image so that the faces are easier to see.

6   Drag the Contrast slider to the right to change the balance between the light and dark areas of the image.

A value of 16 keeps the image from looking washed out.

7   Drag the Saturation slider to the right to intensify the colors.

A value of 60 makes the trees and skin tones richer without looking artificial.

Before

After

8   Adjust the other two images to suit yourself, and then close the Adjust Image window.

> **NOTE** ▸ You can adjust images without fear of making a bad adjustment. At any point, you can click the Reset Image button in the Adjust Image window to remove any adjustments.

Adjusting Framing of Objects

In iWork, you can choose to enclose an image inside a graphical border. These borders are called *picture frames*, and they help draw attention to your photos and reduce visual clutter. The template applies a picture frame to the three photos, and you'll customize that frame.

1   Click the first photo to select it.

2   Shift-click photos 2 and 3 to add them to the selection.

By selecting all three photos, you can adjust them simultaneously.

3   In the toolbar, click the Stroke pop-up menu.

4 Choose the picture frame thumbnail, and choose the black photo-corner-style frame. A simple frame is applied to all three images.

The frames for the three photos change. While the toolbar provides quick access to the picture frames, you can modify them in detail using the Graphic inspector.

5 Open the Graphic inspector and drag the Scale slider to 75% to reduce the size of the frames' corners and border.

6 Save your work by choosing File > Save.

> **TIP** If you want to remove a picture frame, select the media and then choose None from the Stroke pop-up menu.

Using Address Book Cards

Numbers '09 includes several templates that can use information from the Address Book application. By using contact information, Numbers can save you a lot of time when including contacts in your spreadsheets. Instead of retyping contact information, you can drag those contacts directly from Address Book.

For this lesson, you will add contact information from Address Book to your wedding reception spreadsheet. Because you are using your own contacts, your results won't exactly match the figures in this exercise. If you haven't yet added contacts to Address Book, you'll have to enter seven or more contacts to perform this exercise.

NOTE ▶ Numbers looks at a table's header row to map Address Book fields. The header row title should match the field names in Address Book. Make sure that the header row for the table is turned on. You can quickly access this control in the format bar. You can find a complete list of fields in the Numbers online help.

1 Select the placeholder contacts in the table by clicking the first cell and dragging until you've selected cells A2 through E5. Then press Delete to remove the placeholder contacts.

2 Open Address Book.

You may open it from your Dock or from your Applications folder.

3 Under the Group heading, click the Add (+) button to create a new group. Name the group Local Reception.

By using a group, you can organize several contacts.

4 Click All, then drag a contact from Address Book into the Local Reception group.

The contact is added to the group.

5 Drag six more contacts into the group.

6   Position the Address Book window so that you can see it as well as your Numbers spreadsheet.

7   Drag the Local Reception group in Address Book into the Guest List table in Numbers.

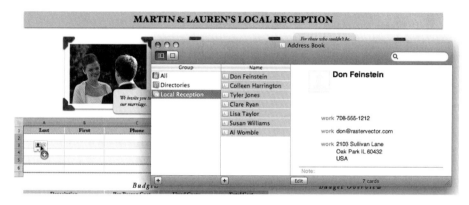

The contacts are added to the Guest List table.

NOTE ▶ You can add a contact's information to a table by dragging a contact or group from Address Book. Dragging a contact into an existing table will import only contact information that matches the table headers.

You can clean the table to properly display the contact information.

8   With the table selected, click column D.

9   Drag the right edge of column D to expand it so that the email addresses fit on a single line.

10   Delete any unused rows from the Guest List table.

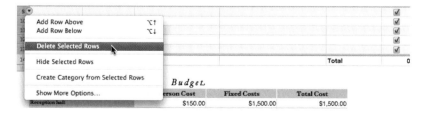

11 Adjust the width of column G so that it matches the page header.

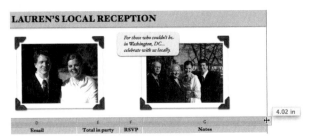

You can use the alignment guides to help judge the correct width.

12 Choose File > Save to save your work.

TIP▶ If you'd like to create a new table with several contacts, just drag their cards onto the canvas. Numbers automatically creates a new table displaying the contact information.

Editing Data in a Table

The data in the spreadsheet can be modified to reflect changes in the reception plans. Fortunately, in Numbers you can quickly add and remove data using intuitive controls that let you adapt your spreadsheet to your needs. In this exercise, you'll make several changes to your spreadsheet that illustrate how to control tables.

1 For the Guest List table, click in cell E2 and type *4*.

This signifies that the first guest will have four people total in his party.

2 Enter data for the remaining guests according to the following figure:

D	E	F
Email	**Total in party**	**RSVP**
don@rastervector.com	4	☑
colleen@photoshopforvideo.com	3	☑
tyler@peachpit.com	2	☑
cryan@rastervector.com	2	☑
lisa@motioncontrol3d.com	4	☑
swilliams@podcastingforacause.com	3	☑
al@vidpodcaster.com	5	☑
	Total	23

The Guest List currently totals 23 guests.

3   Click the Budget table to switch to it.

Numbers allows you to use multiple tables in a sheet for added flexibility. You can modify this table to adjust for event costs

4   Place your pointer over row 3, Band, until the menu arrow appears. From the cell reference pop-up menu, choose Delete Row.

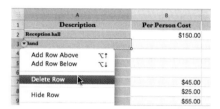

5   Using the same method, delete row 4, "Ceremony location."

NOTE ▸ The costs in the Budget table can be easily modified, but because you have already practiced modifying cell content, you'll use these numbers as is.

6   Remove the yellow comment by clicking the X in the upper right corner.

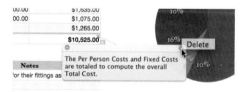

NOTE ▸ You can add your own comments to a table by selecting a cell and then clicking the Comment button in the toolbar. If a cell is not selected when you click the Comment button, a floating comment using the sticky note format will be added to your document.

7   Click the Task List table to switch to it.

8   Remove the task "Book ceremony location" using the cell reference pop-up menu as you did earlier in this exercise.

Let's enlarge the table to include more tasks.

9 In the lower right corner of the table, drag the Column and Row handle to resize the table to 11 rows and 4 columns.

10 Add information to the table as shown in the following figure:

11 Click column D (Notes); then, from the pop-up menu, choose Delete Column.

12 Choose File > Save to save your work.

Sorting Data in a Table

As you build a spreadsheet, it will quickly fill with data that you'll want to organize and present for maximum clarity. Numbers offers predictable data sorting in tables to help you organize lists. Using sorting, you can arrange values in some or all of the cells in a column. You can reorder the information in all rows by sorting a column in ascending or descending order.

NOTE ▶ Header and footer rows are not affected by sorting.

1 Click the Task List table to make it active.

2 Click column B to select it.

This column contains the date of each task. Sorting by date is a logical way to arrange items in a to-do list.

3 Click the pop-up menu for column B and choose Sort Ascending.

The tasks are rearranged by date in ascending order.

4 Click the Guest List table to make it active.

5 Click column A to select it.

Sorting by last name is the most common way to organize a name list.

6 Click the pop-up menu for column A and choose Sort Ascending.

The guests are arranged by last name in ascending order.

7 Save your work by choosing File > Save.

Using Checkboxes, Steppers, and Sliders

If a spreadsheet has a lot of repeated data or requires the entry of a large volume of similar data, Numbers '09 offers an array of checkboxes, steppers, and sliders to accelerate that data entry. Additionally, you can enter data and explore the results interactively by adjusting values. As you adjust cell controls, the formulas and charts update automatically.

1 Click the Guest List to select it.

By default, the Event Planner template uses checkboxes to calculate the total number of guests.

2   Deselect the box in the RSVP column for one guest.

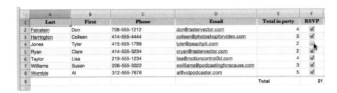

The total number of guests is changed. The Budget and Budget Overview chart are also adjusted dynamically.

TIP To format a cell as a checkbox, click the Checkbox button in the format bar. You can also use a checkbox when a value can have one of two states, such as true or false.

3   Click cell E2 to select the first "Total in party" data cell.

By formatting cells to use stepper controls, you can increase or decrease numbers in a cell by specific increments.

4   Shift-click cell E8 to select cells E2 through E8.

5   Open the Cells inspector.

6   From the Cell Format pop-up menu, choose Stepper.

You now must assign the allowable stepper values for the cells. You want to limit a party to no more than eight members.

7   Set the Minimum value to 1 and the Maximum value to 8.

> **NOTE** ▸ The Minimum and Maximum fields indicate the lowest and highest allowable cell values. You can specify an increment (such as 5) to alter the value by a specific amount with each click (5, 10, 15, 20, and so on).

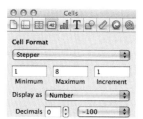

By formatting the "Total in party" cells to use a stepper, you can ensure that only whole numbers with the right formatting are entered.

8   Click cell E3 to select it.

Up and down arrows appear next to the cell so that you can change its value.

9   Click the up arrow to add one more guest to the party.

You've determined you are over budget for the reception. Let's try to trim off a few dollars. You can adjust the budget values to see the impact of modifying individual budget elements.

10 Click the Budget table to make it active.

11 Click cell B2; then Command-click cells B5, B6, and B7 to select them.

12 From the Cell Format pop-up menu, choose Slider.

13 Set the Minimum value to 0, the Maximum value to 300, and the Increment value to 5.

These values allow you to adjust the amount spent on each guest to a value between $0 and $300 in $5 increments.

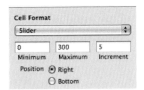

TIP ▶ You should choose to use a slider to quickly make large changes to numbers.

14 Click cell B5 to select the amount budgeted for each meal.

A slider appears next to the cell that enables you to change its value.

15 Change the Catering Per Person Cost to $60.

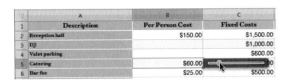

You'll notice that the Budget table and Budget Overview chart both update.

16 Choose File > Save to save your work.

Modifying and Saving Table Styles

Now let's make the spreadsheet look a little nicer so you can print it out and distribute it to others in the family who are helping to organize the wedding. A quick way to format the appearance of a table is to use *styles*. In Numbers '09, table styles can define the font, font size, style, and color for all table elements. A table style can format the background of the table as well as the stroke, color, and border of table cells.

NOTE ▶ Most templates, including the Event Planner, include one or more table styles.

1   Double-click the Guest List title to select it.

When a table title is selected, you can modify its font and style.

2   In the format bar, click the Bold button to change the style of the text.

3   In the format bar, change the size of the text to 18 points.

Phone	**Email**	**Total in party**	**RSVP**
708-555-1212	don@rastervector.com	4	✓
414-555-4444	colleen@photoshopforvideo.com	4	✓
415-555-1789	tyler@peachpit.com	2	

Guest List

NOTE ▶ When you change a table's style, it is called an override. When you assign a different style to a table, you can keep or remove any overrides. To replace a table's style and remove any overrides, click the arrow to the right of the new style and then choose Clear and Apply Style. To replace a table's style but keep the overrides, just click the name of the new style in the Styles pane.

The text for the Guest List table is modified but now does not match the text in the other tables in the spreadsheet.

4   Click the triangle next to the Event Planner style and choose Redefine Style from Table.

The headers on all of the tables update to match the new style.

5   Choose File > Save to save your work.

You can compare your work to the document **14_Event_Planner_Final.numbers** provided in the Lesson_14 folder.

Publishing with iWeb

Now that your spreadsheet is done, let's share it with a few other people involved in the wedding by publishing it to the Internet. You can use iWeb (part of the iLife '09 application suite) to create a website that includes your document. You also can publish a Numbers document directly to your iWeb blog or podcast.

1 Choose Share > Send to iWeb > PDF, or choose Share > Send to iWeb > Numbers Document.

> **NOTE** ▶ You should use PDF if you want to share the file with a broader audience. However, PDF files cannot be easily modified. If you want to share a modifiable document with other Numbers '09 users, choose Numbers Document.

iWeb opens. In the left column, you can choose a theme for your website.

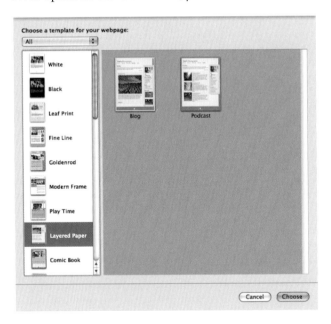

2 Click Layered Paper and choose either a Blog or Podcast template for posting the file. While both templates will work, the Blog format is best for single posts.

3   Click Choose to create the page.

The PDF or Numbers document becomes an attachment that your website visitors can download.

4   Replace all placeholder text in the Blog entry with information about the event or file.

MORE INFO ▶ For more information on publishing your iWeb site, be sure to see the online help and tutorials or *Apple Training Series: iLife '09* (Peachpit Press, 2009).

Lesson Review

1. Name three ways to add media to a table.
2. How can you organize several Address Book contacts?
3. If you want to sort the contents of a table in alphabetical order, which option should you pick?
4. Which cell format can be applied to offer an either/or data state?
5. Which output format should you use when publishing a spreadsheet to the Internet when you want to reach the broadest audience?

Answers

1. You can use the Media Browser to select media, drag the files directly from a Finder window to the Numbers canvas, or choose Insert > Choose.
2. It's a good idea to create a group that contains multiple Address Book contacts.
3. Highlight a row or column; then click the cell reference pop-up menu, and choose Sort Ascending.
4. Use a checkbox when you want to show that a cell has either one value or another.
5. Choose File > Send to iWeb > PDF to create a PDF file for download.

15

Lesson Files   Lessons > Lesson_15 > 15_Team_Roster.numbers
Lessons > Lesson_15 > 15_Time_Log.numbers
Lessons > Lesson_15 > 15_College_Savings.numbers

Time   This lesson takes approximately 60 minutes to complete.

Goals   Freeze a header row
Organize a table using categories and subcategories
Format a table with styles
Filter table data
Change the formatting of cells for special data types
Locate functions with the Function Browser
Replace placeholder arguments in a function

Lesson **15**

Advanced Spreadsheets

In the two previous lessons, we used tables to organize data and analyze and sort information. In this lesson, we'll take data analysis a step further, and dive into the finer points of filtering, categorizing, summarizing, and calculating with Numbers spreadsheets. In particular, we'll use:

▶ Intelligent tables that make it easy to create categories based on your data and summarize the results.

▶ Data filtering, which can help you reorganize data to display specific information.

▶ Powerful formulas, which allow you to calculate a wide range of solutions. With the Function Browser, you can access over 250 functions, including special functions for engineering, statistical, and financial tasks.

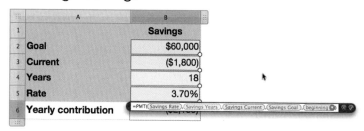

Organizing Information Using Table Categories

Numbers can create useful categories based upon selected columns. In this exercise, we'll use a roster for a youth baseball league to organize a table into several categories.

We'll assume the coaches in the league want to know how many players are available for each position as they're forming teams for the coming season. They also want to sort by the age of the players, so they can start recruiting now for positions where they'll be short of players in future seasons.

Freezing a Header Row

Let's start by opening the league roster and making it easier to read.

Your league roster has a header row across the top of the table, which of course will appear at the top of each page automatically when you print. But it's also something you refer to constantly when organizing your information.

So we'll begin with a handy organizational tool: freezing the header row and header column so that they remain visible while you scroll through the rest of the spreadsheet. By freezing the header row and column, you can always view and refer to those labels, no matter how deep you navigate into your spreadsheet.

1   Open Numbers if it is not already open.

2   Choose File > Open and navigate to the Lesson_15 folder.

3   Select **15_Team_Roster.numbers** and click Open.

Numbers opens a spreadsheet that includes two sheets.

NOTE ▶ Each spreadsheet in this lesson includes a second sheet showing the end result of the exercise. You can compare your own work to these final versions.

4   Select the first sheet Table Categories, and then click on the table, League Roster.

League Roster

	A	B	C	D
1	**NAME**	**AGE**	**FORMER TEAM**	**POSITION**
2	Miguel Garcia	12	Blazers	Catcher
3	Travis Grey	10	Blazers	Pitcher
4	Bradley Cutler	12	Blazers	Pitcher
5	Shawn Craig	11	Blazers	First Base
6	Derek Coe	11	Blazers	Second Base
7	Antonio Milea	10	Blazers	Shortstop

This table contains a roster for a youth baseball league.

5   Scroll down the list to browse the table contents.

As you scroll down, notice that the header row scrolls off the top of the page. It would be more useful if this row were always visible to you as you work.

	A	B	C	D
5	Shawn Craig	11	Blazers	First Base
6	Derek Coe	11	Blazers	Second Base
7	Antonio Milea	10	Blazers	Shortstop
8	Seth Richey	11	Blazers	Shortstop
9	Ian Ramsey	10	Blazers	Third Base
10	Adrian Marshall	12	Blazers	Left Field
11	Jesse Fraser	10	Blazers	Center Field
12	Scott Hayes	10	Blazers	Center Field
13	Dustin Collins	10	Blazers	Right Field
14	Tim Rice	10	Bobcats	Catcher
15	Matthew Robin	12	Bobcats	Pitcher

6   Choose Table > Freeze Header Rows.

	A	B	C	D
1	**NAME**	**AGE**	**FORMER TEAM**	**POSITION**
6	Derek Coe	11	Blazers	Second Base
7	Antonio Milea	10	Blazers	Shortstop
8	Seth Richey	11	Blazers	Shortstop
9	Ian Ramsey	10	Blazers	Third Base
10	Adrian Marshall	12	Blazers	Left Field
11	Jesse Fraser	10	Blazers	Center Field
12	Scott Hayes	10	Blazers	Center Field
13	Dustin Collins	10	Blazers	Right Field
14	Tim Rice	10	Bobcats	Catcher
15	Matthew Robin	12	Bobcats	Pitcher

7   Scroll down the table and notice that the header row remains visible at the top of the table at all times.

Organizing Data Using Categories

You can organize a spreadsheet into categories based upon the values in a single column. For example, in the case of our league roster, you can categorize players by position. This will allow the coaches to organize new teams by viewing how many players they have for each position.

1   Click column D (Position) to select it.

2   Click the cell reference pop-up menu and choose Categorize by This Column.

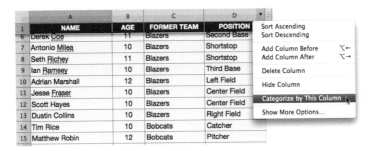

Numbers organizes the data in column D into categories and creates a spreadsheet category for each unique value in the column. The column you used to create categories is the *category value column.*

NOTE ▶ Be sure to remove any empty cells in column D, or they will be organized into a (blank) category.

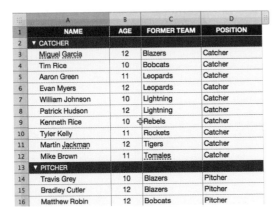

You can take categorizing further by using subcategories. For this table, let's categorize using player age as a subcategory. This will help the coaches distribute players to new teams based upon both position and age, and maintain a fair balance of players on each team.

3   Click column B (Age) to select it.

4   Click the cell reference pop-up menu and choose Sort Ascending to sort the players by age.

5   Click the cell reference pop-up menu and choose Categorize by This Column.

Numbers creates subcategories for the players' ages.

	A	B	C	D
1	**NAME**	**AGE**	**FORMER TEAM**	**POSITION**
2	▼ CATCHER			
3	▼ 10			
4	Tim Rice	10	Bobcats	Catcher
5	William Johnson	10	Lightning	Catcher
6	Kenneth Rice	10	Rebels	Catcher
7	▼ 11			
8	Aaron Green	11	Leopards	Catcher
9	Tyler Kelly	11	Rockets	Catcher
10	Mike Brown	11	Tomales	Catcher
11	▼ 12			
12	Miguel Garcia	12	Blazers	Catcher
13	Evan Myers	12	Leopards	Catcher
14	Patrick Hudson	12	Lightning	Catcher
15	Martin Jackman	12	Tigers	Catcher
16	▼ PITCHER			

The catchers who are 12 years of age are no longer eligible to play in this league, so you have no need to display their names in this roster. You can use categories to address this.

6   Click the disclosure triangle in the 12 Catcher category subheader.

Numbers hides the catchers who are 12 years old, as they will be too old to play next season.

> **TIP** ▶ If you'd like to quickly close all of the categories, click a category's cell reference tab and choose Close All. Conversely, if all categories are closed and you want to open them, choose Expand All.

While this kind of filtering is useful, it can also be applied globally to the table, as you'll discover in the next exercise.

> **TIP** ▶ In this example you categorized first by position, then by age. You can choose to change the priority of any category by clicking its cell reference pop-up menu and choosing Demote or Promote.

Filtering Data

If your table contains information that you'd like to temporarily hide, you can filter it. This hides the data from view but does not remove it from the table.

1   In the toolbar, click Reorganize.

The Reorganize window opens. Notice that the sort controls and the categorizing controls are in use. The middle area of the window is used for filtering.

2   If the filtering controls are not visible in the Reorganize window, click the Filter disclosure triangle to display them.

3   From the "Choose a column" pop-up menu, choose Age.

TIP   You can create new filter criteria by clicking the Add (+) button and defining each column you want to insert.

You can now choose specific data values to display in your spreadsheet.

4   Change the pop-up menu labeled *is* to *is not*; then type *12* in the value field and press Return.

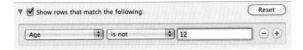

Numbers filters all results to show information for only those rows that do not contain an age value of 12.

NOTE ▶ The subcategory label for age 12 is still visible. If you want to remove any filters, click Reset in the Reorganize window.

5   Close the Reorganize window.

Let's count how many players you have available for each position.

6   Click cell D3 to select the position subcategory.

7   Click the disclosure triangle for D3, and choose Count.

Numbers calculates how many players of each age are available for each position.

TIP ▶ Numbers can also calculate other values automatically, including subtotals and averages for each category or subcategory.

8   Choose File > Close and save your work.

You have formatted a table to show only that information you require. Additionally, when you use categories, the information in your table becomes easier to sort and view.

Formatting a Time Report

As you've seen, table categories make it easier to organize and review information. In the next exercises, we'll use categories and other advanced functions to create a time log. This report is useful for those who bill their time hourly or track time usage.

While Numbers makes your information easy to read, it can also format a table so that it is print ready. By applying table styles and formatting, you can turn a raw spreadsheet into a report that is ready to give to a client.

Let's get started by opening the original time log.

1 Choose File > Open and navigate to the Lesson_15 folder.

2 Select **15_Time_Log.numbers** and click Open.

Numbers opens a spreadsheet with two sheets attached.

3 Select the first sheet, Time Log Start.

This table contains an employee-tracking sheet. Maintaining this sheet is an easy way to track the time spent on specific tasks. Let's clean up the table by removing empty space.

4 Click a cell in the table to select it. Then drag the Column and Row handle up to remove empty rows. You should end up with 30 rows and 4 columns.

5 Click column C (Task); then click the cell reference pop-up menu and choose Categorize by This Column.

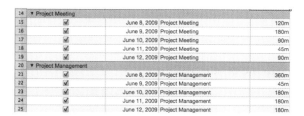

Numbers categorizes the data according to tasks performed. Let's further improve the appearance of the table.

6 In the Styles list, click Beige to reformat the table's appearance.

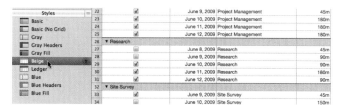

Great—the table looks very professional and easy to read. Let's now use a variable, "billable," to total the number of hours the employee can bill his client.

Performing Calculations with Variables

In the current project, not every hour worked is billable. Some of the employee's time was "internal," which does not produce income but is worth tracking for future planning and analysis. Let's calculate only the number of billable hours.

1 Examine column A.

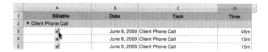

You'll notice that it contains checkboxes for each task. This is a useful way to format a cell so that its value indicates one of two states.

> **TIP** You can quickly format a cell or an entire column to include checkboxes. Select the desired cells, and in the format bar, click the Checkbox button.

2 Click column D to select it.

This column contains the actual time spent. The employee typed the letter *m* after the number data to indicate that the value represents *minutes.*

> **TIP** When entering durations, you can type the full word or use the following abbreviations:

► w—weeks

► d—days

► h—hours

► m—minutes

► s—seconds

► ms—milliseconds

3 Click the cell reference pop-up menu and choose Add Column After.

4 Enter *Billable Time* in the header row for column E.

You now can calculate the number of billable hours by creating a simple formula.

5 Click cell E3 to add a formula because this is the first row with actual data in both the Time and Billable columns.

6 Press the = (equal sign) key to open the Formula Editor.

7 Click cell A3, press the * (asterisk) key, and then click cell D3.

The formula should read =A3*D3.

8   Press Return to apply the formula.

Because the checkbox is selected, it is treated as a value of 1. If the Billable checkbox is deselected, it is treated as a value of 0.

9   Click cell E3 to select it, and then drag the blue Fill handle in the lower right corner through cell E36. Numbers now shows the number of billable hours in column E.

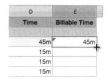   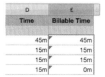

Referencing Data

Now that all of the billable hours are displayed, you can use that information in another table. Let's add a second, reporting table to this sheet so that you can compare the total hours worked with the billable hours.

1   In the toolbar, click the Tables button and choose Sums.

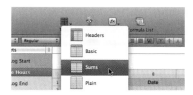

A new table is added to the sheet.

2   In the Sheets pane, double-click the table name to select it and rename the table *Report*.

Let's style this table to match the first table.

3   Click the Beige button to apply the identical table style. Drag the table so that it is aligned with the first table.

4   Label the first three header row cells as follows: Time, Billable Time, and Ratio.

Let's remove the unused column.

5   Select column D; then click the cell reference pop-up menu and choose Delete Column.

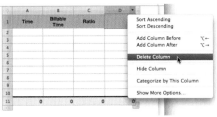

6   In the Report table, click cell A2. This is where the billable time will be added.

7   Press the = (equal sign) key to open the Formula Editor.

8   In the Billable Hours table, drag to select cells D3 through D36.

The formula should read =SUM(Billable Hours :: D3:D36). SUM is a basic function that adds the range of selected cells. You'll explore functions in depth later in this lesson.

9   Press Return. The cell should display a value of 2550 minutes.

Let's perform a similar calculation for the next column.

10   In the Report table, click cell B2, and then press the = (equal sign) key to open the Formula Editor.

11   In the Billable Hours table, select cells E3 through E36.

The formula should read =SUM(Billable Hours :: E3:E36).

12 Press Return. The cell should display a value of 2100 minutes.

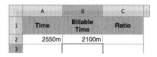

13 Let's remove the unused cells. Drag up the Column and Row handle for the table so that it is three rows by three columns.

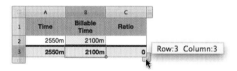

14 In the Report table, click cell C3 and press the = (equal sign) key.

15 Enter the following formula: *=B3/A3*. Press Return.

You have successfully created a new table. By formatting the Report table, you can make displayed values easier to understand.

Formatting Displayed Data

As you create formulas, you'll often want to format the way results are displayed to make the information more clear to the reader. In the current table, it would be useful to see the total time spent displayed as hours and the ratio displayed as a percentage.

1 In the Report table, click cell A3.

Cell A3 is in a footer row and shows the total from the cells in this column. Let's change the calculated totals from minutes to hours and minutes.

2 Open the Cells inspector.

3 From the Cell Format pop-up menu, choose Duration.

You can use the Units control to select the units you want to display for a duration value.

4 Drag the left end of the slider until it's over the Hr unit.

The time total is now displayed in hours and minutes, which is more useful to the manager and the accounting department. Let's reuse this formula in the next column.

5 Drag the blue Fill handle to the right so that the data in column B is displayed with the same formatting.

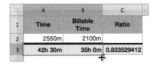

All that is left is to improve the percentage display in column C.

6 Select cell C3.

7 In the format bar, click the Percentage button to change how the cell displays its contents.

The number is now displayed as 82.35%.

8 Choose File > Close and save your work.

You have utilized several advanced features, including formatting irregular units like time, in a table.

Using Advanced Formulas with Functions

As you continue to work with formulas, you'll use functions to perform specific tasks. (For example, you used the SUM and COUNT functions earlier in this lesson.) A function is a predefined, named operation (such as AVERAGE) that can perform a calculation. When writing a formula, you can use multiple functions or just one, depending on the task at hand.

> **MORE INFO ▶** With more than 250 functions to choose from in Numbers, you might overlook a few useful ones; not everyone who uses Numbers has formal training in accounting or statistics. To help you make the most of functions, Numbers includes a dedicated Help module. To use it, choose Help > iWork Formulas and Functions Help. It contains several example formulas and a detailed reference guide.

Let's use a function to determine a financial goal for college savings.

1 Choose File > Open and navigate to the Lesson_15 folder.

2 Select **15_College_Savings.numbers** and click Open.

Numbers opens a spreadsheet with two sheets attached.

3 Select the College Planning sheet.

The table on the sheet outlines a target for savings. A family has determined that it wants to set aside $60,000 toward the cost of a daughter's tuition. Let's break down the contents of the table.

College Savings

	Savings
Goal	$60,000
Current	($1,800)
Years	18
Rate	3.70%
Yearly contribution	

The family's savings goal is $60,000, and it currently has $1,800 in the bank. (According to accounting practice, investments are shown in parentheses to represent negative numbers.) The family has 18 years toward its goal because the savings started as soon as a child was on the way. It is expected that an interest rate of 3.7% can be realized by investing the savings.

What the family wants to determine is how much money it has to save each year to realize the college savings goal. Let's find a function to calculate the annual investment.

4   Click on table and select cell B6, and in the toolbar, click the Function button. Choose Show Function Browser.

The Function Browser is a convenient way to add a function to a formula.

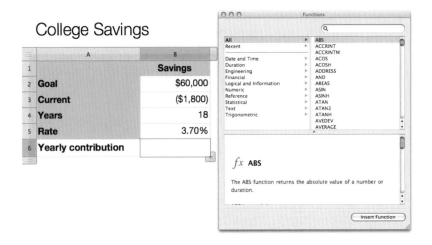

The browser is organized as follows:

▶   The left pane lists categories of functions so that you can browse by the type of function.

▶   The right pane lists individual functions. Click a function to select it and view information about how to use it.

▶   The lower pane contains detailed information about the selected function.

5   In the left pane, click Financial; then scroll to examine your choices in the right pane.

The appropriate function choice is PMT, which, according to the explanatory text, returns the fixed periodic payment for an annuity based on a series of regular periodic payments of a constant amount at constant intervals with a fixed interest rate.

6   Choose PMT and then click the Insert Function button.

The function is added to cell B6. Several argument placeholders are located in the function by default. To use the function in your formula, let's replace those placeholder arguments with actual data. Move your pointer and hold it over each placeholder. Numbers will explain what type of information is needed to complete the formula.

7   Click the periodic-rate argument.

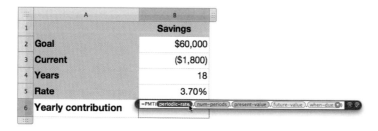

8   Click cell B5 (Rate) to update the argument to use that data.

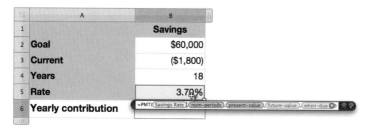

You'll want to replace all the arguments with actual data.

9   Click the num-periods argument and click cell B4 (Years).

10   Click the present-value argument and click cell B3 (Current).

11   Click the future-value argument and click cell B2 (Goal).

12   The last argument is when-due. This argument is light-colored because it is an optional step that is not critical to the calculation. Click the when-due disclosure triangle and choose beginning.

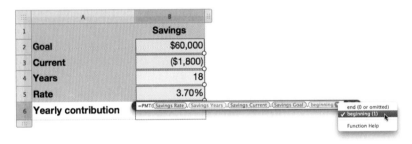

This means the payment is due at the start of the year (and that the money would be available before the student enrolled in college).

13   Press Return to calculate the formula.

Numbers informs you that the family must deposit $2,185 each year to save its goal of $60,000 by the end of an 18-year period.

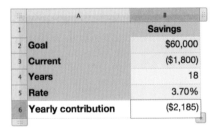

14   Choose File > Close and save your work.

You've used a complex function to analyze variables and determine a correct value. Functions are very useful for a variety of tasks, and you'll want to fully explore the Function Browser to locate other helpful functions for your typical data scenarios.

MORE INFO ▶ Be sure to check out Help > iWork Formulas and Functions User Guide for a detailed user's manual for each function. It also offers helpful advice on the construction and use of formulas and functions.

Lesson Review

1. How do you freeze a header row?
2. How can you filter data automatically?
3. How do you reference a value from one sheet to another?
4. Define a function.
5. In a formula, how do you insert actual data into a placeholder argument?

Answers

1. Choose Table > Freeze Header Rows.
2. In the toolbar, click the Reorganize button to open the Reorganize window. In the central filter area of the window, set the filtering values.
3. In the destination sheet, select the cell in which you want to place the calculated value. Press the = (equal sign) key to open the Formula Editor. Create a formula based on cells in the source sheet. Press Return to calculate the value and place it in the destination sheet cell.
4. A function is a predefined, named operation that can perform a calculation.
5. In the Function Browser, choose the desired function and click Insert Function. Click the desired argument; then click the cell in which the actual data appears. Do this for every placeholder argument in the function. Press Return to accept and calculate the formula.

16

Time   This lesson takes approximately 60 minutes to complete.

Goals   Customize a bar chart's display options

Combine two sets of data into a single bar

Display a margin of error

Explore several data display methods

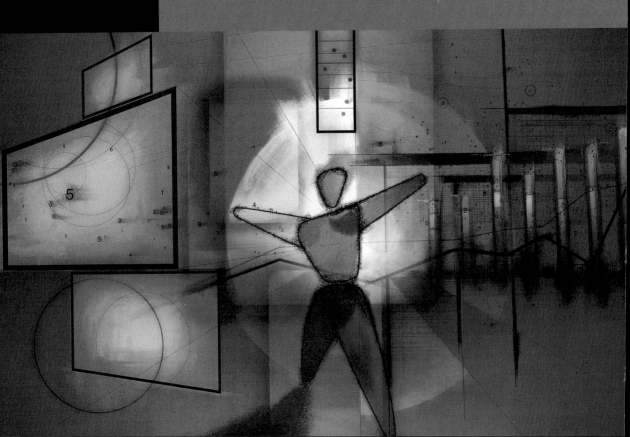

Lesson 16

Advanced Charting

When building a chart, your objective is to make complex data easy to understand. At times, however, multiple data sets seem impossible to represent in a simple chart. Fortunately, the sophisticated charting tools shared by all iWork applications will help you do the impossible. Using a wealth of chart types and visual styles in iWork, you can turn intricate data relationships into clear, quickly comprehensible imagery.

In this lesson, you'll use Numbers to explore the many chart types in iWork and build charts with five of the most powerful charting options.

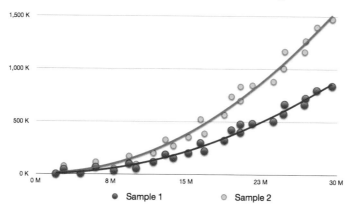

▶ Choosing the Right Chart for the Job

So far, you've looked at the most common chart types: bar, column, and pie. But iWork offers much more. You'll find 19 different chart types inside iWork: 11 two-dimensional and 8 three-dimensional. Knowing which type of chart to use can be tricky as certain charts are designed for certain situations or data types.

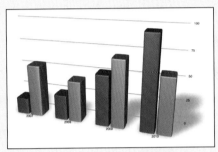

Column and Stacked Column

The column chart is a popular option and is frequently used to present data that was arranged in the rows and columns of a table or spreadsheet. This chart type is excellent when showing changes in data over time, such as comparing year-end financial results over a decade. The most common column layout places categories of information along the horizontal (x) axis with the value entries along the vertical (y) axis.

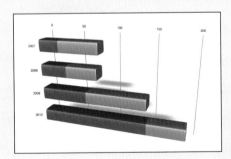

Bar and Stacked Bar

A bar chart can translate data from rows and columns into plotted bars, a useful design when comparing two or more individual items. The bar chart is a suitable choice when you must display long axis labels or when you are comparing duration values. You can also combine multiple values for a single period into a stacked bar.

▶ Choosing the Right Chart for the Job *(continued)*

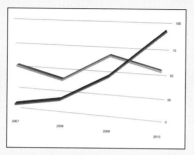

Line

Like column charts, line charts work well for data that is arranged in columns or rows. What differentiates line charts is that they are effective for displaying continuous data over a range of time, which makes them excellent for charting trends. For a line chart to work effectively, category data must be available in even increments (such as months or quarters) and be represented along the horizontal axis. The value data is also evenly represented along the vertical axis. The points on the graph are connected with a line, and multiple colors are used to distinguish between multiple trends.

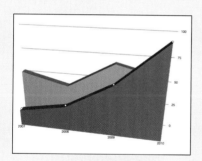

Area and Stacked Area

Area charts also clearly show data from rows and columns but are particularly well suited to track the magnitude of change over time, which makes them appropriate for showing financial or population growth. An area chart can convey both the change in individual values and a cumulative change in total value.

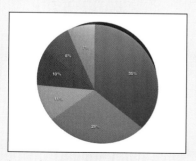

Pie

A pie chart works well to show the proportionate relationships of data in a single column or row of a table, such as the results of a survey. The pie chart represents individual data values as a percentage of the whole pie (which adds up to 100 percent). A pie chart works very well when the goal for the chart is to show a relationship between entries (such as the results from a survey). Pie charts can be displayed in 2D or 3D, depending on the style of your slides.

continues on next page

▶ Choosing the Right Chart for the Job *(continued)*

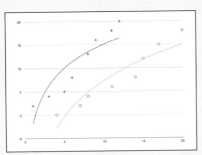

Scatter

To create a scatter chart, you will require at least two columns or rows of data, which makes the scatter chart a useful way to represent the relationships between the values of one or more tables, such as comparing statistical or scientific data. A scatter chart uses a two-value axis with number values on both the x- and y-axes. Before creating a scatter chart, make sure you've entered x and y point values for each of the data series you want to plot. The data tends to be displayed in uneven intervals (scattered) across the chart.

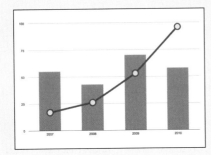

Mixed

Mixed charts are preferred for combining two series of data in a single chart and displaying them in different chart types. For example, you may choose to display one set of data as a line chart and use columns for the other data series. In a Mixed chart, each chart type used can represent only one data series. This is a good way to compare actual versus estimated data (such as projections).

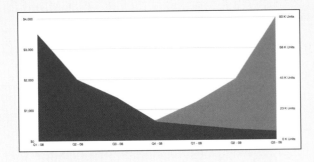

2-Axis

Charts with two axes can be easily charted with iWork. A 2-axis chart is really a Mixed chart with different values for each chart's y-axis. For example, you may chart data such as temperature and snow accumulation over a period of time.

Creating a Stacked 3D Bar Chart

While a standard bar chart allows you to compare two sets of data represented by multiple bars, the stacked bar chart lets you combine two or more sets of data into a single bar.

In this exercise, you'll analyze a restaurant's delivery fleet over a four-year period, creating a stacked bar chart that shows how many motorcycles and scooters are in service. At the same time, your chart will compare the total vehicles in use for each year. Using Numbers, you'll chart two sets of data in one bar and then customize the bars to achieve a 3D look.

1   In Numbers, choose File > Open and open Lesson_16 > **16_Cylinder Chart .numbers**.

   You'll find a table showing the yearly count of scooters and motorcycles in the delivery fleet.

	2007	2008	2009	2010
Scooters	27	36	63	143
Motorcycles	55	43	80	48

2   Select the table. In the toolbar, from the Charts pop-up menu, choose Stacked Bar.

   The chart is assigned a default title, which is centered above the chart. These default titles work well, but Pages also allows you to add additional text boxes as desired.

3   In the format bar, click the Chart Options pop-up menu and select Show Title to deselect it and remove the default title.

   You can create a text box in which to freely position a title.

4   In the toolbar, Option-click the Text Box button.

   Option-clicking lets you drag in the canvas to choose where the text box should be placed.

5 Double-click in the new text box, and type *Delivery Vehicles in Corporate Fleet.*

You have created a text box for your chart title so that you can customize the font settings in the format bar and drag the title into a new position.

6 Format the text box to use Helvetica Neue, Bold, 24 pt.

7 Resize and position the title, legend, and chart. You can use the following figure for guidance:

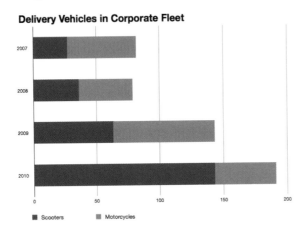

Formatting a 3D Bar Chart
While 2D charts are clear, 3D charts use the added feature of depth to display your Numbers data. They offer more display options and can add a sense of perspective that makes your data easier to understand.

1 Select the chart on the canvas.

2   In the format bar, from the Chart Type pop-up menu, choose 3D Stacked Bar.

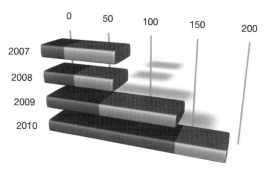

The chart changes to a 3D representation. Let's customize its appearance.

3   Open the Chart inspector; then click Chart and make the following changes:

▶   Bar Shape—Cylinder.

▶   Lighting Style—Soft Fill.

▶   Drag the arrows in the 3D Scene controller or 3D Chart arrowhead on the canvas to change the viewing angle.

▶   Adjust the size and position of the chart so that it resembles the following figure:

Delivery Vehicles in Corporate Fleet

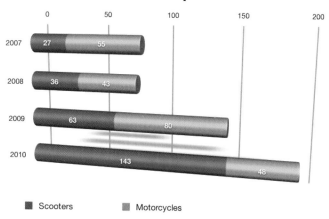

To ensure that the numbers of scooters and motorcycles are clearly understood, you can insert the actual data values inside each cylinder.

4   Open the Chart inspector and click Series.

5   Select the Value Labels checkbox and choose Center for Position. You may change the labels, but you must select them.

6   Click the motorcycle label on a bar, then Shift-click the scooter label so that both objects are selected.

You can use keyboard shortcuts to quickly reformat the text.

7   Press Command-B to make the text bold; then press Command-+ (plus sign) four times to increase the point size from 11 pt to 15 pt.

A few more refinements could make the chart more visually compelling.

8   To customize the cylinder colors for each data set, click a cylinder for the first data set; then, in the format bar, click the Fill well. Set Scooters to red and Motorcycles to purple.

Let's make a few more changes to improve the chart's appearance. A trend in modern graphic design is a subtle use of opacity.

9   Open the Graphic inspector and lower the Opacity to 70%.

The lines behind the cylinders seem to be visible through the shapes. Let's also make the cylinders bigger and easier to read.

10 Open the Chart inspector and click Chart. Change the Gap between bars to 50%.

This makes the bars bigger and reduces the space between each bar. For additional clarity in reading the data, you can add another set of gridlines.

11 Select the entire chart by clicking it in the Sheets pane.

12 In the format bar, from the Y Axis pop-up menu, choose Show Gridlines.

You've created and formatted a stacked bar chart using advanced 3D controls. For reference, you can compare your chart with the chart on the second sheet.

13 Save your work and close the document.

Displaying a Margin of Error

When dealing with survey-based data, you'll often have a *margin of error*, a number that indicates the amount of error possible in a random sample. A common situation in which you have to deal with margin of error is when processing surveys or polls. The greater the margin of error, the less accurately the data represents the real-world values. To fully represent a survey, you'll want to display that error margin in your chart.

Using Numbers, you can place error bars around data points in all 2D charts (except pie charts) to indicate how much error might surround a particular data point.

1 Open Lesson_16 > **16_Error Bars.numbers**.

This table includes two columns of percentages: Approval Rating and +/−. You will use this polling data to create a chart showing a politician's approval rating by month, along with the monthly margin of error. A column chart with error bars will fit the bill.

2   Select the B column header; then, in the toolbar, click the Charts button and choose Column.

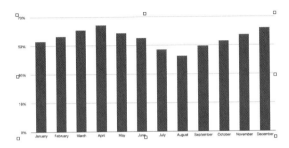

3   Drag the chart's edges to resize as desired.

Numbers allows you to customize several display parameters. Let's start by changing the chart grid and background.

4   With the chart selected, click the Fill well in the format bar and choose a bright color such as a light orange.

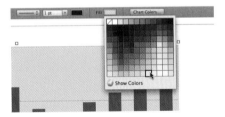

5   To add a border to the chart, in the format bar, click the X Axis pop-up menu and choose Show Chart Borders.

6   In the format bar, click the Y Axis pop-up menu and choose Show Minor Gridlines.

When displaying the full data range between 0 and 100%, the chart could be hard to read. You can narrow the chart's data range to focus on just the active area (between 40 and 70 percent).

7   In the Chart inspector, click Axis; then enter the following values for Value Axis (Y):

▶   Max—0.7

▶   Min—0.4

▶   Steps—3

▶   Format—Percentage

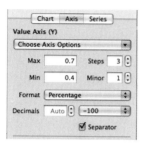

Now that the chart is tighter in focus, let's improve its appearance. One way to enhance the look of a 2D chart is to use gradient fills instead of solid colors.

1   Select the data series by clicking any column in the chart.

2   Open the Graphic inspector; then, from the Fill pop-up menu, choose Gradient Fill.

3   Click each color well and choose the desired colors.

For this chart, use a dark and light orange, as in the following figure:

4   In the Stroke area, choose Line from the pop-up menu. Set a point size of 2 pt and choose a dark red color.

The results should resemble the following figure:

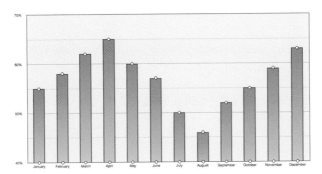

Now that the chart appears more polished, let's create the error bars for each month. Margin of error is generally expressed as a +/− value, which means that the actual data value may be above or below the displayed value within a certain percentage. Adding an error bar visually shows that range on the chart.

1   In the Chart inspector, click the Series button. Near the bottom of the inspector window, click the disclosure triangle to open the Advanced section.

2   Click the Error Bars button; then, from the Error Bars pop-up menu, choose Positive and Negative.

3   To use margin-of-error values from the table, change the next pop-up menu (currently labeled Fixed Value) to Custom.

4   Click the Positive text field; then, in the table, drag over the +/− cells from January to December to select them.

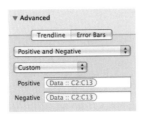

5   Click in the Negative text field; then click in the table and drag across the same +/– cells from January to December.

You can customize the look of the error bars, including color, size, and endpoints.

6   Click any error bar in the chart to select all of the error bars.

7   In the format bar, increase the Stroke to a size of 3 pt (points) and change the Stroke Color Well to a dark brown.

8   From the "Error bar" pop-up menu, choose the arrowheads.

9   Select the Shadow checkbox.

For reference, you could compare your chart with the one on the second sheet.

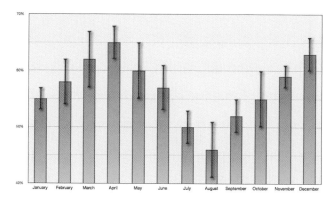

10   Close your document and save your work.

Building a Mixed Chart

Let's look at another advanced chart type that works well for comparing similar units on one chart. In a quarterly sales meeting, management needs to compare projected shipments with actual shipments. Both values can be expressed by the same value type, number of units. You compare both data sets within the same chart using a Mixed chart type.

1   Open Lesson_16 > **16_Mixed Chart Type.numbers**.

This file contains a table and a column chart. The table includes three years of quarterly projected shipment and actual shipment data. The chart, however, displays only the projected shipment values. You will use the actual shipment values to chart a second data series.

2   Select the chart and verify that the data series in the table is highlighted. Drag the fill handle to expand the data series to include the Actual Shipments cells.

	Q1-07	Q2-07	Q3-07	Q4-07	Q1-08	Q2-08	Q3-08	Q4-08	Q1-09	Q2-09	Q3-09	Q4-09
Projected Shipments	32 M	42 M	50 M	59 M	40 M	44 M	55 M	68 M	48 M	60 M	62 M	73 M
Actual Shipments	28 M	30 M	41 M	49 M	36 M	45 M	52 M	71 M	45 M	56 M		

TIP ▶ An alternative to using the Fill handle is to drag a selected row of data onto the chart. This will add the second series of data.

3   Click in the legend and rename the second data series *Actual Shipments*. Resize and reposition the legend as necessary.

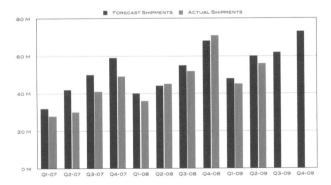

Your chart currently displays both data series as columns. To further distinguish one data set from another, let's change the chart to overlay the data series on top of each other in contrasting chart types.

4 Select the entire chart; then, in the format bar, click the Chart type pop-up menu and choose Mixed.

> **NOTE** ▸ Some of your columns may automatically become a line graph. You'll set the appropriate data values to the proper chart types shortly.

5 In the chart, select the Forecast Shipments data series.

6 In the format bar, change the Series Options pop-up menu to Line.

7 In the chart, select the Actual Shipments data series.

8 In the format bar, change the Series Option pop-up menu to Column.

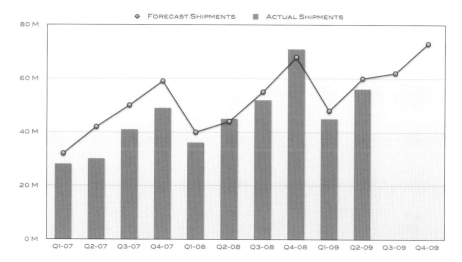

Comparing Data in a 2-Axis Chart

When you created the 3D cylinder bar chart earlier in this lesson, the two data sets (numbers of scooters and motorcycles) were organized by year, and both data sets were expressed in whole numbers. But what if the data sets utilized two different value types, such as currency and percentages? If you wish to chart this style of relationship, Numbers includes a 2-axis chart to compare data of two different types.

1   Open Lesson_16 > **16_2-Axis Chart Type.numbers**. In the toolbar, click Charts and choose 2-Axis.

	Q1 - 08	Q2 - 08	Q3 - 08	Q4 - 08	Q1 - 09	Q2 - 09	Q3 - 09
Unit Cost	$3,500	$2,000	$1,400	$600	$475	$350	$275
Unit Sales	3 K Units	5 K Units	9 K Units	15 K Units	28 K Units	45 K Units	90 K Units

This table contains two data series (Unit Cost and Unit Sales). Though both series are categorized quarterly, the two series utilize different data values: dollar amount and thousands of units. This is the perfect situation in which to use a 2-axis chart type.

2   Select the data in the table.

3   In the toolbar, click the Charts button and choose 2-Axis.

Numbers displays the two data sets in a 2-axis chart; first seen as in the left chart below and, after formatting, as in the right chart.

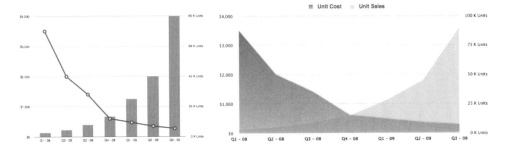

Notice that the 2-axis chart maps the Unit Cost values in the left axis (Y1) and the Unit Sales values in the right axis (Y2).

If you'd like more practice with 2-axis charts, here are a few tips for modifying this table:

▶   The settings in the Chart inspector and the format bar influence both data series when you select the chart. You can customize each series separately by selecting an individual data series in the chart before making changes.

▶ In the Chart inspector, you can choose Column, Line, or Area from the Series Type pop-up menu.

▶ Customize the Value Axis (Y1 and Y2) by choosing Minimum and Maximum values and the number of steps.

▶ When using the Area plot type, you can include data points by selecting a data series; then, in the Chart inspector, click the Data Symbol pop-up menu and choose a symbol.

Making a Scatter Chart

There's one more advanced chart type to explore: the scatter chart. A scatter chart can be used to visualize multiple data sets, each represented by a different symbol; and it can include any number of data points. You'll use a scatter chart when you want to show possible relationships between two variables.

1   Open Lesson_16 > **16_Trendlines_Scatter.numbers**.

Population	Data Sample 1	Sample 2
2 M	0 K	0 K
3 M	44 K	77 K
5 M	6 K	11 K
6 M	66 K	116 K
8 M	33 K	58 K
9 M	99 K	173 K
10 M	55 K	96 K

Here you see the number of successful sales listed by population. Two samples were taken within the population.

2   Select the table.

3   In the toolbar, click Charts and choose Scatter.

4   To add trendlines, open the Chart inspector. Click Series, then click the disclosure triangle to open the Advanced section near the bottom of the Inspector window.

5 Click Trendline and click the Trendline type pop-up menu to select the shape for the trendline.

Numbers displays the data as a scatter chart. With some additional formatting, your chart can resemble the following figure:

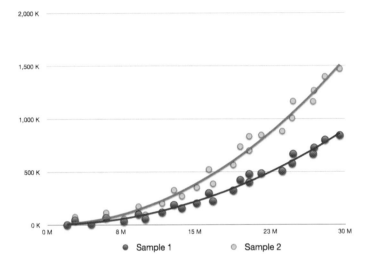

Here are a few tips to use when working with a scatter chart:

▶ A data pair is required for positioning a data point. You can share a single column or row as the X value for multiple Y values, as seen with this chart.

▶ Select a symbol or line before trying to change its look in the format bar or inspector. Some items are altered in the Chart and/or Graphic inspectors.

▶ You can include trendlines, error bars, and connect points of a series using the Chart inspector.

You have utilized the advanced features of Numbers for creating sophisticated charts. Remember that you can copy a chart from Numbers and paste it into a Keynote presentation or Pages document. In fact, charts pasted from your saved Numbers document are linked so that you can then click the Refresh button to implement those changes in Pages or Keynote. Knowing how to harness the full charting abilities of Numbers will help you to create clear and attractive charts in iWork.

The Road Ahead

If you've worked your way through the complete book, then this brings your journey to an end. While you may have completed this first journey, there's a lot more to discover. The best thing about iWork is as you grow stronger in one application, you grow stronger in all three. Be sure to explore the many options and paths iWork offers.

Lesson Review

1. Which chart type might be best suited for displaying annual financial data for a ten-year period? For comparing the execution speeds of multiple computer processors? For displaying two different types of data?

2. How do you choose a chart type to create?

3. How can you make chart elements translucent?

4. How do you format two sets of data to create a Mixed chart?

Answers

1. Column or stacked column chart. Bar or stacked bar chart. Mixed chart.

2. In the Numbers toolbar, click Charts and choose a chart type.

3. In the Graphic inspector, reduce the Opacity to a value less than 100%.

4. Choose the first set of data; in the format bar, from the Series Options pop-up menu, choose a chart type. Then repeat that method for the second data set.

Index

Apple Certification
Fuel your mind.
Reach your potential.

Stand out from the crowd. Differentiate yourself and gain recognition for your expertise by earning Apple Certified Associate certification to validate your iWork '09 skills.

How to Earn Apple Certified Associate Certification

As a special offer to owners of *iWork '09,* you are eligible to take the certification exam online for $45.00 USD. Normally you must pay $65.00 USD to take the exam in a proctored setting at an Apple Authorized Training Center (AATC). To take the exam, please follow these steps:

1 Log on to ibt.prometric/apple, click Secure Sign-In (uses SSL encryption) and enter your Prometric Prime ID. If you don't have an ID, click First-Time Registration to create one.

2 Click Continue to verify your information.

3 In the Candidate Menu page, click Take Test.

4 Enter iWork09EUPP in the Private Tests box and click Submit. The codes are case sensitive and are only valid for one use.

5 Click Take This Test, then Continue to skip the voucher and enter your credit card information to pay the $45 USD fee.

6 Click Begin Test at the bottom of the page.

7 When you finish, click End Test. If you do not pass, retake instructions are included in the results email, so do not discard this email. Retakes are also $45.

Reasons to Become an Apple Certified Associate

- **Raise your earning potential.** Studies show that certified professionals can earn more than their non-certified peers.

- **Distinguish yourself from others in your industry.** Proven mastery of an application helps you stand out from the crowd.

- **Display your Apple Certification logo.** Each certification provides a logo to display on business cards, resumes and websites. In addition, you can publish your certifications on Apple's website to connect with schools, clients and employers.

Training Options

Apple's comprehensive curriculum addresses your needs, whether you're an IT or creative professional, educator, or service technician. Hands-on training is available through a worldwide network of Apple Authorized Training Centers (AATCs) or in a self-paced format through the Apple Training Series and Apple Pro Training Series. Learn more about Apple's curriculum and find an AATC near you at training.apple.com.

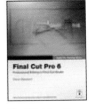